By Sharon Donohue

The Bible Clicks in 365 Stories:

The Bible Clicks, A Creative Through-the-Bible Series
Book One: Stories of Faith, Vision, and Courage from the Old Testament

The Bible Clicks, A Creative Through-the-Bible Series
Book Two: Stories of Faith, Hope, and Love from the New Testament

The Bible Clicks, Avatar Edition at www.TheBibleClicks.com

The Bible Clicks

A Creative Through-the-Bible Series
Book One

Visit The Bible Clicks at www.TheBibleClicks.com

The Bible Clicks

A Creative Through-the-Bible Series
Book One

*Stories of Faith, Vision, and Courage
from the Old Testament*

Compiled and retold by
Sharon Donohue

ABridge Press

The Bible Clicks, A Creative Through-the-Bible Series
Book One: Stories of Faith, Vision, and Courage from the Old Testament

Nihil Obstat: Douglas Culp
Censor Librorum
March 31, 2010

Imprimatur: Most Reverend Ronald W. Gainer
Bishop of Lexington
March 31, 2010

The nihil obstat and imprimatur are official declarations that a published work is free of doctrinal or moral error. No implication is contained therein that those who have granted the nihil obstat or imprimatur agree with the contents, opinions, or statements expressed, nor do they assume any legal responsibility associated with publication.

Published by ABridge Press

Paperback ISBN 978-1-7350722-0-3

With love

to my daughter, Katie,
who inspired me to write The Bible Clicks,

to my husband, Kevin,
who encouraged me to publish The Bible Clicks,

to my patron, Saint Angela Merici,
who prays we run with perseverance the race marked out for us,

and to Mom D,
who proved that God's Word changes lives,
The Bible Clicks for all ages.

CONTENTS

The Bible Clicks

A Creative Through-the-Bible Series
Book One

INTRODUCTION

"Who is this for," the publisher asked, "kids or adults?"

"It's for people—people read books!"

It was the middle of my interview with author Madeleine L'Engle, and I smiled as she recounted to me her exasperating journey in publishing *A Wrinkle in Time*. The scenario she portrayed could just as easily apply to *The Bible Clicks*. Like Madeleine, I know that people—of all ages—are captivated by compelling stories, and no stories are more intriguing than those portrayed in Scripture, God's storybook for all generations.

The Bible has sold more copies than any other book in the world, yet how many people have read that book cover-to-cover? It is a daunting task because Scripture is like a library, comprised of many smaller books and various genres of writing. But Scripture's rich stories are a gift to all of us, a treasure that should not be buried on dusty shelves. Why not unpack those gems?

The Bible Clicks takes you on a journey through Scripture, traveling from Genesis through Revelation in 365 episodes—stories that appeal to all ages of readers, for all ages of time, using these two portals:

Book One
Stories of Faith, Vision and Courage from the Old Testament

Book Two
Stories of Faith, Hope, and Love from the New Testament

When you travel through Scripture by way of stories, the Bible clicks.

Enjoy the journey!

God's Creation

TBC Book One, Chapter 1
Genesis 1:1-2:3

It is hard to imagine how our world came into being, because no one was there to watch it—except God. People today have a lot of ideas to explain how the world came to be. They also have a lot of questions. But the first people on earth brought their questions to God, and God explained it this way. . . .

In the beginning, the earth looked nothing like it does now. It was dark and empty. But my Spirit was upon it. So when I said, "Let there be light, there was light." Yet I did not remove the darkness. The light I called "day," the darkness "night."

At that time, all you would have seen was water. I decided to draw up some of the water to hold it above the earth. So I made a special area for that water, the sky. That was my second step in creating the world. And I liked what I saw.

On the third day, I took the waters that were below the sky and gathered them to one place. That made room for dry ground. The dry ground I called "land," and the waters I called "seas." I commanded the land to produce seed-bearing plants and trees.

The fourth day I said, "Let there be lights in the sky to separate the day from the night. They will mark the days, the seasons, and the years. From now on it is their job to give light on the earth." The sun lights the earth by day, the moon by night. I also made the stars you see in the sky at night. They are like lights in the heavens, maintaining day and night and separating light from darkness.

Then I looked at all that I had made thus far, and I thought to myself, *This is good.*

The fifth day I made creatures that could live in the water. I also made birds that would soar across the sky. After making the sea creatures and birds, I saw that this, too, was good. So I blessed them and said, "May you have offspring and fill the earth."

On the sixth day I commanded the land to produce living creatures that would reproduce and bear offspring that looked like their parents—

livestock, creatures that move along the ground, and wild animals. So out of the dust I made them, and that, too, was good.

Then I said, "Let us make a being whose nature resembles God. He will rule over the fish, the birds, and the animals—over the whole earth." So from the dust of the ground, I made a man, and his image differed from the animals. I could have friendship with him.

I blessed all the creatures and said, "You will have young ones like yourselves who will grow up and have little ones of their own. In time you will fill the earth." To the man I said, "You and your descendants will rule over them. The plants and trees will provide you with food."

As for the animals, the beasts, the birds, the creatures that move on the ground—in fact, every being that has the breath of life in it—I gave them every green plant to feed on. They were happy with that. And when I watched them, I was happy, too.

By the seventh day I was finished. So I rested on that day and made it a special one. Now you, the people of my creation, must follow my example. If you keep that day holy, that is, if you set aside your work that day and worship me, I will bless you.

And that was just the beginning. . . .

TBC 1

The First People

TBC Book One, Chapter 2
Genesis 2:4-25; 1:28; 3:20

Of all God's creation, one creature stood out above all. Man held a special place in God's heart. The Creator prepared a place for him to live, a beautiful garden called "Eden." The river that watered it separated into four headwaters: the Pishon, Gihon, Tigris, and Euphrates. Today those rivers flow a different course; we can only guess where the Garden of Eden was located, somewhere near the eastern Mediterranean gulf. It was there that man began to serve God, by working in the garden. And it was there that he began his life's journey.

In the center of the garden stood two trees unlike any others. Every time Adam saw them, he could hear a voice within, the words God had spoken on their first walk: "Adam," he said, "I have made all this for you. You may eat from any of these trees. But there is something you must know about those two trees—the ones in the middle of the garden. The first is the tree of the knowledge of good and evil. The one beside it is the tree of life. I forbid you to eat from the tree of the knowledge of good and evil. If you eat from that tree, you will surely die."

Adam was never sure what to think about those words. He was so innocent that he never even thought about doing bad things. All he knew for sure was that the Creator loved him, and he loved the Creator. And that was enough. He would keep away from that strange, beautiful tree.

Day after day the Lord God would enter the garden to meet with Adam. The two of them would walk together in the cool of the day. How Adam loved those walks! So did the Creator.

Then one day the Lord said, "Adam, you have a name because I gave you one. None of the animals have a name. I have made you caretaker over Eden. What would you name each of these creatures?"

This was a new job, deciding what to call each living creature. At God's command, the animals eagerly approached them. As Adam began to give them names, he noticed something unusual. For every kind of animal God had made, there was more than one. In fact, he had never realized it until now. Every creature had a partner—except him.

Adam found himself feeling something he had never experienced before, such a strange feeling that he didn't even know how to describe it. For the first time in his life, he felt alone.

As Adam pondered this, he lay down. A few moments later, he was sound asleep. As he slept, he began to dream. . . . It was as if he had left his own body and was watching himself lying on the ground. There before him, the Lord God opened up his side and took one of his ribs. From that one rib, the Creator fashioned a new creature. In a way, she looked like man. But then again, she looked so different that even the animals stared in amazement. My, she was beautiful!

Adam sat up groggily, wishing he could return to that wonderful dream. Then he turned, and there beside him sat the most gorgeous being he had ever seen—the creature of his dreams!

He reached out to touch her soft, lovely cheek. "What shall I call you?" he said. "You are not at all like the other creatures." She smiled, and his heart soared.

"Ah, I know," he said. "Your bones were made from my bones and your flesh came from my flesh. So I shall call you 'woman,' for you came from man."

From the very beginning, God created the man and the woman to need each other. The woman was made from the man's body to show that he meant for them to be one. And that is why a young man leaves his parent's home—to be joined to his wife to start a new home.

The Lord God blessed the couple and said to them, "May you have many children, and may your children also be blessed with many children. Fill the earth with people and take charge over it." When Adam thought of those joys that lay ahead of them, he named his wife Eve, for he knew she would become the mother of all people.

TBC 2

The Beginning of Sin

TBC Book One, Chapter 3
Genesis 3:1-24

Of the animals the Lord God had made, the serpent was certainly the slyest of them all. Perhaps that is why an evil spirit named Satan hid himself inside the serpent's body. Satan was the most beautiful angel God had created. He was also the most powerful, appointed as arch angel to rule above the others. But something had changed all that. Satan had rebelled against the Lord. And now, this fallen angel stared with keen interest, watching the new creature that God had made.

Eve stood in the middle of the garden, staring at the trees. They were pleasant to look at, and the fruit tasted good. In the middle of the garden God placed two special trees, "the tree of life" and "the tree of the knowledge of good and evil." As Eve stared, the serpent edged near.

"Did God really tell you not to eat from any tree in the garden?" he asked.

"Oh no," she said, "we may. But not from that one in the middle. If we do, we will die."

"Oh, surely you would not die," the serpent said. "Haven't you wondered why God won't let you have that fruit? He knows you will become like God himself in knowing good and evil."

The woman stared at the fruit, admiring its beauty. She wondered what it would be like to be like God, to have his wisdom. So she reached out and took a piece of fruit from the limb.

Nothing happened. Maybe the serpent is right, she thought. *Why did my husband tell me I must not touch it?* Slowly she brought it to her lips. She took a small bite, then another, and another.

Meanwhile, Adam came near. Eve turned around, and when she saw him, she held out the fruit. He could see that she had eaten from it. "Have some," she said. "It's very good."

I wonder why nothing happened? Adam thought. He put the fruit to his mouth and took a bite. At that moment he knew the truth—something did happen. The eyes of both of them were opened in a new way. They had new thoughts and feelings—but the joy was gone. So was their glory. It was as though something within them had died. They suddenly felt embarrassed and ashamed over their nakedness. So they sewed fig leaves together to cover themselves.

Later that day, Adam and Eve heard the Lord God walking in the garden in the cool of the day. But instead of meeting him, they hid. "Adam," the Lord called. "Where are you?"

At first Adam did not answer. He felt torn. Again the Lord called. Finally, Adam called back.

"I heard you walking," he said, "and I was afraid because I was naked. So I hid."

"Who told you that you were naked? Have you eaten from the forbidden tree?"

"The woman you put here with me—she took some first. Then she gave some to me and I ate it." Both of them now appeared. The Lord turned to Eve and said, "What have you done?"

"The serpent deceived me," she said, "and I ate fruit from the forbidden tree."

The serpent was nearby. So the Lord said to the creature, "Because you have done this, I will curse you more than all the animals. From now on you will crawl on your belly and eat dust all your life. I will put hatred between you and the woman, and between your offspring and hers.

"As for you," the Lord said to Eve, "when you bear children, I will greatly increase your pains in giving birth. Since you led your husband to disobey me, from now on he will lead you."

Now he turned to Adam. "Because you disobeyed me by eating the forbidden fruit, I will also curse the ground. You will have to work hard to grow your food, from now until the day you die. I made you from the dust of the ground, and to dust you will one day return."

No longer were Adam and Eve clothed with glory. So the Lord made them clothes from animal skins. But how to repair the broken trust was another matter. And what if they ate from the tree of life? Should they live forever in a fallen world now under his curse? So God drove them out of the Garden of Eden. His holy angels guarded the entrance, and a flaming, flashing sword would remind them of this new, sobering truth— they could never return.

TBC 3

The First Children

TBC Book One, Chapter 4
Genesis 4:1-26

God kept his promise to Eve. After enduring the pains of childbirth, she felt a tremendous new joy. She had given birth to a son and named him Cain. Of course, there were no doctors to help them. But the Lord himself had calmed her fears and helped her through it all. She gave praise to God, saying: "With the Lord's help, I have brought forth a baby boy."

When she became pregnant again, she and Adam now knew what to expect—or so they thought. They had yet to learn that every child is unique. Again her pain was great, but so also was the overwhelming joy. This time she gave birth to another son, and she named him Abel.

Adam and Eve taught their sons to worship the Lord. Regularly they brought offerings to him. The boys learned from an early age that all they received, including the creation of nature, was a gift from God. As they grew older, Abel tended flocks as a shepherd while Cain worked the soil and grew crops.

But one day something tragic happened. It was after the boys, who were now young men, had brought their offerings to the Lord. It began when Cain brought some of the fruits he had grown. Abel, on the other hand, brought fat portions from one of the best firstborns of his flock. The problem came when only one of the offerings was accepted by the Lord.

The Lord was pleased with Abel and the offering from his flock. For some reason, however, God was not pleased with Cain and his offering. When Cain saw that God accepted Abel's offering but rejected his, he became angry. The look on his face showed his resentment.

The Lord noticed this, and he said to Cain, "Why are you angry and disappointed? If you do the right thing, won't you and your offering will be accepted? But if you do not, watch out. Even now you are tempted to do the wrong thing, but you must say no to those feelings."

But Cain had already made up his mind. He was still feeling angry at his brother and jealous because God liked Abel's offering. So Cain listened to his feelings instead of listening to God.

"Abel!" he called. "Let's go out to the field."

Cain led his brother far out into the field where no one could see them. Then he attacked Abel and killed him. He thought no one had seen him do it. But he was wrong.

When he returned from the field, a voice called out to him.

"Cain!" the Lord called. "Where is your brother Abel?"

"I don't know," he answered. Still feeling bitter, he added, "Am I my brother's keeper?"

"What have you done?" the Lord said. "Listen! Your brother's blood cries out to me from the ground. I know what you have done. The ground has opened its mouth to receive your brother's blood. But it will reject you, for I have placed a curse on you.

"You must leave," the Lord commanded. "From now on, whenever you work the ground, no matter where you are, no crops will grow for you. You will wander from place to place, but you will never find peace within you. You will always be a restless wanderer."

Cain cried out in anguish. "My punishment is more than I can bear," he said. "Today you are driving me from this land, and I will be away from you, unable to sense your presence. I will always be a restless wanderer on the earth, and whoever finds me will kill me."

"No," the Lord said, "if anyone kills you for what you have done, I will punish him seven times harder than I am punishing you." Then God put a mark on Cain, and no one would interfere with the Lord's discipline: Cain left God's presence, traveling east to the land of Nod.

Adam and Eve were heartbroken. In a single day they lost both their sons. But God knew their pain. In time, Eve became pregnant again. She gave birth to another son.

"I will name him Seth," she said, "for God has granted me another son to take Abel's place." As Seth grow up, he held a special place in their hearts—and in the heart of God.

TBC 4

Noah and the Ark

TBC Book One, Chapter 5
Genesis 5:1-32; 6:1-8:19; Hebrews 11:5,6

Adam and Eve had no idea God would bless them with many other children besides Seth. After knowing the joys, and heartaches, of being parents, they now discovered a new pleasure— they were grandparents. Their sons and daughters grew up and had children of their own. Generation after generation was born. Some think people in those days lived much longer than we do today. One man, Methusaleh, is said to have lived 969 years.

Methusaleh's father, Enoch, was special not only to the people around him, but also to the Lord, for Enoch walked with God. The two of them enjoyed each other's company the way friends look forward to being together. Enoch eagerly spent time with God, and that pleased the Lord very much. In fact, God was so pleased that he did something he had never done for any other person. When Enoch was 365 years old, the Lord took him from earth—Enoch never died.

But in those days, few people were devoted to God like Enoch. Instead of spending time with God, they spent their time dreaming up evil schemes. Their behavior had grown so terrible the Lord became grieved that he had made man, and his heart was filled with pain.

Because man's wickedness was so terrible and so widespread, the Lord made a grave decision. He said, "I will wipe out mankind from the face of the earth. This world is filled with violence because the people are totally corrupt. For that reason I will destroy both them and the earth."

But there was one man who was different. Noah was a righteous man: No one had anything bad to say about him. And like Enoch, he walked with God. So the Lord decided he would reveal his plans to Noah. He would still destroy the world, but he would save Noah and his family.

God told Noah that he would also spare some of the animals—two of every kind of creature, one male and one female, and seven pairs of the birds and animals used for sacrifices in worship, animals that chewed the cud and had a split hoof, like the cow.

God had a special plan. The Lord commanded Noah to build an ark out of cypress wood and to coat it with pitch. It would be a triple-decked boat, 450 feet long, 75 feet wide, and 45 feet high—large enough to house Noah's family, the animals, and all the food they would need.

This was an overwhelming task. It would take years to build a boat like that. And what would people say? After all, this couldn't be done in secret. But God knew that; it was all part of the plan. So Noah obeyed the Lord. By the time he was 600 years old, the ark was finished.

Noah gathered his family and led them up the ramp and into the massive boat. His sons, Shem, Ham, and Japheth, had helped him build it. They and their wives gathered the food that they and the animals would need. The eight of them now watched as God sent to the boat the animals he would spare. Seven days later, the Lord shut them in, and it began to rain.

Rain fell on the earth 40 days and nights, for God had released the floodgates of water from the sky and the springs of water on earth. The waters rose quickly, covering the mountains by a depth of 20 feet. It was a tragic flood. Every animal, every bird, and every person died.

When the rain finally stopped, the waters continued to flood the earth for 110 more days, and then the water started to go down. By the fifth month the ark rested on Mount Ararat, in what is today the country of Turkey. Two months later the mountaintops could be seen.

After 40 more days Noah opened the window and sent out a raven. It kept flying back and forth. Then Noah sent out a dove, but it soon flew back. Seven days later he sent it out again, and it returned with a freshly plucked olive leaf!

A week later, Noah sent the bird out once more. This time it did not return. Finally, the waters had completely receded. So now, after slightly more than a year in the ark, Noah could remove the covering. God told the family it was time to come out. The ground had dried.

TBC 5

Man's Plan Versus God's Plan

TBC Book One, Chapter 6
Genesis 8:20-22; 9:1-17; 10:1-32; 11:1-9

When Noah and his family stepped out of the ark, they were awestruck by the stillness. With all the animals now off the ark, they suddenly realized that they were alone. Were they really the only people God had chosen to spare? This new realization was hard to imagine.

They were grateful God spared their lives, but the thought of those who had died brought pain. Noah had warned them, just as God had prompted him, but they had refused to listen.

The family piled stones to build an altar, and the aroma of the sacrifices pleased God. As they bowed in worship, the Lord said, "Never again will I curse the ground because of mankind, even though his heart is filled with wickedness. Never again will I destroy all of earth's living creatures."

Then God blessed Noah and his sons. "May you bear many children and fill the earth. All the animals will fear you. You may take them for food, just as you eat the plants. But do not eat meat with its blood in it. And from now on, I will hold you accountable: If anyone commits murder, he will pay for it with his own life and his own blood. For you are made in God's image.

"I now establish my covenant—my agreement—with you, your descendants, and every living creature. Never again will all life be cut off by flood waters, and I have set this as my sign in the clouds." They all looked up, and there in the sky they saw a magnificent rainbow.

Eventually the family began doing things they had done before the flood. Noah grew crops, just as he had done in years past. He planted a vineyard, and when the grapes ripened, he made some wine. At first he drank just a little. But the more he drank, the more he craved.

Now he was lying down, for the wine made him drunk. He didn't know that his youngest son, Ham, had walked into his tent. Ham looked at the wine, realized his father was drunk, and saw that he was naked. But instead of covering him, he boasted to his brothers that he had seen their father naked. His brothers were alarmed. They knew they must find a way to protect their father's dignity. So they walked into the tent with their backs turned and covered him with a blanket.

When Noah woke up and learned what Ham had done, he was enraged. He cursed both Ham and his descendants, who would come to be known the Canaanites.

From Noah's three sons, God began to repopulate the earth. The oldest son, Japheth, became the father of those who eventually traveled north, into the coastal parts of what is today Europe and Asia. His second son, Shem, became the father of the Semitic peoples in the East. Noah pronounced a special blessing on Shem and his descendants, predicting that in the years to come, Shem's descendants and Japheth's descendants would rule over the Canaanites.

As the population grew, various dialects developed, but people could still understand one another. They began to move eastward and settle in the plains of Shinar, later called Babylonia. They baked bricks, which were superior to stone, and they learned to use tar as mortar.

In time the people gathered and said, "Let's work together to build a city, with a tower reaching to the heavens. Then we will become famous and keep from being scattered." So instead of spreading outward, as God had commanded, they began building upward.

Their plans, of course, were no secret to the Lord. As he watched them work, he thought: *If as one people with one language they have begun to do this, then nothing will be impossible for them. Let us go down and confuse their language.*

The people made tremendous progress, until something bizarre happened. One day, quite suddenly, the tribes were unable to understand one another—they were speaking different languages. When they could not understand one another, it became impossible to work together, and they stopped building their tower, which became known as "Babel," meaning "confusion." For the Lord had caused confusion with their language, and God's plan prevailed.

TBC 6

The Greatest Man on Earth?

TBC Book One, Chapter 7
Job 1:1-22

A story is told of a remarkable man named Job who lived in an ancient land called Uz. Many things were unusual about Job, but most noteworthy of all was his reputation for choosing to do what was right—for respecting God and hating evil.

God had blessed him with seven sons and three daughters. He had tremendous wealth, included thousands of sheep and camels, hundreds of oxen and donkeys, and countless servants. No one doubted he was one of the greatest men who lived in the East.

Job's sons regularly held banquets in their homes and invited their sisters to these feasts. And after each banquet, Job would sacrifice a burnt offering on his children's behalf, in case any of them had sinned and silently cursed God.

One day, unbeknown to Job, the angels came to present themselves before the Lord, and Job's whole life was about to change. The rebellious angel, Satan, had come with them, and the Lord said to him, "Where have you come from?"

Satan answered, "From roaming through the earth and going back and forth in it."

Then the Lord said to Satan, "While you were roaming the earth, did you notice my servant Job? There is no one like him on the whole earth. The man is faultless—he always chooses to do what's right. He respects God and turns away from anything that's evil."

"Does Job respect God for nothing?" Satan replied. "You have you put a hedge around him, protecting him, his household, and everything he has. You have blessed everything he does. His flocks and herds spread throughout the land. So of course he blesses you. But if you were to stretch out your hand and strike everything he has, surely he would curse you to your face."

Satan sneered, daring the Lord to meet his challenge.

"Very well," the Lord replied. "Everything he has is in your hands to do with as you wish, but you may not lay a finger on Job himself."

Then Satan departed from the Lord's presence.

Not long after that, a servant came running to Job and he could hardly catch his breath.

"What's wrong?" Job asked.

"While your sons and daughters were feasting," he said, "Sabaeans attacked us in the field. They killed all the other servants and stole the oxen and donkeys!"

While the servant was still speaking, another messenger came running up to Job. "The fire of God has fallen from the sky!" he shouted. "It burned up your sheep and your servants. I'm the only one who escaped death!"

While he was still explaining what had happened, yet another messenger ran up to them. "The Chaldeans formed three raiding parties," he said. "They swept down on your camels and carried them off. All your servants were put to the sword, except me, for I escaped!"

While he was still speaking, a fourth messenger came racing up. His news was so urgent that he blurted it out: "While your sons and daughters were feasting, a mighty desert wind swept in and struck the house. It collapsed on them and they all died. I am the only one who survived!"

At this, Job tore his robe and wailed. Then he shaved his head, for there was no greater way to show the grief he was feeling and the loss he now mourned.

Finally, Job fell to the ground. With his face buried in his hands, he worshiped God.

"O Lord!" he cried. "Naked I came from my mother's womb, and naked I will leave. The Lord gave me much, and now the Lord has taken it away. May the Lord's name be praised."

Meanwhile, all heaven watched and listened. In all that had happened to him, Job did not sin by accusing God of wrongdoing.

TBC 7

The View from Heaven

TBC Book One, Chapter 8
Job 2:1-42:17

Another day, the angels came again to present themselves before the Lord, and once again, Satan came with them. "Where have you come from?" the Lord asked. "

From roaming through the earth," Satan replied, "and going back and forth in it."

Then the Lord said to him, "Have you watched my servant Job? There is no one on earth like him. He is faultless, choosing only what is right. Here is a man who fears God and turns from evil. And he still maintains his integrity, even though you incited me against him."

"Skin for skin!" Satan replied. "A man will give all he has for his own life. But if you were to strike his flesh and bones, he would surely curse you to your face."

"Very well," the Lord said to Satan. "He is in your hands, but you must spare his life."

Then Satan went out from the Lord's presence and afflicted Job with painful sores. They itched so miserably that Job scraped himself with a piece of broken pottery as he sat among the ashes. His wife cried bitterly, "Are you still holding on to your integrity? Curse God and die!"

"You speak like a foolish woman," Job replied. "Shall we accept good from God and not trouble?" She glared and walked away. But in all that happened, Job did not sin in what he said.

Word spread of Job's misfortunes, and three friends came to comfort him. For seven days they sat with him, not saying a word. Finally, Job spoke. He cursed the day of his birth.

His friend Eliphaz confronted him. "Has God ever destroyed anyone for being innocent? Surely you must have sinned. Appeal to God. Confess your sins and accept his discipline."

Job was appalled. "Are you 'friends' calling me a liar? If I sinned, what have I done?"

At this, Bildad's face grew red with anger. "Do you regard us as stupid cattle, unable to give counsel? When your children sinned, God judged them! You have trusted in your wealth."

Job shook his head. "I despise my life," he said, "although I am blameless. If only I had someone to stand as a mediator and plead my case before God. . . ."

Now Zophar spoke up. His words held a cutting edge: "You talk if you were faultless! How I wish God himself would rebuke you. In the end the wicked get what they deserve."

Job dropped to his knees. Then he raised his hands and cried out, "Though God slay me, yet will I trust him. Surely I will defend myself to his face and be delivered."

During this time another man came and sat among them. Elihu was much younger than they. For that reason, he said nothing. But now, he too felt flushed with anger. Finally, he spoke.

He turned to Job's friends and said, "Do you realize what you have done? All of you have condemned this man. Yet no one has produced any evidence to prove these accusations."

Job was impressed with the young man's wisdom—until he turned to Job. "And you, sir," he said. "Listen to yourself! Do you realize you have justified yourself rather than God?"

As soon as the young man finished rebuking them, a storm suddenly arose. From this fearful storm, the Lord himself called out to Job with a voice that sounded like thunder.

"Brace yourself, and I will question you. Where were you when I laid earth's foundation? Do you question my justice? Would you condemn me to justify yourself? God reigns over the proud." They were terrified.

Job shook as he cried out, "How can I reply? I repent in dust and ashes."

The Lord now turned his attention to Job's friends. He rebuked all three of them. Then God commanded them to make sacrifices so Job could pray for them.

Finally, the Lord did something that far surpassed Job's desires. He blessed him with ten more children and double his livestock. And he honored Job by granting him a long, full life.

Job was a rich man indeed—rich in the mercies of God.

TBC 8

God Chooses Abram

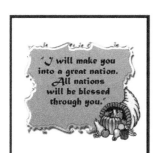

TBC Book One, Chapter 9
Genesis 11:27-12:20

God continued to take a special interest in the descendants of Shem. One man, Terah, stood out as someone who knew what it meant to have friendship with God. Yet he was also influenced by the pagan gods that his family worshiped.

Now Terah had three sons: Haran, Nahor, and Abram. Haran, the oldest, had a son named Lot and a daughter named Milcah. But he died in Ur of the Chaldeans, when his children were young. His younger brother Nahor eventually married Haran's daughter, Milcah. In those days, it was not unusual to marry within one's family, and Abram married his half-sister, Sarai. She, too, was a daughter of Terah.

Terah knew the Lord was prompting him to move away from their homeland, known for its pagan moon-god. So he took his youngest son, Abram, his daughter, Sarai, and his grandson, Lot. Together they set out for the land of Canaan. But they stopped in Haran, for it offered great opportunities to buy and sell and to grow prosperous. Here, too, people worshiped the moon-god. Terah was content to settle there, and there he remained until his death at age 205.

During those years, the Lord began to speak to Terah's son, Abram. "Leave this country," the Lord urged him. "Leave your people, even your father's household. Go to the land that I will show you, and I will make you into a great nation and bless you. I will bless those who bless you and curse those who curse you. And all peoples on earth will be blessed through you."

Me, the head of a great nation? Abram thought. This was hard to imagine. It appeared that his wife, Sarai, was not able to get pregnant. Still, Abram could not resist the voice of the Lord. So at age 75, he set out for Canaan with his wife, Sarai, his nephew, Lot, and all of their possessions, for in Haran they had acquired much wealth and many servants.

After many days they arrived in Canaan, near the great tree of Moreh at Shechem. Many Canaanites were in the land, and Abram began to wonder whether this was really a wise idea. That's when the Lord appeared to him.

"To your offspring," the Lord said, "I will give this land." So in that very spot, Abram built an altar to worship the Lord.

Then Abram went to another part of Canaan, the hills of Bethel. There he pitched his tent, with Bethel on the west and Ai on the east. He built another altar and proclaimed that the Lord is God. Some time later, Abram continued his journey toward the Negev.

Now there was a famine in the land, and it was so severe that Abram's household was forced to travel to Egypt, where there was more food. But as they headed for Egypt, Abram thought, *My wife, Sarai, is so beautiful. . . . What will happen if the Egyptians are attracted to her?*

"Sarai," he said, "I know what a beautiful woman you are. When the Egyptians see you and realize you are my wife, they might kill me to take you. So say that you are my sister. Then they will treat me well for your sake and my life will be spared."

Abram was right. When they arrived in Egypt, the Egyptians did indeed notice she was a remarkably beautiful woman. When Pharaoh's officials saw her, they told Pharaoh. Soon thereafter, Sarai was invited into his palace. The Pharaoh wanted her for a wife in his harem.

Meanwhile, Abram was treated well because of her. Pharaoh gave him sheep and cattle, male and female donkeys, menservants and maidservants, and camels. But the Lord punished Pharaoh by inflicting serious diseases on him and his household.

Why is this happening to us? Pharaoh wondered. When he finally realized he was being judged by God, he summoned Abram.

"What have you done to me?" Pharaoh said. "Why didn't you tell me she was your wife? Why did you say she was your sister? Here is your wife. Take her and go!"

So the Lord prompted Pharaoh to send Abram away with all the belongings he had acquired. And Abram was grateful for the mercy of God.

TBC 9

Parting as Friends

TBC Book One, Chapter 10
Genesis 13:1-14:24

Abram breathed a sigh of relief as he left Pharaoh's court. He could now return to the Negev in Canaan with his wife, his nephew, Lot, and all his possessions. While he was in Egypt, he had become very wealthy in livestock and in silver and gold.

When Abram reached Bethel, he found the altar that he had built when he first arrived in Canaan. Once again he worshiped and declared to the people around him that the Lord is God.

During their time in Egypt, Lot also had acquired great herds and flocks and tents. Now the land where they sojourned could no longer support them both, and quarreling arose between their herdsmen. Abram knew he must deal with the situation.

"Let's not quarrel," he said to Lot, "for we are brothers. Let us now part. You go one way, I'll go the other."

Lot looked out in the distance. The plain of the Jordan was well watered, like the garden of the Lord and the land of Egypt near Zoar. There was no doubt which land was better. So Lot pitched his tents near Sodom. Abram went the other way and lived in Canaan.

Soon after Lot had left, the Lord spoke to Abram. "Lift up your eyes," he said, "and look in every direction. All the land that you see I will give to you and your children forever. I will make your offspring as numerous as the dust of the earth. Now go and walk throughout the entire land that you see, for I am giving it to you." So Abram moved his tents and traveled to the great trees of Mamre at Hebron. There he built another altar and worshiped the Lord.

At this time a conflict arose between some of the tribes living near Sodom and Gomorrah. Kedorlaomer, the king of Edom, faced a struggle with his vassals, five tribal kings who had been forced to pay tribute. It was not unusual for a dominant tribal leader to force the smaller tribes into paying him gold or silver or other things of value. This was the price they paid for peace. The agreement also offered them protection from other tribal chiefs who might wage war.

After 12 years of serving Kedorlaomer, these five smaller tribes decided to break away. So Kedolaomer made plans to regain his control. Within two years, he joined forces with three other kings. Their forces conquered territory that stretched from the hill country of Seir to the desert of Paran. When they reached the Valley of Siddim, the tribes who rebelled were waiting.

What the five tribal kings did not know was that the valley was full of tar pits. So when they turned to retreat, many fell into the pits. The rest of them fled to the hills. Then the four conquering kings seized all their goods, including the wealth from Sodom and Gomorrah. They captured the people and took them as their slaves. Among those taken captive was Abraham's nephew, Lot.

When Abram learned of this, he called out his 318 men that he had trained for battle. With his local allies, the tribal leaders Mamre, Eshcol, and Aner, Abram set out to rescue Lot.

During the night Abram divided his men to attack the four kings. Caught off guard by that maneuver, the king's army fled. Abram pursued them as far north as Hobah, north of Damascus. There he found Lot and all the other captives, as well as their possessions. All the stolen goods had been recovered. Together with his allies, Abram escorted them back to Sodom.

In the Valley of Shaveh, Abram was greeted by Melchizedek, king of Salem. He was priest of God Most High, who created heaven and earth. Melchizedek brought out bread and wine. Then he blessed Abram and God. Abram, in turn, gave him a tenth of everything.

The king of Sodom also came to meet Abram. "I will make an agreement with you," he said. "Give me the people you rescued, and I will allow you to keep the goods for yourself."

This wasn't the first time Abram had been tempted by wealth. But now he did not waver.

"No," Abram said. "I have taken an oath before the Lord. I will accept nothing from you, so you can never say, 'It was I who made Abram rich.'" Then Abram and his people returned home.

TBC 10

God's Promise to Abram

The Lord reminded him of the plan God had for his life.

TBC Book One, Chapter 11
Genesis 15:1-21

Some time after Melchizedek had met with Abram, the Lord spoke to Abram in a vision, which was like a dream. Perhaps Abram had been feeling troubled, for the Lord said to him, "Do not be afraid, Abram. I am your shield, your very great reward."

Abram sighed. "O Sovereign Lord," he said, "what can you give me since I am childless?" Abram called him "sovereign" because he believed that God rules over all that happens in our lives. Yet he spoke to God the way one speaks to a friend, pouring out his heart.

"You have given me no children, so all I own will one day go to my servant, Eliezer."

"No, he will not inherit your possessions. You will have a son, and he will be your heir."

Taking Abram outside, the Lord said to him, "Look up in the sky and count the stars—if you can. That's how numerous I'll make your off-spring."

Abram gazed up at God's creation in the heavens. He believed the Lord, just as he had believed him years ago when he left Ur. Because Abram had taken God at his word, the Lord accepted him as a friend, for that is the kind of faith God desires.

As Abram gazed at the stars, the Lord reminded him once again of the plan God had for his life. The Lord knew that Abram must not lose sight of what God was calling him to do.

"I am the Lord," he said, "who brought you out of Ur of the Chaldeans. I have brought you here to give you this land. I want you to take possession of it."

The task before him seemed impossible. How could he take possession of a land filled with other people? Many questions came to mind as he pondered God's words. Again he sighed.

"O Sovereign Lord, how can I know I will gain possession of it?"

The Lord replied, "Bring me a heifer, a goat, and a ram, each three years old. Then bring me a dove and a young pigeon."

Abram did as the Lord commanded him. He sensed what the Lord was about to do. Animals like these were used as sacrifices; they were also used to seal an agreement.

His hunch was right. The Lord would confirm his promise. So Abram took the heifer, the goat, and the ram and cut each of them in half. Then he arranged the halves opposite each other. The birds he left whole. A few moments later, some birds of prey flew down on the carcasses, but Abram drove them away.

As the sun began to set, Abram fell into a deep sleep. A thick and dreadful darkness now swept over him. Then the Lord spoke.

"Know for certain that your descendants will be strangers in another country for 400 years. They will be enslaved and mistreated. But eventually I will punish that nation. After that time, your people will come out with great possessions.

"As for you, I will bless you, and you will live a long, peaceful life. Then I will take you home to be with your fathers who died before you."

That night, a smoking firepot with a blazing torch suddenly appeared. God caused the torch to pass between the pieces. Abram understood the meaning behind those objects and the reason why they appeared in the thick darkness. They symbolized God's holiness in the midst of a sinful world. The Lord was choosing a special people for himself. Like these symbols, they would be set apart as a holy people.

Abram would never forget this ceremony and the covenant it represented: "To your descendants I give this land, from the Wadi River of Egypt to the great river, the Euphrates." The people in Canaan would never accept this. But that, too, was part of God's plan. . . .

TBC 11

Sarai and Hagar

TBC Book One, Chapter 12
Genesis 16:1-16

Ten years passed since the Lord made his promise to Abram, and Sarai was beginning to lose hope. God had blessed them with many possessions and many servants. But with each new baby born to their servants, Sarai felt a twinge of pain and regret. Abram was now 85; Sarai was in her 70s. What woman her age had ever gotten pregnant? Sarai knew the promise God made to her husband. But what about her inability to conceive? Deep in thought, she stared at the servant with her infant, and an idea came. *Perhaps there is another way.*

Later, when she was alone with Abram, Sarai brought up her idea. "Since the Lord has kept me from having children, why don't we build our family through my maidservant?"

In those days, it was not uncommon for a barren woman to have children through a servant. Her husband would take the servant as another wife. Once she got pregnant, the baby was considered the child of her mistress. Sarai reasoned she could adopt the baby as her own.

As long as Sarai lived, Abram would never have taken another wife. But since this was her idea, he agreed. After all, God did say he would bless him with children. Perhaps this is what he had intended all along. So Abram took the Egyptian servant Hagar as his wife.

It wasn't long before Hagar became pregnant, and she began to lord it over Sarai. *Surely I am more than just a servant now,* Hagar thought. *I have given my master a child; my mistress could never do that.* Hagar's joy took on a haughty disposition and tensions mounted. And now the only thing Sarai regretted more than her barrenness was her decision to give Hagar to Abram.

Sarai's feelings of anger grew until one day she lashed out at Abram. "You are responsible for the wrong I am suffering!" she cried out. "I gave you my servant as a wife. But now that she is pregnant, she despises me. May the Lord judge between you and me!"

Abram had enough of this bickering. Angrily, he replied, "Hagar is still your maidservant, subject to you. So do whatever you wish."

That was all Sarai needed to hear. Now that Abram confirmed her authority over Hagar, Sarai began to mistreat her. Hagar realized she was still a slave in the eyes of Abram. And Sarai would never let her forget that. She wished she had never been given to Abram.

Sarai made her life so miserable that Hagar slipped out of their camp and ran away. She took the road to Shur, which would lead to her homeland, Egypt. But all this while, the Lord had been watching. Both Sarai and Hagar had forgotten that nothing escapes his notice.

Hagar finally reached a spring in the desert, and there the angel of the Lord spoke to her. "Hagar, servant of Sarai, where have you come from, and where are you going?"

At first, Hagar thought this was just a stranger. But when she realized he knew her, she was amazed. She was still in awe as she answered him: "I'm running away from my mistress."

The angel of the Lord spoke gently. "Go back to your mistress and submit to her. I will give you so many descendants that you can't even count them. The child you carry is a son. You shall name him Ishmael (God hears) for the Lord has heard your misery." In their culture, names were significant, and the meaning of a name often revealed something about that person.

The angel of the Lord also revealed what the future held for him. "When your son grows up, he will father a wild tribe of people, living in hostility with the neighboring peoples."

From that time on, Hagar referred to the Lord as, "You are the God who sees me." For she said, "I have now seen the One who sees me." She even gave a name to the well where he spoke, "Beer Lahai Roi," meaning "well of the Living One who sees me."

So Hagar obeyed the Lord and returned to her mistress, Sarai. What was spoken to her did came true. When Abram was 86 years old, Hagar bore a son, and they named him Ishmael.

TBC 12

The Sign of God's Covenant

TBC Book One, Chapter 13
Genesis 17:1-27; 18:1-15

Thirteen years after Ishmael was born, the Lord once again appeared to Abram. Twenty-four years had passed since God first made his promise. Abram was now 99 years old, and he was startled by the voice he heard so clearly: "I am God Almighty. Walk before me and be faultless. I will confirm my covenant with you and increase your numbers."

Abram fell facedown as the Lord continued to speak to him.

"This is my everlasting covenant. Your name will now be Abraham (father of a multitude), for I have made you a father of many nations. Your descendants will be kings, and I will give you the land of Canaan. I will be your God and the God of your descendants.

"Now you must keep my covenant. As the sign of this agreement, every boy among your household must be circumcised. He must have his foreskin cut off when he is eight days old.

"As for your wife, Sarai, you must no longer call her by that name. From now on you are to call her Sarah (meaning "princess"). I will bless her, and surely I will give you a son by her. She will become the mother of nations; kings of peoples will come from her."

Once again, Abraham fell down in worship. But he laughed within. *Will a son be born to a man who is 100 years old? Will Sarah bare a child at age 90? And what about Ishmael?* Finally, Abraham spoke up: "If only my son Ishmael might live under your blessing!"

"Yes," said the Lord, "I hear what is on your heart. But my promise is through Sarah. This time next year she will have a son, and you will name him Isaac. As for Ishmael, I will surely bless him as well and make him into a great nation. He will become the father of twelve rulers. But my covenant is not with him. It is with Isaac."

So Abraham circumcised every male among all the servants in his household. Not long after this, three strangers appeared to him near the great trees of Mamre. Abraham saw them coming as he sat near the opening of his tent. So he stood up and hurried to greet them.

Bowing low, he said, "If I have found favor in your eyes, my lord, may you and your companions stop here for a while. This heat is unbearable. I will have water brought to you so you can wash your feet. Then you can rest under this tree while I get you something to eat."

"Very well," the first man answered.

Abraham hurried to call Sarai. While she arranged for the servants to bake bread, he selected a choice calf and ordered a servant to prepare it as quickly as he could. Then Abraham served his guests some curds and milk. When the meat was ready, he brought it out to them.

He stood in the shade while his guests ate. "Where is your wife, Sarah?" the leader asked.

"She is there, in the tent," he said.

The guest looked at her tent, then turned back and continued to speak. "I will surely return to you this time next year, and by then, Sarah will have a son."

Now the whole time the men were speaking, Sarah was listening to them from the entrance of her tent, which was behind them. When she heard what he said about having a son, she began to laugh, for she was well past the age of childbearing. She thought to herself, *After I am worn out and my husband is old, will I now have this pleasure?*

By now Abraham was beginning to realize this was no ordinary guest. He watched in silence as the man turned around. "Sarah, why did you laugh?" the man asked. "Is anything too hard for the Lord? I will return at the appointed time, and you will have a son."

It startled Sarah to realize he heard her laughing. Embarrassed and afraid, Sarah replied, "No, my lord, I wasn't laughing." But the Lord said, "Yes, you did laugh." And from that moment on, Sarah took his words to heart.

TBC 13

A Severe Judgment

TBC Book One, Chapter 14
Genesis 18:16-19:38

Abraham grew quiet when he realized that his three guests were no ordinary strangers. As they rose to leave, the leader turned to his two companions and said, "Shall I hide from Abraham what I am about to do? No, I will not, for I have chosen him to keep the way of the Lord. You go on ahead of me." The Lord turned to Abraham and said, "The outcry against Sodom and Gomorrah is so great and their sin so grievous that I am about to see it for myself."

Abraham knew what that meant. Those cities were known for their wickedness. Surely God would judge them. But that thought brought a pang to his heart. Lot was living in Sodom.

Abraham glanced at the two who had left for Sodom. He knew this was his only chance. "Lord, I have a question for you. Would you destroy Sodom if it had 50 righteous people?"

"No, he replied, "I would not."

"What if there were only 45?" "No," he answered.

"And if there were only 40?" "No."

"What if there were only 30?" "No."

"And if only 20?" "No."

"Please, my Lord, bear with me. What if there were only ten righteous people?"

"No," he said. "For the sake of those ten I would spare it." Then he turned to leave.

Abraham's heart felt heavy, watching him go. He doubted they had ten righteous people.

Meanwhile, the two angels traveled ahead to Sodom, arriving in the evening. Lot was sitting at the city gate. He greeted them and invited them to his home. They declined, saying that they would sleep in the city square. When Lot heard that, he begged them to come to his home.

The men finally agreed to come. After finishing their meal, they heard a great commotion. Every man in the city had surrounded the house.

"Send out those strangers!" they shouted. The men were demanding to have sexual relations with Lot's two guests.

Lot went outside by himself. "No, my friends," he pleaded. "Don't do this wicked thing."

"You're just a foreigner!" one man shouted. "Who are you to judge us? Get out of the way!" As the crowd surged forward one of the angels pulled Lot inside and struck them with blindness.

The angel now turned to Lot. "If you have any other relatives here, get them out quickly. The outcry to the Lord against these people is so great that he has sent us to destroy this city."

Lot slipped out the door and ran to tell his sons-in-law. But they thought he was joking.

At dawn, the angels urged Lot to hurry and leave. Yet Lot was hesitating. So they grabbed his hand and the hands of his wife and two daughters. Then they led them out of the city, for the Lord was merciful, and he knew what was on Abraham's heart.

"Run to the hills," they warned, "and don't look back."

"No, my lords," Lot begged, "please—I won't be able to make it that far, and I'll be swept away. Couldn't we just flee to Zoar? It's such a small town, isn't it?"

"Very well," one of them answered. "We will spare Zoar. But you must hurry."

By the time Lot's family reached Zoar, the Lord had rained down burning sulfur on Sodom and Gomorrah. Everything was destroyed. The smoke was dense, like that of a burning furnace. The stench was awful. Lot's wife kept thinking of all they had left behind. She stopped suddenly and turned around to see what had happened. In that instant, she became a pillar of salt.

Early the next morning, Abraham returned to place where he had stood before the Lord. As he looked toward Sodom and Gomorrah, all he could see was the dense smoke.

The devastation was so great that Lot was afraid to stay in Zoar. So he took his two daughters and went to the hills, where they lived in a cave.

TBC 14

The Promised Child

TBC Book One, Chapter 15
Genesis 21:1-34

A year after the Lord visited Abraham, something wonderful happened to Sarah. At the age of 90, she gave birth to a son. Abraham named him Isaac, just as the Lord commanded. For Sarah, the name held a double meaning. The word "isaac" means laughter. Sarah's face got red just thinking about that day when the stranger spoke, how she had laughed at his prediction. But she explained the baby's name by saying, "God has brought me laughter, and everyone who hears about this will laugh with me. Who would have said I would nurse children? Yet I have borne Abraham a son in his old age."

Indeed, this baby's birth was truly a gift from God. Not only had Sarah been barren, but both she and Abraham were well beyond child-bearing age. By the time Isaac was born, Abraham was 100 years old. Yes, the Lord had kept his promise. And Abraham would also keep his. When the baby was eight days old, Abraham circumcised him just as God had commanded. This was the sign of God's agreement, the covenant he made with Abraham.

The next special day in Isaac's life came when he was a toddler, the day he would be weaned from drinking his mother's milk. On that day, Abraham held a great feast. Isaac, of course, was the center of attention, for this feast was being held in his honor.

Everyone was having a wonderful time, until Sarah noticed what Ishmael was doing. The young teenager was mocking little Isaac. Sarah knew he was acting out of jealousy, but the thought of what he had done galled her. What might he do when both the boys grew older?

The feast was barely over when Sarah cornered Abraham and told him what Ishmael had done. "So get rid of that slave woman and her son! Never will he share my son's inheritance."

Abraham felt as though a dark cloud were hanging over his head. Ishmael was his son, his own flesh and blood. How could he possibly send him away?

But in the midst of his turmoil, he could hear the Lord speaking to him: "Do not worry, Abraham. This time I want you to listen to Sarah.

She is right when she says my covenant will be kept through Isaac. Do not be afraid for Ishmael. Because he is your offspring, I will make him into a nation, too."

Early the next morning, Abraham took some food and a flask of water and gave them to Hagar. His son was a prince in Abraham's tribe, but Hagar was still just a slave woman. So he set the pack on her shoulder as he sent the two of them away.

It was a painful time for Ishmael. What he didn't know was that it was even more painful for his father. Ishmael kept wiping tears from his eyes as they left Abraham's tents and set out in the desert of Beersheba.

They wandered in the desert until they ran out of water. Hagar told her son to lie down and rest under one of the bushes. Then she slipped off and sat down about a bowshot away from him. *I can't bear to watch him die*, she thought. And all at once, she began to sob.

By this time, the young man Ishmael was also crying.

Suddenly Hagar heard a voice calling to her. It sounded familiar. "What is the matter, Hagar? Do not be afraid. God has heard the boy crying. Go now and comfort him. Do not worry, for I will make him into a great nation."

When she looked up again, she saw a well of water in front of her. She reached out and touched it. No, it wasn't a mirage. Quickly she filled her flask and brought a drink to her son.

As Ishmael grew up, it was evident that God was providing for him. He became known as a skilled archer. And when it was time for him to marry, his mother found him a wife from Egypt. Ishmael's life was not easy, but the Lord was with him.

TBC 15

Abraham's Greatest Test

TBC Book One, Chapter 16
Genesis 22:1-19; Hebrews 11:17-19

Sometimes God brings tests into a person's life. Often the test involves a choice, and the choice one makes reveals whether that person really trusts God. One day, God brought such a test into the life of Abraham.

"Abraham!" the Lord called.

"Here I am," he replied.

"Abraham, I want you to take your son, your only son Isaac, whom you love, and go to the region of Moriah. When you arrive there, I will direct you to a certain mountain. Then I want you to sacrifice Isaac as a burnt offering."

This was one time Abraham wished he had not heard the Lord's voice. All night long he lay awake, wondering what he should do. *Why is God asking me to do this?* he thought. *And what about His promise?* The Lord had spoken clearly on that—he would keep his covenant through Isaac. *That can only mean one thing. . . .* thought Abraham.

He got up early the next morning and saddled his donkey. No one knew what he was planning to do. He called for his son Isaac and two of their servants. The servants were to cut enough wood for a burnt offering. Then they bundled the wood and set out toward Moriah.

They had traveled for three days when Abraham finally saw their destination in the distance. "Stay here with the donkey," he told his servants, "while the boy and I go over there. The two of us will worship on that mountain. Then we will meet you back here."

Abraham took the bundles of wood and placed them on Isaac's shoulder. Then he took the fire and the knife, and they walked away. As they continued their journey, Isaac said, "Father, the fire and the wood are here, but where is the lamb for the offering?"

"God himself will provide the lamb, my son." And Abraham really believed that. For the past three days, he had consoled himself by remembering that God's promise to him would be fulfilled through Isaac. He reasoned that if God wanted him to kill his son, then surely God would raise Isaac from the dead.

When they reached the place God had designated, Abraham and Isaac built an altar for the sacrifice. Carefully they arranged the wood on it. Then Abraham did something that shocked his son. He tied him up and laid him on the altar, on top of the wood.

Abraham loved his son deeply, but he also loved the Lord. His hands shook as he took the knife and raised it in the air. Just as he was about to bring it down, the angel of the Lord called out. "Abraham! Abraham!" he called.

"Here I am," he replied.

"Do not lay a hand on the boy," he said. "Do not do anything to him. Now I know that you fear God, because you have not withheld from me your son, your only son."

Abraham looked up, and there in a thicket he saw a ram caught by its horns. God had indeed provided the sacrifice. Abraham named that place "The Lord Will Provide." From then on came this saying: "On the mountain of the Lord, the Lord will provide."

After the offering was made, the angel of the Lord again called out to Abraham: "I swear by myself, the Lord, that because you have done this and not withheld your only son, I will surely bless you and make your descendants as numerous as the stars and the sand. They will indeed take possession of the cities of their enemies. And through your offspring, all nations on earth will be blessed, because you have obeyed me."

Then Abraham and Isaac rejoined their servants, and they all returned to Beersheba. As Isaac grew into manhood, he often recalled that day, and he learned from watching his father what it meant to love and fear the Lord.

TBC 16

A Wife for Isaac

Shyly Rebekah lowered her veil . . .

TBC Book One, Chapter 17
Genesis 24:1-67

A time of great mourning had now fallen upon Abraham, Isaac, and their entire household. At age 127, Sarah passed away. Isaac was now 37. He had been very close to both his mother and father. An emptiness pierced his soul as he sat alone and pictured her warm smile of approval.

Abraham often thought of how God had blessed him with his beautiful wife. Now he wanted that same joy for his son. So he called his most trusted servant into his tent.

"Put your hand under my thigh to take an oath. You must find a wife for Isaac. Swear that the woman you select will not be from the Canaanites, but from my own relatives."

"What if she is not willing to come?" he asked. "Should I then take your son there?"

"No," Abraham said, "you must not. The Lord will send his angel before you to guide you. If the woman is unwilling to come, you will be released from this oath."

So the servant left the tent and prepared for his journey. He selected ten camels and many gifts from his master's possessions. For one who seeks a bride must not come empty-handed.

The journey took him many days. When he reached a spring near Nahor, he prayed, "O Lord, God of my master Abraham, may you show him kindness in this way: Bring the right girl into my presence. Reveal it by prompting her to say, 'Have a drink, while I water your camels.' "

Before he had finished praying, a girl appeared, and she was beautiful. When the servant asked for a drink, she gave it to him. Then she said, "I'll water your camels, too."

As the servant watched her, his heart began to pound. *This is the one! Wait—I must find out one more thing. . . .*

"Young woman, if I may ask, whose daughter are you?"

"I am Rebecca, the daughter of Bethuel. My father's parents were Milcah and Nahor."

Immediately, the servant bowed down in worship.

"Praise you, Lord, God of my master, Abraham! For you have indeed shown him kindness by leading me to his relatives."

Then he rose and explained why he came.

"Let me run tell my family," Rebekah said.

As Rebekah came running into the house, her brother Laban said, "Where did you get that ring and those bracelets?" With excitement she told her family all about Abraham's servant.

Laban's eyes lit up when he saw the gifts. He rushed to meet the caravan and greet them. "Come, you who are blessed by the Lord! I've prepared a place for you and your camels."

So the caravan continued toward the family's house. But the servant refused to eat until he could explain his mission: "The Lord has blessed my master with great wealth. And it will all go to his son Isaac, born to him in old age by Sarah. I have been sent to find a wife for Isaac, a woman from your household." Then he explained how God had answered his prayer.

Laban and his father Bethuel knew this was not by chance.

"What can we say?" Bethuel replied. "This is obviously from the Lord."

The servant bowed to the Lord in gratitude. Then he gave the family members more gifts.

The next morning, however, Rebekah's brother and mother urged the servant to wait a number of days. But the servant was insistent. He feared that they might change their minds.

"Let's ask Rebekah what she wishes," Laban suggested. But he and his mother were surprised by her response. The servant had told her how terribly Isaac missed his mother. Surely it would please him if she came right away. So she left that day with her family's blessing.

As they traveled, the servant told Rebekah about Isaac. When they finally neared the tents of Abraham, they saw someone in the fields all alone, just meditating. "Who is that?" Rebekah asked. The servant smiled. "That is your husband." Shyly, Rebekah covered herself with her veil.

So Isaac married Rebekah, and he loved her dearly. The loss he had been feeling suddenly began to ease, for she brought him great comfort and much joy.

TBC 17

Jacob and Esau

While Esau hunted with his father,

Jacob stayed close to his mother.

TBC Book One, Chapter 18
Genesis 25:19-34

At the age of 40, Isaac married Rebekah, and both of them now looked forward to the day when they would have a child. But as time went on, it was apparent that Rebekah was barren. This troubled her greatly, and now it was Isaac's turn to comfort her.

"Don't worry," he said. "My own mother was said to be barren, and look, here am I!"

With a heart full of faith, Isaac prayed, and the Lord granted his request. After 20 years of marriage, Rebekah became pregnant. But the pregnancy was not at all what she had imagined it.

She called out to the Lord and asked, "What is happening to me?"

She could hear his voice as though he were speaking within her: "Do not worry," the Lord said. "You have two babies inside your womb. I will make each of them into a nation of people. One nation will be stronger than the other, and the older child will serve the younger."

So at age 60, Isaac became the proud father of twin boys. The first baby to come out of Rebekah's womb was red and hairy. So his parents named him Esau. When he came out of the womb, his brother was grasping his heel. They named that one Jacob, meaning "heel grabber."

As the boys grew, it became obvious their personalities and interests were as different as their appearance. Esau was an outdoorsman. At a young age, he became a skillful hunter, like his father. Isaac always had a taste for wild game, so it surprised no one that he favored Esau.

Jacob, on the other hand, was a quiet man who preferred to stay among the tents. While Esau hunted with his father, Jacob watched his mother and enjoyed doing the things she taught him. He was his mother's son, for Rebekah favored him above Esau.

One day when Jacob was by himself, cooking some stew, his brother Esau came in from the open country. Today he had nothing to show for his labors. Now he was tired and very hungry. The smell of Jacob's cooking drew him near.

"Let me have some of that red stew! I'm famished!" Jacob knew that was one of his favorite meals. It wasn't only his red hair that earned him the nickname him "Edom" (red).

Jacob smiled and said, "Just how hungry are you?"

"Very hungry!" he replied. "Now give me some stew."

"Are you hungry enough to sell me your birthright?"

"What do you mean?"

"I mean, sell me your birthright. Pledge me your birthright and I'll give you some stew."

Esau waved his hand in disgust. "Look, I just told you, I'm starving. So what good is the birthright to me?" To ensure that Esau wouldn't change his mind later, Jacob said, "Swear to me first." So Esau promised on oath to give Jacob his birthright.

Jacob now gave him bread and lentil stew. When Esau finished eating and drinking, he got up and left, as if nothing had happened. That was how little he valued his birthright.

The birthright, however, was important in their culture. It signified the privileges and responsibilities given to the firstborn son. When a father was close to death, he would evenly divide all that he owned among his sons. But the firstborn son received a double portion, for he also held twice as much responsibility for their family. He would care for his widowed mother and any unmarried sisters. He would lead the family in decisions and in guiding them spiritually.

Sometimes a father would not give his firstborn the birthright. If his eldest was unworthy of the privileges or unable to handle the responsibilities, he could select another son.

The birthright brought more than wealth. It also brought the father's spiritual blessing, a prayer to invoke God's favor upon that son. Sometimes the blessing took the form of a prophetic prediction. Jacob had now acquired the birthright, but not the blessing—at least, not yet. . . .

TBC 18

Jacob Tricks Isaac

TBC Book One, Chapter 19
Genesis 27:1-40

Signs of old age weighed heavy on the heart of Isaac, who was now blind. He worried he might slip off in his sleep. He must put his household in order. So he called for his first-born son.

"Esau, my son, get your quiver and bow and go out to the open country to hunt some wild game. Prepare it the way I like it. Then bring it to me so I may give you my blessing."

Rebekah was secretly listening to what Isaac had said. She was afraid this would happen. Immediately she sent for Jacob. When he arrived, she motioned with her hand and whispered.

"We must be careful that no one hears us. Your father is about to give his blessing to Esau. Your brother is out in the fields now, hunting for game so he can bring your father a meal. Here is what I want you to do: Get me two young goats. I'll prepare the meat the way your father likes it. Then you take it to him, as if you are Esau, so he will give you his blessing.

"But Esau is hairy," Jacob said, "and I have smooth skin. What if my father touches me? If he realizes I'm trying to trick him, I will surely bring down a curse rather than a blessing."

"Just do as I say," she insisted, "and let the curse fall on me."

Jacob brought her the goat meat, and she prepared it the way Isaac liked it. Then she gave Jacob some of Esau's clothes, for they carried Esau's scent. *Jacob is right,* she thought. *We must do something to make his skin feel hairy.* So she covered his hands and neck with goat skins.

Jacob took a deep breath as he reached his father's tent. "My father!" he called out.

"Yes, my son," Isaac answered. "Who is it?"

"I am Esau, your firstborn. Sit up and eat your meal so you may give me your blessing."

"How did you get it so quickly?" he asked.

Jacob could feel his face turning red. "The Lord your God gave me success."

"Come near me," Isaac said, "so I can touch you to know whether you really are Esau." Jacob stepped closer and held his breath. Isaac reached out to touch him.

"The voice is Jacob's," he said, "but the hands are Esau's. Are you really my son Esau?"

"I am," Jacob replied. He could feel his heart pounding in guilt.

So Isaac ate and drank. Then he gave Jacob his blessing: "May God give you an abundance of grain and new wine. May nations serve you. May you be lord over your brothers. May God curse those who curse you and bless those who bless you."

After Isaac had blessed him, Jacob left right away. A few moments later, Esau returned from his hunting trip. He, too, prepared some tasty food and brought it to Isaac.

"My father," he said, "sit up and eat so that you may give me your blessing."

Isaac trembled violently. "Who was it that hunted game and brought it to me just now?" he demanded. "I ate it just before you came, and I blessed him—and indeed, he will be blessed!"

"What!" Esau exclaimed. Then he gave a loud and bitter cry. "Bless me too, my father!"

"Your brother came deceitfully," Isaac said. "It is too late. He has taken your blessing."

"His name fits him!" Esau shouted. "First he took my birthright and now my blessing!"

"Father," he wailed, "have you no blessing for me?"

"I have made him lord over you," Isaac said. "All his relatives will be his servants. And I have sustained him with grain and new wine. So what can I possibly do for you now, my son?"

Esau cried out, "My father, have you only one blessing to give?" Then he wept aloud.

Isaac sighed as he felt his son crying on his chest. He put his hand on Esau's shoulder. God's Spirit welled up within him, and he gave this prophecy: "Your dwelling will be away from the earth's richness, away from the dew of heaven. You will live by the sword and you will serve your brother." Then he added, "But when you grow restless, you will throw off his yoke."

TBC 19

Jacob's Dream

TBC Book One, Chapter 20
Genesis 27:41-46; 28:1-22

Sorrow turned to rage as an angry young man stormed out of Isaac's tent. *I'll kill him,* Esau thought, *after our father dies.* His vengeance gave way to angry boasting, and rumors began to spread. When Rebekah heard what he was planning to do, she feared for Jacob's life.

So she called for Jacob and spoke to him privately. "Esau's grudge is much worse than I thought. He is consoling himself by planning to kill you once your father dies. You must flee to my brother in Haran. When Esau calms down and his anger subsides, I will send for you."

"But what about my responsibilities here?" Jacob asked.

"Don't worry. I will talk to your father so that you may leave with his blessing."

Then Rebekah went to Isaac. She knew what would persuade him. "Isaac, I'm disgusted with living because of these Hittite women that Esau has married. If Jacob takes a wife like these Hittite women, my life will be worth nothing!" Isaac sighed. They brought grief to him, too.

Her plan worked. Isaac called for Jacob. He entered the tent and knelt at his father's side.

"My son, I want you to go at once to Paddan Aram, to the house of your mother's father, Bethuel. Take a wife for yourself from among the daughters of Laban, your mother's brother."

Then Isaac reached out and put his hand on Jacob's head. "May God Almighty bless you and increase your numbers until you become a community of peoples. May he give to you and your descendants Abraham's blessing, to take possession of this land, which God gave to Abraham."

As he prepared for his journey, Jacob feared for his life. *What if Esau sees me leaving and he follows me? He could kill me and no one would know. I must leave quickly.*

Jacob covered many miles before his brother learned that he had left. It was the servants who later told Esau that Jacob had left. They said that Isaac had blessed him and sent him to Paddan Aram to take a wife.

Not until then did Esau realize how much his Canaanite wives had displeased his father. *So my father has blessed him again, has he?* That gave Esau an idea.

He traveled to see his uncle, Ishmael, the first son who was born to Abraham. Ishmael had a number of daughters. So Esau arranged to take one of them, Mahalath, as his third wife. He would give special honor to her. Esau was eager to take her to his father and tell him what he had done. *And who knows,* Esau thought, *perhaps I will gain my father's blessing after all.*

But once a blessing was given, it could not be revoked. Jacob would still remain the heir.

As Jacob left Beersheba he set out toward Haran. When the sun began to set, he stopped for the night. Taking one of the stones nearby, he put it under his head as a pillow and lay down.

When he finally fell asleep, Jacob had a dream. He saw a stairway stretching to heaven. The angels of God were ascending and descending on it. At the top of the stairs stood a glorious figure. "I am the Lord," he said, "the God of your father Abraham and the God of Isaac.

"All peoples on earth will be blessed through you and your offspring. I am with you and will watch over you wherever you go, and I will bring you back to this land. I will not leave you until I have done what I have promised you."

When Jacob awoke, he thought, *Surely the Lord is in this place!* Fear gripped his heart. *How awesome is this place. This is none other than the house of God and the gate of heaven!*

The next morning, Jacob took the stone that was under his head and set it up as a small pillar. Then he poured oil on it. That was his way of setting apart that area as a special place. Before then, people called that area Luz. But Jacob renamed it Bethel, meaning "house of God."

Then he prayed a vow. "O Lord, be with me and watch over me on my journey. Give me food to eat, clothes to wear, and a safe return to my father's house. If you do this, then you will be my God, and I will give you a tenth of all you give me." And the Lord heard his prayer.

TBC 20

Jacob's New Family

TBC Book One, Chapter 21
Genesis 29:1-30

After many days of weary travel, Jacob breathed a sigh of relief. He saw a well in the distance and three large flocks grazing nearby. Surely he must be close to Paddan Aram, the homeland of his mother's relatives.

Jacob called out to the shepherds, "My brothers, where are you from?"

"Haran," one of them replied.

"Do you know Laban," Jacob asked, "Nahor's grandson?"

"Yes, we know him."

"Is he well?" Jacob asked.

"Yes, he is. Here comes his daughter Rachel."

As Rachel came with Laban's flock of sheep, Jacob wondered why no one had moved the stone covering from the well. So he walked over to the shepherds and began to talk with them. "The sun is still high," he said. "It can't be time to gather the flocks. Why not water the sheep now then take them back to pasture?"

"We can't," said one of the shepherds. "Not until all the flocks have come." Once all the flocks arrived, the shepherds would roll the heavy stone off from the well and water the sheep. When they were finished they would roll back the covering.

While they were discussing the situation, Rachel arrived with her father's flock. Jacob couldn't help but notice how much she resembled his mother. Without waiting for the others to come, he went to the well, rolled away the stone, and watered his uncle's sheep.

As Rachel thanked him, tears welled up in his eyes. "I am a relative of yours," he said, "the son of your aunt, Rebekah." Then Jacob kissed her and wept aloud. God had led him safely to the very place where his relatives were living.

"I must run and tell my father!" Rachel said. And she raced away to her home.

As soon as Laban heard the news, he ran to meet his nephew. Laban embraced Jacob and kissed him on each cheek. "Come," Laban said. "You have had a long journey. Let's go home." As they walked along, Jacob told him about his family. Laban just kept staring and smiling. Finally, he said, "You are my own flesh and blood. Stay with us as long as you like."

After Jacob had stayed with them for a month, Laban said. "Just because you are a relative of mine, should you work for me for nothing? Tell me what your wages should be."

Now Laban had two daughters. The older one, Leah, had weak eyes. But the younger one, Rachel, was beautiful, and Jacob was attracted to her. So he said, "I'll work seven years in return for your younger daughter, Rachel."

Laban smiled. Then he replied, "It's better that she goes to you rather than some other man. It's a deal. Stay here with me."

Those next seven years seemed like only a few days to Jacob because of his great love for Rachel. At the end of that time, he asked Laban for his wife.

So Laban invited all their friends and gave a marriage feast. But when evening came, he called his other daughter, Leah, and placed the wedding veil over her instead of Rachel. With her face covered, according to custom, he presented her to Jacob, along with Zilpah the maidservant.

Not until the light of morning did Jacob realize he had slept with Leah. Angrily, he raced to his uncle's home. "Why have you deceived me like this?" he shouted.

"It's not our custom to give the younger daughter first," Laban replied. "But I will make you a deal. If you agree to work another seven years, I will give you Rachel as well."

So after he finished Leah's bridal week, Jacob took Rachel as his second wife. Laban gave her Bilhah as a maidservant. For the next seven years, Jacob continued to work for Laban.

TBC 21

Jacob's Children

TBC Book One, Chapter 22
Genesis 29:31-35; 30:1-24

Within a week after her wedding, Leah's joy turned to heartache. She had hoped that, in time, Jacob would learn to love her. But it was obvious Rachel had won his heart. When the Lord saw Leah was not loved, he opened her womb, but let Rachel remain barren. Leah gave birth to a son, naming him Reuben, which meant "a son." For she thought, *The Lord has seen my misery and given me a son. Surely now my husband will love me.*

Leah became pregnant again and gave birth to a second son. She thought her husband would be so pleased that he would begin to love her. "Because the Lord has heard that I am not loved," she said, "he gave me this one, too." So she named him Simeon, meaning "he hears."

After Leah became pregnant a third time, she gave birth to yet another son. She thought, Now at last my husband will become attached to me, for I have borne him three sons. So she named him Levi, meaning "attached."

Leah conceived yet again, and when she gave birth to a fourth son, she said, "This time I will praise the Lord." So she named him Judah, which means "let Him be praised." But after Judah's birth, Leah stopped having children.

When Rachel realized she was not getting pregnant, she became jealous of Leah. She lashed out at Jacob, "Give me children, or I'll die!"

Jacob replied in anger, "Am I in the place of God, who has kept you barren?"

If I can't get pregnant, Rachel thought, *I'll have children through my maidservant.* So Rachel gave Bilhah to Jacob as another wife, to have children through her. Bilhah soon got pregnant and bore him a son. Rachel named him Dan. Then Bilhah gave birth to another son, and Rachel named him Naphtali.

When Leah saw she was having no more children, she did the same thing Rachel did. She gave Jacob her maidservant as another wife. Zilpah became pregnant and gave birth to a son. Leah named him Gad. Then Zilpah bore Jacob another son, and Leah named that one Asher.

Many years had now passed since Jacob married Leah and Rachel. Seeing the infants that were born to their maidservants made both women wish they were pregnant.

One day, during wheat harvest, Reuben found some mandrake plants and brought them to his mother. Leah thought they might help her to get pregnant once more, for the people of that region believed mandrakes would help a woman become more fertile. When Rachel saw the plants, it gave her an idea. She decided to make a deal with her sister. "Give me some of your son's mandrakes," she said, "and Jacob can sleep with you tonight."

So when Jacob returned from the fields, Leah met him and said, "You must sleep with me tonight." Then, with a tone of sarcasm, she added, "I have hired you with my son's mandrakes." So he slept with her that night.

While Rachel was tasting her mandrakes, Leah was praying. And God listened to her.

When the time came for Leah to give birth to her fifth son, she thought, *God has rewarded me for giving Jacob my maidservant.* So she named him "Issachar" for "reward."

In time, Leah bore Jacob yet another son, and she was thrilled. *God has given me a precious gift,* she thought. *Now my husband will treat me with honor because I've borne him six sons.* So she named him Zebulun. Then she bore him a daughter and named her Dinah.

Finally, God heard Rachel's pleas, and he opened her womb so she could conceive. She became pregnant and gave birth to a son.

"God has taken away my disgrace," she said.

She named him Joseph, meaning "may he," hoping God might give her yet another son.

TBC 22

Jacob Flees

They decided to leave without telling Laban.

TBC Book One, Chapter 23
Genesis 30:25-43; 31:1-55

Now that Rachel had given birth to their son, Jacob decided it was time to leave. He met with Laban to tell him about his decision. "I wish to take my wives and my children away from here," he said, "so I can return to my homeland."

Laban was afraid this would happen. *How can I get him to stay?* he wondered.

"I know the Lord has blessed me because of you," Laban said. "Please, I want you to stay. Name your wages, and I will pay them."

Jacob sighed. Perhaps he should consider Laban's offer. "All right," he said. "But don't pay me anything. Instead, let me remove any speckled or spotted sheep or goats from your flocks. They will serve as my wages."

Laban agreed. Then he raced out to his fields and removed all the spotted animals before Jacob could take them.

But God blessed Jacob in spite of Laban's deceitfulness. Jacob took freshly cut branches from poplar, almond, and plane tree. Then he placed them near the watering troughs. The flocks mated there, and when they gave birth, they bore speckled and spotted young.

So Jacob kept those animals for himself. From then on, he took the strongest of all the animals and placed them near the troughs to mate. Those animals continued to bear speckled livestock. Meanwhile, Jacob left the weak animals to mate with Laban's flock.

Jacob soon grew prosperous, owning large flocks and many servants. When Laban's sons saw how wealthy he had become, they grew jealous and complained to their father. Jacob noticed Laban's attitude toward him had changed. And the Lord told Jacob it was time to leave.

So he sent for Rachel and Leah. As they stood in the fields where no one could hear, Jacob broached his plan.

"Your father's behavior toward me has changed. Each time God blessed my livestock, he changed my wages. It was the Lord who gave me the idea about the branches. He revealed it in a dream. Now he has also revealed that we must leave."

Rachel and Leah agreed. "Our father has used all the wealth that was paid for us. Surely the wealth God took away from our father belongs to us and our children. Do what God has told you."

They decided to go without telling Laban. As they prepared to leave, Rachel slipped into her father's home and stole his household idols. No one knew she had done this, not even Jacob.

Jacob and his family traveled ten days before Laban caught up with them. But God had warned him to say nothing good nor bad to his son-in-law. So he simply said, "Why didn't you let me say goodbye to my family? And why did you steal my household gods?"

Jacob replied, "I was afraid you would take your daughters from me. But as for your household gods, I swear to you, if you find anyone here with them, that person shall not live."

Laban searched their tents. But Rachel had hidden the little statues in her camel's saddle bag. Then she sat on it. When her father entered her tent, Rachel pretended she had cramps and could not stand. So Laban could not find the statues that were hidden, and Jacob rebuked him for his accusation.

Laban lashed out in anger: "The women are mine, the children are mine, the flocks are mine! Yet what can I do? Since you are leaving, let's make a covenant, an agreement of peace."

So they set up a pillar and agreed that neither one would cross that border to harm the other. Both of them pledged their oath before God. Then Jacob offered a sacrifice, and he invited Laban and those with him to join them for a feast.

Early the next morning, Laban kissed his grandchildren and his daughters and blessed them. Then he returned to his home. Jacob thought that his troubles were now behind him. Little did he know that they had only just begun. . . .

TBC 23

Jacob Meets Esau

TBC Book One, Chapter 24
Genesis 32:1-32; 33:1-20; Hosea 12:4

Jacob had been away from his homeland for so long that he had almost forgotten why he left—his brother, Esau, wanted revenge. Jacob's mother had reassured him she would send word when Esau calmed down. That message had never come. Could it be that, after all these years, his mother had died? Or did this mean that Esau had never forgiven him? Perhaps it meant both.

Jacob continued his journey with his family, his servants, and his livestock. Finally he reached a familiar place, and the Lord confirmed it with a host of angels to meet him. Yes, the Lord was here. It reminded him of that day years ago, when God's angels visited him in a dream.

With a touch of fear, Jacob sent messengers to Esau. "Tell him I've been with Laban. Explain that I have my own livestock and servants and that I hope to find favor in his eyes."

When the messengers returned, Jacob sensed there was bad news. "Esau is coming to meet you," they said. "He has 400 men with him." Afraid and distressed, Jacob divided all his flocks and herds into two groups. *If one group is destroyed,* he thought, *the other can flee.*

Then Jacob fell to his knees and prayed: "O God of my fathers Abraham and Isaac, O Lord who has told me to return to my home. I know I am not worthy of all your kindness and faithfulness. Save me, I pray, and save the mothers and children from the hand of my brother."

That night Jacob selected some possessions to send ahead of him as a gift to Esau: He sent 200 female goats and 20 males, 200 ewes and 20 rams, 30 female camels with their young, 40 cows and 10 bulls, 20 female donkeys and 10 males. He divided them into separate herds with distance between each group. Then he told each servant, "When my brother meets you and asks where you are going, tell him, 'These belong to your servant Jacob. They are a gift to you.'"

That night Jacob sent his family and possessions across the ford of the Jabbok River. Later, while he was alone, a man came up to him, and they wrestled all night. Finally, the man said, "Let me go, for it is now daybreak." But Jacob refused. So the man touched his hip socket and wrenched it. Still, Jacob clung to him. "I will not let you go unless you bless me," he said.

The man smiled, then he spoke: "Your name will no longer be Jacob, but Israel, for you have struggled with divine and human beings and have prevailed."

"What is your name?" Jacob asked.

"Why do you ask my name?" the man replied. Then he blessed Jacob.

So Jacob named that place Peniel because he had seen God face-to-face and was spared. And from that day on, Jacob walked with a limp.

When morning dawned, Jacob saw Esau coming with his 400 men. Quickly, he divided his family into three groups so some could escape if attacked. Jacob led the way, bowing to Esau as he went. But Esau ran to meet him, threw his arms around him, and kissed him.

When Esau looked up, he said, "Who are they?"

"The children God has graciously given your servant."

"What do you mean by all the droves I met?" Esau asked.

"They are yours," Jacob said. "Please, accept them as my gift."

"I have plenty, my brother," Esau replied. "You keep the droves."

But when Jacob insisted, Esau accepted them. Then he offered to escort Jacob's family.

"No," Jacob said, "you needn't do that. You go on ahead of me. I have to travel slowly with the children." The truth was, Jacob was still fearful.

So Esau returned to Seir, assuming he would meet Jacob there. Jacob, however, went to Succoth, where he built shelters for his livestock. When he arrived within sight of Shechem, he pitched his tent. Then he built an altar, and with a grateful heart, he worshiped the Lord.

TBC 24

Jacob's Favorite Son

TBC Book One, Chapter 25
Genesis 37:1-35

After all he had been through, Jacob should have known better. His mother had favored him, just as Isaac had favored Esau. And what had favoritism brought? Years of painful separation. God had blessed Jacob with a large family and much wealth. But by the time he returned to Canaan, it was too late to share those joys with his mother. So Jacob turned his attention to the family God had given him, but the apple of his eye was his youngest son, Joseph.

Almost 17 years had now passed since Jacob returned. He was no longer the same man. He had even changed his name. He wanted to be called Israel, the name the Lord had given him.

Joseph was a baby when they arrived in Canaan, but now he was a young man, and his father treated him like a prince. Born to Israel in old age, he was the son of Israel's favorite wife. His brothers knew their father loved Joseph most. They recalled him giving Joseph a beautifully orna-mented robe, a sign of his favor, a hint of the birthright. From that day on, they hated him.

As for Joseph, he only made matters worse. His father would send him to the fields with his brothers, the sons of Bilhah and Zilpah. As Israel's youngest children, it was their job to tend the flocks. But when they returned home, Joseph would give his father a bad report about them.

Then there was the day when Joseph told his brothers about a dream he had. "We were binding sheaves of grain," he said, "and mine stood up-right while yours bowed down."

"What?" they said. "Do you think you will rule over us?" And they hated him even more.

But Joseph didn't take the hint. He later told them about another dream. "The sun, moon, and eleven stars were bowing down to me," he said. This time, however, he also told his father about the dream.

Israel was angry. "Will your mother, brothers, and I all bow down to you?"

Sometime later, Israel sent Joseph to Shechem to see how his brothers were. But Joseph could not find them. Finally, someone told him they had gone to Dothan to graze the livestock.

As Joseph approached Dothan, one of his brothers saw him in the distance. "Here comes that dreamer," he said, mockingly. "I suppose his father has sent him here to spy on us."

"I know how we could stop those reports," said another brother. "If we did away with him, no one would ever know. Let's throw him into that cistern and say an animal killed him."

When Reuben heard this, he said, "Let's not take his life. Don't shed any blood. Just throw him into the cistern." They didn't know Reuben planned to rescue him and take him home.

When Joseph reached their camp, his brothers pinned him down and stripped off his robe. Then they threw him into the empty cistern. Joseph begged them to let him out, but they ignored him. As they sat down to eat, they saw a distant caravan of Ishmaelites traveling to Egypt.

That gave Judah an idea. "What will we gain if we kill our brother and cover up his blood? Let's just sell him to the Ishmaelites; after all, he is our own flesh and blood." So they pulled him out of the well and sold him to the Ishmaelites for 20 shekels of silver.

Reuben was not there at the time. When he later returned, he slipped away to the cistern. Joseph was gone! Reuben tore his clothes in distress. Quickly he ran back to his brothers.

"The boy isn't there!" he exclaimed.

When they told him what they did, he let out a wail. "Oh no! Where can I turn now?"

But the brothers had already planned their cover up. They picked up the robe they had taken off Joseph. Then they slaughtered a goat and dipped the robe in its blood. When they arrived home, they took the robe to Israel. "We found this. Is it your son's robe?"

Israel recognized it right away. "It is!" he cried. "Oh, my son!" Their plan had worked. Israel thought an animal had attacked him. He put his head down and wept mournfully. When his sons realized no one could comfort him, they regretted what they had done. But it was too late.

TBC 25

A Slave in Egypt

TBC Book One, Chapter 26
Genesis 39:1-23; 40:1-23

While Israel mourned the death of his young son, Joseph stood on a platform in Egypt, wondering about his fate. He was to be sold as a slave. The only question was, to whom?

An Egyptian named Potiphar took Joseph and led him away. He was the captain of Pharaoh's guard, and as far as he was concerned, this was a bargain. The young man was strong and handsome. He had a sharp look in his eye, and something set him apart from the other slaves.

Potiphar's hunch proved right. Joseph had quickly learned the language and customs of Egypt. What's more, Potiphar found he could trust him. Whatever Joseph did seemed to flourish, for the Lord's favor rested on him and God blessed him. Potiphar was so pleased with Joseph that he placed him in charge of his entire household.

It was during this time that Potiphar's wife first saw Joseph. She smiled and flirted with him, but he walked away. One time she slipped near him whispered, "Come to bed with me." Joseph pulled away.

"Come," she urged softly.

"No," he said. "My master has entrusted me with everything he owns. He's withheld nothing from me—except you, his wife. How could I do such a wicked thing? I'd be sinning against my master and against God."

But she refused to give up. Day after day she tried to entice him. One day Joseph walked into the house and no one was home. He felt relieved. Then he heard footsteps approaching. Potiphar's wife wrapped her arms around him. "We're alone," she said. "Come to bed with me!"

Joseph turned to pull away, but she grabbed his cloak in both hands. So he slipped out of his robe and ran out of the house. When she realized her plan had failed, she was furious.

She stared at the robe. *I know what I'll do. . . .*

Suddenly she screamed. A servant raced in.

"That Hebrew tried to force me to go to bed with him! Look—here is his robe!"

When Potiphar arrived, she told him her story, and he believed her. Angrily, he threw Joseph in prison.

But the Lord was with Joseph. God gave him favor with the warden, and soon he was put in charge of the prisoners. The warden trusted him completely, for God always gave him success.

While Joseph served as the warden's assistant, the king's chief cupbearer and chief baker had offended the king. So he sent them to prison, where they were assigned to Joseph's ward.

One night, they each had a dream. The dreams bothered them so much that even Joseph noticed something was wrong. "Why are your faces so sad today?" he asked.

"We both had troubling dreams," one man said, "and we don't know what they mean."

Joseph smiled and said, "Don't interpretations belong to God? Tell me your dreams."

So the cupbearer began: "I saw a vine with three branches. It budded and blossomed, then its clusters ripened. So I squeezed out the grape juice and put the cup in Pharaoh's hand."

"The three branches stand for three days," Joseph said. "At that time, you will be restored to your position as cupbearer." The man was relieved. Joseph said, "Now you must do something for me. Remember to mention me to Pharaoh, for I have done nothing to deserve being here."

When the chief baker saw that Joseph had given a favorable interpretation, he also told his dream. "On my head were three baskets of bread. The top basket held all kinds of baked goods for Pharaoh, but birds were eating from them."

Joseph looked serious. "The three baskets stand for three days," he said. "At that time, Pharaoh will call for you. But he will have you hung. And the birds will eat your flesh." The baker put his head into his hands. He could only hope that Joseph's predictions were wrong.

Three days later it was Pharaoh's birthday. He gave a feast for his officials and called both the cupbearer and baker. Then he restored the cupbearer. The baker, however, was hung.

Joseph hoped the cupbearer could get Pharaoh to free him. But the man had forgotten his promise.

TBC 26

From Bondage to Blessing

TBC Book One, Chapter 27
Genesis 41:1-57

Pharaoh tossed and turned in his sleep, for he was deeply troubled by what he was seeing. Two years had now passed since Pharaoh's cupbearer was restored to his position, the time when the cupbearer had seen a vision in his sleep. Now it was Pharaoh who had a startling dream. He saw seven sleek and fat cows coming out of the Nile River and grazing among the reeds. Then he saw seven gaunt, ugly cows come out and eat the fat ones.

Pharaoh awoke briefly and sat up in bed. *It was only a dream,* he thought. But as he drifted off, Pharaoh had a second dream. Seven heads of good, healthy grain grew on a single stalk. Then seven other heads grew, thin and scorched, and they swallowed up the healthy, full heads of grain.

The next morning Pharaoh was even more troubled by the dreams. They were so unusual and so similar. . . . So he sent for his magicians and wise men, but none of them were able to interpret Pharaoh's dreams. Finally, when the cupbearer heard what had happened, he remembered Joseph and told Pharaoh about him.

Immediately, Pharaoh sent for Joseph. When Joseph appeared before him, Pharaoh looked down from his throne and said, "I had a troubling dream and no one can explain its meaning. I understand that you are able to interpret dreams."

Joseph said, "I cannot do it on my own. But God will give Pharaoh the answer he seeks."

So Pharaoh recounted his dreams. "I was standing on the bank of the Nile when seven fat, sleek cows came out of the river, only to be eaten by seven gaunt, ugly cows. Then I saw seven healthy heads of grain swallowed by seven scrawny heads."

Pharaoh now turned to Joseph, waiting for his response.

"The two dreams have the same meaning," Joseph said. "God is revealing what he is about to do. The good cows and healthy grain stand for seven years of abundance in Egypt. But they will be followed by seven years of severe famine. The dream came in two forms to show that God has firmly decided this, and it will occur soon. May Pharaoh now find a wise, discerning person to assist him. And may that person take charge of storing surplus food over these next seven years, to prepare for the years of famine."

The plan seemed good to Pharaoh and his officials. Then Pharaoh said, "Can we find anyone as wise and discerning as this man, in whom is the spirit of God?"

So Pharaoh appointed Joseph to take charge of his palace and to govern over the people of Egypt. Only Pharaoh himself would be greater in power.

Pharaoh gave Joseph his signet ring, dressed him in fine robes, and paraded him in a chariot to signify his authority. Then he gave him Asenath, the priest's daughter, as his wife.

Joseph was 30 years old when he began to serve Pharaoh. He traveled throughout Egypt during those first seven years and stored the surplus food. So much grain was gathered that he eventually stopped keeping records because it was beyond measure.

During that time, two sons were born to Joseph. He named his first son Manasseh, saying, "It is because God has made me forget all my trouble and my father's household." His second son he named Ephraim, for God had made him fruitful.

After those seven years of plenty, the people cried out to Pharaoh. Famine had begun to spread over the whole country. So Joseph opened the storehouses and sold grain.

The other countries near Egypt also suffered famine, and many people came to Egypt for food. It did not dawn on Joseph that the famine had spread even to his homeland, the land of Canaan.

TBC 27

Saved by Egypt

TBC Book One, Chapter 28
Genesis 42:1-38

A severe famine had swept over the land, including Canaan, and Israel found himself in a desperate situation. Word spread, however, that Egypt held an abundance of food. When Israel heard that, he sent his sons to Egypt, that is, all except the youngest one. Israel kept Benjamin with him. He held a special place in his heart, for his mother Rachel had died giving birth to him.

Meanwhile, in Egypt, Joseph ruled as its governor. When the sons of Israel arrived to buy grain, they bowed down to him, not recognizing he was their brother. But Joseph recognized them. Pretending not to know them, he harshly asked, "Where do you come from?"

"We came from Canaan to buy food," they said.

Then all at once, Joseph remembered his dreams. But he continued to act like a stranger. "You are really spies!" he shouted.

"No, my lord," one of them replied, "we are twelve brothers. The youngest one is with our father; the other is dead."

Joseph was surprised to hear their response, but he did not show it. He wanted to know more about the other brother. "No," he insisted, "I believe you are spies. Here is how I will test you: You will not leave here unless one of you goes back to Canaan and returns here with your other brother." And for three days they were all held in custody.

On the third day Joseph called for them and said, "Since I fear God, here is what you may do: To prove you are honest men, let one of your brothers stay here in prison while the rest of you go back to Canaan. Then return with your youngest brother."

Joseph turned away. He had used an interpreter to speak to them, so they didn't realize he understood what they were saying.

"Surely we are being punished by God because of our brother Joseph," Reuben said. "Didn't I tell you not to sin against the boy? But you wouldn't listen!"

Joseph walked away so that no one would see his tears. Then he returned and commanded that Simeon be bound before them. As he left the room, he whispered these orders: "Give all of them supplies for their journey. Fill their bags with grain and put the silver back in their bags."

The brothers anxiously began their journey home, relieved at the chance to prove themselves. That night, however, when one of them opened his bag, he saw his silver. "Look!" he shouted. "Here is the silver I brought to pay for the grain. How did it get back in my sack?"

When his brothers saw it, they trembled. "What's going on?" one of them cried out. "What has God done to us?"

As soon as they arrived home, they told their father all that had happened. "The man who is Lord over Egypt accused us of spying and treated us harshly. He kept Simeon in custody. He has told us to return with our youngest brother to prove we are not spies."

Israel put his head in his hands. As his sons emptied their sacks, each man found his pouch of silver! Now all of them were frightened.

Israel lifted his hands in the air and said, "You have deprived me of my children! Joseph and Simeon are no more, and now you want to take Benjamin. Everything is against me!"

Then Reuben, his oldest son, spoke up. "Let me make the journey with Benjamin. I swear that you can trust me. You may put both of my sons to death if I fail to bring him back to you. I promise, I will bring him back."

"No!" Israel said. "My son will not go there with you. His brother is dead and he is the only one left of Rachel's sons. If harm were to come to him on the journey, you would bring my gray head down to the grave in sorrow."

Israel had spoken. The matter was settled . . . or so he thought.

TBC 28

Egypt's Best-kept Secret

TBC Book One, Chapter 29
Genesis 43:1-34; 44:1-34; 45:1-3

Death threatened every family in Canaan, including the tribe of Israel. His family had eaten all the grain they purchased from Egypt, and the famine was still severe. Israel summoned his sons and told them to get more food in Egypt. They knew it wasn't that simple. Only Judah had the boldness to reason with his father.

"We can't do that. The man in Egypt solemnly warned us to bring Benjamin. We won't go unless we can take him.

"Listen," Judah urged, "by now we could have gone there and back, if only you had let us! Send the boy with me, and I will bear the responsibility. But let us go at once, before our children starve to death."

Israel sighed. "All right," he said. "Bring gifts from our land and twice as much silver as before. May God grant you mercy."

So Israel's sons set out for Egypt, and Benjamin went with them. When they arrived, they asked to see the governor. Joseph appeared and saw that Benjamin was with them. Then he ordered that they be taken to his house to dine with him.

His brothers were surprised by this invitation. As they pondered it, they began to fear his motives. What if he were taking them there to make them his slaves? After all, they had never paid for the grain they were given. Afraid for their lives, they went to Joseph's steward and told him about the silver they had found in their sacks.

"It's all right," the steward said. "I received your silver. Your God has given you the treasure in your sacks."

Then he left. When he returned, Simeon was with him.

When Joseph came home they presented their gifts to him. He greeted them and asked them about their father.

Then he looked at Benjamin and said to him, "God be gracious to you, my son."

Joseph became so moved that he had to slip away into a private room, and there he wept.

After washing his face, Joseph returned. "Serve the food," he said.

The brothers ate at a separate table and were surprised to see they were seated in order according to their age. And Benjamin's portion was five times larger than anyone else's.

The next morning, Joseph gave his steward strict orders concerning them: "Fill their sacks with grain and return their silver with it. Put my silver cup in Benjamin's sack. When they leave, go after them. Say, 'Why have you repaid good with evil by stealing my master's cup?' "

The brothers had not traveled far when Joseph's steward caught up with them and confronted them. "We haven't stolen anything," they said. "If any of us is found to have the cup, may that person die, and may we become your slaves."

"Very well, but only the guilty person will become my master's slave."

The steward searched each man's sack, from the oldest to the youngest. And when he came to Benjamin's sack, there was the cup. When the brothers saw it, they tore their clothes in grief. They all returned with him and threw themselves on the ground before Joseph.

"What have you done?" Joseph demanded. "Don't you know I can discern such things?"

"What can we say?" Judah said. "God has uncovered our guilt. We are your slaves."

"No," Joseph said, "just the youngest. The rest of you may leave."

"Please, my lord," begged Judah. "Though you are equal to Pharaoh, allow me to speak. My father's life is closely bound up with the boy, and I guaranteed his safety. Please, let me remain as your slave, and let the boy return to his father."

Joseph could no longer control himself. "Out of my presence!" he yelled to his servants. Then Joseph revealed who he was. As he spoke, he wept so loudly the Egyptians heard him, and they told Pharaoh. His brothers were stunned—and terrified. What would happen to them now?

TBC 29

The Big Surprise

TBC Book One, Chapter 30
Genesis 45:4-28; 46:1-34; 47:1-12

Joseph's brothers trembled as they stood before him. "Come closer," Joseph said. "Yes, it is I, your brother Joseph—the one you sold into Egypt, 22 years ago! But do not be distressed. God permitted this to happen to save your lives. He sent me here to preserve a remnant for you."

The brothers were so shocked that they were speechless.

"Now hurry back to my father," Joseph said, "and tell him that God has made me lord of Egypt. Bring him back here with your families, your flocks, and your herds. There will be five more years of famine, and I will provide for you so you won't perish."

His brothers were still just standing there in dismay when Joseph stepped forward and threw his arms around Benjamin. The two brothers held each other and wept.

Then Joseph kissed each of his brothers and wept as he embraced them. With great joy they now talked with him and told him of their families back in Canaan.

When the news reached Pharaoh and his officials, they were pleased. Pharaoh summoned Joseph. "Tell your brothers to load supplies so they can return to Canaan to get their families. I will give them the best of the land here in Egypt. Have them take carts with them to carry back their children and wives."

Joseph then gave his brothers carts and provisions as well as new clothing. But to Benjamin he gave 300 shekels of silver and five sets of clothes. He also prepared gifts for his father. As he sent them off, he added, "Don't quarrel on the way!"

When they finally reached their home, all of them wanted to be the first to tell the good news. "Father, the most wonderful thing has happened! Joseph is alive! He is ruler of all Egypt!"

Israel was so stunned he didn't believe them. But when he saw all that they brought from Egypt, the truth of their words began to sink in, and his spirit revived.

"I will go to Egypt," he said, "and see my son."

So Israel's whole family set out on their journey. At Beersheba, Israel offered sacrifices. Then God spoke to him in a vision. "Don't be afraid to go," the Lord said. "I will make you into a great nation and bring you back again, and Joseph himself will close your eyes."

Renewed by God's promise, Israel left Beersheba, along with his children and their wives, his grandchildren, and all their livestock and possessions. All of Israel's descendants, including Joseph and his sons, now totaled 70.

As they approached Egypt, Israel sent Judah ahead to get directions to Goshen, where they would settle and tend their herds. Then Joseph got in his chariot and returned with Judah to meet them. When he saw his father, he ran to meet him. He threw his arms around him and wept.

Joseph chose five of his brothers to present to the king. "When Pharaoh asks you about your occupation, just say, 'Your servants have tended livestock from our youth.' You will be allowed to live in Goshen, for shepherds are detestable to Egyptians."

So Joseph's brothers appeared before Pharaoh and responded to him as Joseph had instructed them.

Then Pharaoh said to Joseph, "Let them live in the best of the land, in Goshen, and if any have special ability, let them take charge of my livestock."

Then Joseph presented his father, and his father blessed Pharaoh.

"How old are you?" Pharaoh asked.

"The years of my pilgrimage are 130," Israel said. "They have been few and difficult, fewer than my fathers."

Though his life had been difficult, Israel enjoyed his final years with his family reunited. Joseph's years of suffering were now bearing fruit. God had used him not only to rescue all of his family, but also to preserve millions more in the land of Egypt.

TBC 30

A Time to Mourn

TBC Book One, Chapter 31
Genesis 47:28-31; 48:1-22; 49:1-28; 50:1-26

With the time of mourning completed they feared for their lives.

From the moment Israel felt his son's warm embrace, God poured new life into his soul. Who would have guessed that 130-year-old Israel would enjoy 17 years in Egypt? The years Jacob had lost in mourning for Joseph were replaced with the joy of being a grandfather to Joseph's sons.

With each year that passed, Israel wondered if it were his last. So one day, he decided to send for Joseph. "Put your hand under my thigh," he said. "You must promise me on oath that you will bury me in Canaan, not in Egypt. Bury me where Abraham, Sarah, and Leah are buried."

When his time to die drew near, Israel again called for Joseph. By now Israel was nearly blind. He did not recognize Joseph's sons, but he promised to bless them as if they were his own.

Israel kissed the boys and embraced them. Then Joseph placed Manasseh to the right of Israel because he was Joseph's firstborn, and Ephraim stood to the left. Israel, however, crossed his arms to put his right hand on the younger son, Ephraim. Joseph thought his father was confused. So he reached out to put Israel's right hand on Manasseh. But Israel refused his help.

"I know what I am doing, my son," Israel said. "Don't worry; Manasseh, too, will become a great people. But Ephraim will be greater and will father a group of nations."

Israel then called all his sons and prophesied over each of them.

"Reuben, my firstborn, you will no longer excel in honor and power, because you defiled my bed. As a young man you once took one of my wives as your own. Though I said nothing at the time, it did not escape my notice.

"Simeon and Levi, cursed be your violent anger. Your people will surely be scattered.

"Judah, you are like a lion that crouches. Your brothers will bow down to your sons. The scepter will not depart from your descendants.

"Zebulun, your people will live by the sea. As for you, Issachar, you are a rawboned donkey who will submit to forced labor.

"Dan, your sons will provide justice for their people. Gad, your tribe will be attacked by raiders, but then they will turn back and strike their enemies.

"As for you, Asher, your rich food will provide delicacies fit for a king. And Naphatali, you are a doe set free, who gives beautiful words."

Then Israel said, "Joseph is a fruitful vine, climbing over a wall. He overcame the attackers' hostility because of the Mighty One of Jacob. He, the Rock of Israel, gives you all the greatest blessings. Benjamin, you are a ravenous wolf, devouring the prey, dividing the plunder."

When he finished speaking, Israel breathed his last, and God gathered him to his forefathers. Joseph threw himself upon his father and wept. Soon all the brothers were weeping.

Joseph ordered the physicians to embalm their father to prepare him for burial. All of Egypt showed sympathy for Joseph's family, mourning his death 70 days. Then Joseph fulfilled his oath to his father. He arranged to bury him in Canaan, in the cave of Machpelah, near Mamre. They held a solemn ceremony, mourning Israel's death, and Pharaoh's officials joined them.

With the time of mourning now completed, Joseph's brothers feared for their lives. What if Joseph now decided to retaliate? So they made a plan among themselves, and all of them but Benjamin met with Joseph. Judah spoke on their behalf: "Before your father died, he asked that you would forgive us." Then they all threw themselves down and said, "We are your slaves."

Joseph wept. "Don't be afraid," Joseph said. "That was God's plan, meant for our good."

In the years that followed, Joseph continued to provide for them in Egypt. He lived to 110 years old and knew the joy of seeing his great-great-grandchildren. When his own death finally drew near, he, too, made his family take an oath: "When God comes to your aid and takes you from this land, carry my bones with you." One day they would all return to Canaan.

TBC 31

Baby Moses

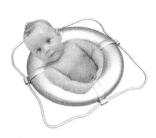

TBC Book One, Chapter 32
Exodus 1:1-22; 2:1-10

Joseph's generation had long passed, but their descendants became so numerous that they drew the attention of Pharaoh. Of course, this was not the same Pharaoh who appointed Joseph as governor. Hundreds of years had passed since then, and few knew of Joseph. What they did know was that these Hebrews were multiplying like grasshoppers. Soon they would outnumber the Egyptians. No one was more worried about that than the Pharaoh who now ruled Egypt.

For this reason, Pharaoh forced the Hebrews into slavery. He oppressed them by making them serve as his laborers, building storage cities. The Egyptians worked them ruthlessly, having them make bricks and mortar. But the more the Hebrews were oppressed, the more they multiplied.

Pharaoh knew he must do something to stop their growth. So he summoned the midwives who helped the Hebrew women in childbirth. The two leading midwives, Shiphrah and Puah appeared before Pharaoh. "Kill all the baby boys born to the Hebrews," he commanded. But the midwives feared God more than they feared Pharaoh, and they let the babies live.

When the king learned what they were doing, he demanded to know why they disobeyed him. So they lied to pacify him: "Hebrew women are not like Egyptian women," said one of the midwives. "They are more vigorous and give birth before the midwives arrive."

God was pleased with these courageous women who had chosen to do the right thing. And he decided to show his kindness to them, for they had risked their own lives by refusing to kill the babies. So the Lord blessed the midwives by giving them families of their own.

The Hebrew people now became even more numerous. Pharaoh realized their population was mounting. In his desperation to stem the tide, he gave this order to all his people: "Every baby boy born to the Hebrews must be thrown into the Nile River. The girls, however, will remain alive." Pharaoh reasoned that if the girls were permitted to live, the Hebrews would be forced to intermarry. In time they would lose their identity as a nation of people.

Shortly after this edict was given, a Hebrew couple from the tribe of Levi gave birth to a son, and there was something about this baby that was different. Even as an infant, it was obvious he was exceptional. This was their third child, born after their daughter, Miriam, and their son, Aaron. Somehow they must keep the Egyptians from learning about their baby.

When they could no longer hide him, the mother took a papyrus basket and coated it with tar and pitch to make it waterproof. Then she lay the baby inside and put it among the reeds of the Nile River. Her daughter, Miriam, stood at a distance to watch what would happen.

Just then, Pharaoh's daughter went down to the Nile to bathe. While she was there, she saw the basket among the reeds. When she opened it, she saw the baby crying and felt sorry for him. "This is one of the Hebrew babies," she told her attendants.

Immediately, Miriam ran to Pharaoh's daughter. She said to the princess, "Shall I go and get one of the Hebrew women to nurse the baby for you?"

"Yes, that would be good," she said. So Miriam brought her own mother to the princess.

"Take this baby and nurse him for me," the princess commanded, "and I will pay you for your services." So the woman took the baby, her own son, and kept him at home to nurse him.

When the child grew old enough to be weaned, the woman took him back to Pharaoh's household. The princess then adopted the little boy as her own son. She smiled as she held him in her arms. "I will give you the name Moses," she said, "for I drew you out of the water."

The baby's birth mother left quickly to hide her tears. It was painful to let him go. But she had done the right thing. Better he should live as another woman's son than not to live at all. Was it only a coincidence that Pharaoh's daughter had rescued him? No, this was the hand of God.

TBC 32

Moses in Exile

TBC Book One, Chapter 33
Exodus 2:11-25; 3:1-12

Who would have guessed an orphaned Hebrew baby would be raised as the son of Pharaoh's own daughter? Moses grew up in Pharaoh's household, showered with the privileges of a prince. And he received the finest education the world had to offer.

From an early age, Moses knew he was a Hebrew, and he grew up with a fascination for those people who served his grandfather, Pharaoh. One day when he watched them work, he saw an Egyptian beating a Hebrew slave. Moses felt his blood boil. He followed the Egyptian until he reached a secluded place. Then Moses attacked him and killed him. Quickly he hid the body.

The next day Moses returned to the place where the slaves worked. He saw two Hebrews quarreling, and soon it turned into a fight. No foreman was nearby, so Moses stepped in. He grabbed hold of the aggressor and said, "Why are you hitting your fellow Hebrew?"

"Who made you ruler and judge over us?" one man said. "Are you going to kill me, too?"

Moses dropped his grip. Suddenly fear pierced his soul. Someone must have seen him!

When Pharaoh learned what Moses had done, he was furious, and he vowed to have him killed. But Moses had already fled. He traveled to Midian, a land of flocks and herds—a land with no Egyptians. There he sat by a well. Then he noticed seven shepherdesses being driven away by some shepherds. So he came to the women's rescue and watered their flock.

Then the girls returned to their father, Reuel, who was a priest of Midian. He frowned when he saw them. "Why have you returned so early?"

"Some shepherds drove us away, but an Egyptian rescued us and watered the flock."

"Where is he?" Reuel asked. "Go and invite him to join us." So Moses dined with them.

Reuel was so impressed with Moses that he invited him to stay there. The idea appealed to Moses. This was the last place Pharaoh would look for him. In time Reuel repaid Moses for his service by giving him his oldest daughter in marriage. So Moses married Zipporah. When she gave birth to a son. Moses named him Gershom, meaning "a stranger," for he was now an alien.

During that time, Pharaoh died. His son, the prince, now reigned in his place. But the Israelites' lives had grown even more miserable in their slavery. So they cried out to God, and the Lord heard their cries. He remembered his covenant and watched over them with concern.

Meanwhile, Moses tended the flock for his father-in-law. One day, he led the flock to the far side of the desert and noticed something odd— a bush was on fire, yet it did not burn up.

Moses stared, wondering, *Why doesn't it burn up?* He walked closer to get a better look.

Then a figure appeared in the flames. The angel of the Lord called out, "Moses! Moses!"

Moses' heart raced within him. "Here I am," he said.

"Don't come any closer," the Lord said. "Take off your sandals. This is holy ground."

Moses stopped and slipped off his sandals.

"I am the God of your fathers," the voice said, "the God of Abraham, Isaac, and Israel."

At this, Moses hid his face, afraid to look at the Lord.

"I have seen the misery of my people," the Lord said. "I have heard them crying out, and I am concerned about their suffering. So I have come down to rescue them from the Egyptians, to bring them out and take them to a land flowing with milk and honey, a land where they will prosper. Now go, for I am sending you to Pharaoh to bring my people out of Egypt.

Moses was stunned. "Who am I to go to Pharaoh and bring the Israelites out of Egypt?"

"I will be with you," the Lord reassured him. "And I will give you a sign to know I the Lord have sent you: When you have brought my people out, you will worship God on this mountain."

Moses stood in his bare feet, wondering, *What should I do now?*

TBC 33

God's Dynamic Duo

TBC Book One, Chapter 34
Exodus 3:13-22; 4:1-31

One doubt after another swept over Moses as he beheld the figure in the flames. Had the Lord really chosen him to lead God's people out of Egypt? Who would ever believe that? Why, he could hardly believe it himself. But the image remained before him and did not disappear.

Moses took a deep breath. "Suppose I tell the Israelites you have sent me. They will ask me, 'Who has sent you? What is his name?' What shall I say?"

"Say 'I Am' has sent you, the God of your fathers Abraham, Isaac, and Israel. Now go and call together the elders of Israel. They will listen. Then all of you go to the king of Egypt. Ask him if your people may take a three-day journey to make sacrifices. He will refuse, but then I will stretch out my hand against him and his people. When I have finished, he will let them go."

Moses sighed. "What if the elders do not believe me?"

"What is in your hand?" the Lord asked. "A staff," Moses replied.

"Throw it on the ground." Moses threw down the staff. As soon as it hit the ground, it turned into a snake, and Moses ran. The Lord said, "Pick it up by the tail, and it will return to a staff. When the elders see this, they will believe the God of their fathers has appeared to you.

"Now put your hand in your cloak, then take it out." Moses put his hand in his robe then took it out—it was diseased with leprosy. But when he put it in and out again, it was restored.

"If they don't believe these signs, take water from the Nile and it will turn to blood."

"O Lord," Moses said, "I have never been eloquent. I'm not a good speaker."

The Lord replied firmly, "Who gave man his mouth? Is it not I, the Lord? Now go. I will help you speak and teach you what to say."

"Please, Lord," Moses begged, "send someone else to do it."

At this, the Lord grew angry. "What about your brother, Aaron? He can speak well. He is already on his way to meet you, and he will be glad when he sees you. You will tell him my words and he will speak to the people for you. I will help both of you and guide you."

As the vision began to fade before him, Moses heard his final words. "Go back to Egypt now, for all the men who wanted to kill you are dead."

So he knew, Moses thought to himself. *He knew why I was afraid.*

Moses had a lot to explain to his father-in-law. But the older man did not seem surprised. He put his hand on Moses' shoulder and gave him his blessing. Then Moses packed for the journey. Putting his wife and sons on a donkey, he left for Egypt.

At a lodging place, the Lord appeared to Moses, and he became deathly ill. Zipporah knew why. The Lord told Moses to circumcise their sons, but Zipporah was reluctant. Now she had no choice. She found a sharp flint knife. Then she cut off the foreskin on both sons and pressed the bloody strips against Moses feet. "You are a bridegroom of blood to me," she said disgustedly. But she had done the right thing. The Lord relented, and Moses was soon well.

Meanwhile, Moses' brother Aaron had also begun a journey, for the Lord had prompted him. "Go into the desert," the Lord had whispered, "and there you will meet Moses."

After years of separation, the two brothers met at the mountain of God. They greeted each other with a kiss and a hug. Moses explained to Aaron why he had returned. He told him about the vision and what the Lord had said. Then he showed him the miraculous signs.

Aaron helped Moses contact all the Israelite elders, and the elders agreed to meet with them. Together, the two men explained what the Lord had said. Then they performed the miracles. To Moses' surprise, the people believed they were sent from God. And when the elders heard that God was concerned about their misery, they bowed down and worshiped the Lord.

TBC 34

Judgment on Egypt

TBC Book One, Chapter 35
Exodus 5:1-6:12; 7:1-8:19

Memories suddenly flooded his heart as Moses stepped into Pharaoh's palace. The last time he walked these halls, he was a prince, a Hebrew-born Egyptian. Now, after 40 years in the desert of Midian, he looked nothing like an Egyptian. He looked like a shepherd. Nothing but his relationship to these Israelite elders allowed him to appear before Pharaoh.

The king motioned to him and said, "Speak. I am listening."

With Aaron and the elders by his side, Moses said, "We have a message from the Lord our God. The Lord says, 'Let my people go to hold a festival to me in the desert.' "

"Who is the Lord that I should obey him?" Pharaoh shouted. Seeing a group of Israelites with him, he added, "Look, you have stopped my laborers! All of you, get back to your work!"

When they left, Pharaoh summoned the slave drivers. "The slaves are getting lazy. You have been too easy on them. Stop providing the straw for bricks. Make them get it themselves."

So the slave masters refused to provide straw. But they demanded just as many bricks as before. The Hebrews watched in disbelief. How could they possibly make as many bricks as before? Of course, they could not, so the slaves who served as foremen were beaten.

When the Hebrew foremen appealed to Pharaoh, they realized that Moses' visit had triggered these new orders. As they left the palace, they saw Moses and Aaron. "May the Lord judge you," they shouted, "for making us a stench to Pharaoh!"

Moses felt terrible. He found a place where he could be alone, and there he fell on his knees. "O Lord," he said, "ever since I went to Pharaoh it has only brought trouble."

The Lord said, "I am the Lord. I will indeed free my people and take them to their land."

So Moses rose and arranged for a meeting with the elders. But when he told the people what the Lord had said, they refused to listen.

Moses and Aaron returned to Pharaoh by themselves. Pharaoh's officials thought they were two of Israel's elders, for Moses was 80 and Aaron was 83. As they entered Pharaoh's court, Aaron threw down his staff, and it became a snake. To his surprise, Pharaoh's magicians did the same thing. But then, something happened that surprised all of them: Aaron's staff swallowed up all the others. Yet Pharaoh showed no surprise. He had hardened his heart, as God had predicted.

The next morning Moses and Aaron went to the bank of the Nile. They waited until Pharaoh appeared. Then Moses said, "Because you have not listened to the Lord, he will turn the Nile to blood." And so he did. Fish died, the river stunk, and no one could drink its water.

The Pharaoh's magicians used their secret arts to do the same thing. So Pharaoh turned and walked away. Then the Egyptians dug along the Nile to get fresh drinking water.

Seven days later, Moses and Aaron returned to Pharaoh with a message. "The Lord says, 'Let my people go to worship me. If you refuse, I will plague the country with frogs.' " So Aaron stretched out his staff and frogs appeared. But the magicians did the same thing. Frogs were now everywhere. They were such a nuisance that Pharaoh agreed he would let the people go if they stopped the plague of frogs. But when the frogs died, Pharaoh refused.

Moses and Aaron were not surprised. The plagues reminded people of the false gods they worshiped—the Nile River, frog goddesses, healing gods, sun gods. . . . The Lord showed that the Egyptians' earth god was false when he commanded Aaron to stretch out his staff and strike the ground. The dust turned to gnats, and they were everywhere, covering both men and animals.

Again the magicians called upon their secret arts. By imitating each miracle, they hoped to prove that the plagues were just magic tricks. But when they realized they could not imitate this feat, they were surprised and sent a message to Pharaoh: "This is the finger of God."

TBC 35

The Man with the Hard Heart

TBC Book One, Chapter 36
Exodus 8:20-9:35

Something dramatic was about to happen in the land of Egypt, a miracle unlike any other sent by God. Up to this point, the plagues had clearly affected everyone in Egypt, and still, Pharaoh stubbornly refused to release the Hebrews. So now, the Lord would show all Egypt that the Hebrews were a distinct people, set apart by the Lord God.

Once more, Moses confronted Pharaoh. "The Lord says, 'Let my people go to worship me. If you refuse, I will send a plague of flies, but I will spare my people in Goshen.' " The king ignored them. The next day flies appeared, and they ruined the entire land—except for Goshen.

Pharaoh now summoned Moses. "You and your people may sacrifice to your God, only you must not go far to do it."

But Moses was insistent: "Our God says we must make a three-day journey. If we were to make offerings in the presence of Egyptians, they would stone us for sacrificing animals that they hold sacred. So we must do as the Lord our God commands us."

"You may go," Pharaoh replied. "Now pray for me and remove these flies."

So Moses left and prayed to the Lord. But once the flies had disappeared, Pharaoh hardened his heart and broke his promise.

The Lord sent Moses to Pharaoh once more, with yet another message. This time the Lord would bring a terrible plague on Egypt's livestock.

Pharaoh ignored the warning, and the next day God struck the livestock in Egypt. The plague killed many of their horses, donkeys, camels, cattle, sheep, and goats. But the Israelites' animals remained untouched—not one of them died.

The Lord then commanded Moses and Aaron to take handfuls of soot from a furnace and toss it into the air in Pharaoh's presence. Immediately it became fine dust that caused festering boils to break out on both people and animals. The Egyptians had believed they could appeal to a god who would heal them of such infirmities. But that god proved false, as even Pharaoh's magicians were tormented by the boils and unable to stand in his presence.

The next day, the Lord sent Moses to Pharaoh with another message: "Let my people go to worship me, or I will send the full force of my plagues against you and your people. Then you will know there is no one like me in all the earth. By now I could have sent a plague that would have wiped out you and your people from the face of the earth. But I have raised you up for this very purpose, that I might show my power, that my Name might be proclaimed in all the earth.

"Since you still resist, I will send a devastating hailstorm. Have your remaining livestock brought to a place of shelter, for every man and animal outside will die."

By now, many of Pharaoh's officials had begun to fear God. Even if Pharaoh did not heed Moses, they would. Quickly they sheltered their slaves and animals.

Moses left Pharaoh's presence, and once outside, he stretched out his staff. Thunder roared and lightning flashed as the Lord rained hail on Egypt. It was the worst storm the Egyptians had ever seen, striking men and animals, and destroying trees and crops. But the Israelites in Goshen were spared.

Pharaoh summoned Moses and Aaron. "This time I have sinned," he said. "The Lord is right; I and my people are in the wrong. We have had enough thunder and hail. I will let you go."

"Very well, I will pray to the Lord. But I know that even now, you still do not fear God."

Moses went out of the city and spread his hands toward the heavens. The thunder and hail stopped. So did the rain. When Pharaoh saw that the storm had stopped, he changed his mind once again and refused to let the Hebrews go.

TBC 36

'Let My People Go'

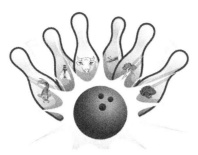

TBC Book One, Chapter 37
Exodus 10:1-12:30

By now Moses and Aaron were both well-known among the Egyptians, and Pharaoh's officials personally escorted them to the king. Moses told Pharaoh that they had yet another message from the Lord: "How long will you refuse to humble yourself before me? Let my people go or I will send massive swarms of locusts."

The two brothers left without waiting for his reply. Immediately, the officials stepped forward to reason with Pharaoh. "Let the Hebrews go. Already Egypt is ruined. How can we possibly stand any more of these plagues?"

So Pharaoh summoned Moses and Aaron to return. "You may go worship the Lord your God." he said. "Now tell me, just who will be going?"

With a strong unwavering voice, Moses replied, "Everyone, along with our herds."

"No!" Pharaoh said. "I will not permit that. Only the men. Now go." Then he ordered that they be driven from his presence.

As they stood outside the palace, Moses stretched out his staff. A powerful east wind picked up and blew across Egypt. The next morning, the land was filled with locusts. Their swarms were so dense the ground looked black. They devoured every plant and every tree's fruit.

Pharaoh quickly summoned Moses and Aaron. "I have sinned," he said. "Forgive my sin and pray to the Lord to take away this deadly plague."

Moses prayed, and a strong west wind carried the locusts into the Red Sea.

After all this, Pharaoh still refused. So the Lord told Moses to stretch out his hand toward the sky. Suddenly, darkness covered the land, a darkness that could be felt. For three days it remained dark, and no one dared to leave his home. But in Goshen, the Israelites had light.

Once more, Pharaoh called for Moses. "I have decided that you may go to worship the Lord. You may take your women and children but leave your herds." When Moses insisted that they needed the livestock for sacrifices, Pharaoh refused.

"Get out of my sight!" he shouted, "And don't come back!"

"May it be as you said," Moses replied. "Never again will I appear before you. And now, the Lord says to you, 'At midnight I will kill every firstborn in Egypt, whether person or animal. But the Israelites will be spared. Then you will say, "Go." ' " Then Moses left, hot with anger.

The Lord commanded Moses to have the people ask the Egyptians for objects of silver and gold. The Egyptians willingly gave them all that they requested, for they feared what would happen if they did not, and they now held Moses in high regard.

"After this plague," said the Lord, "Pharaoh's officials will beg you to leave. You will never forget that day. From now on, this will be the first month of your year. Commemorate this day for generations to come. On this day I will judge Egypt, but I will pass over you and bring you out. For seven days you must use no leaven in your bread. Eat nothing made with yeast."

Then Moses called a meeting with all the elders. "Each family must select a choice year-old lamb and slaughter it at twilight. Place some of its blood on the top and sides of your doorposts. Roast the meat and eat it, along with bread made without yeast. This will be a lasting ordinance for all generations. When your children ask you, 'What does this ceremony mean?' tell them, 'It is the Passover sacrifice to our Lord, who spared us when he struck the Egyptians.' "When Moses finished speaking, the people bowed down and worshiped the Lord.

At midnight the Lord fulfilled his promise. All of Egypt's firstborns were killed, both people and animals. Loud wailing was heard throughout all Egypt. But the angel of death passed over the Israelites, for he saw the blood on their doorposts, the sign that they had been spared.

TBC 37

Free at Last!

TBC Book One, Chapter 38
Exodus 12:30-14:31

Loud wailing was heard from every home in Egypt. Every family mourned the death of their firstborn. In the middle of the night, Pharaoh sent for Moses and Aaron.

"Leave us," he said. "Go, worship your Lord. Take your families, your flocks, and your herds. And bless me."

The Egyptians urged the Israelites to hurry and leave, fearing they would all die. So the Hebrews, also known as Israelites, obeyed the Lord's command: They took their dough before the yeast was added, wrapped it in cloths, and carried it on their shoulders in kneading troughs.

The Israelites had lived in Egypt for exactly 430 years, since the time of Joseph, when Israel moved his tribe of 70 descendants. Now their numbers reached more than a million, and the Lord was sending them back to their homeland. Moses took Joseph's bones with them, as the sons of Israel had sworn to do. Everything was happening just as God had predicted to Abraham.

Before they began their journey, the Lord gave Moses a message for his people: " 'From now on,' the Lord says, 'every firstborn male among you is mine, whether man or animal. Each year at this time, you must redeem every firstborn son by sacrificing a lamb.' "

Six hundred thousand men, besides women and children, traveled with their livestock from Rameses to Succoth, then on to Etham. The Lord went ahead of them, leading them in a pillar of cloud by day and a pillar of fire by night.

God led the Israelites through the desert. He avoided the shorter route, through Philistine country. Had they gone that way, they might fear an attack then change their minds and return to Egypt.

The Lord now ordered Moses to turn the people back, to camp between Migdol and the sea, explaining to Moses his strategy: "Pharaoh will think that you are wandering around in confusion, hemmed in by the desert. Again I will harden his heart, and he will pursue you. But in the end I will gain glory."

After the Israelites had fled, Pharaoh and his officials began to have second thoughts. "What have we done?" they said to one another. "We have lost the services of our slaves!"

So once again, God hardened Pharaoh's heart. Taking more than 600 chariots, Pharaoh and his soldiers pursued the Israelites.

As Pharaoh's army approached, the Israelites looked back in terror. One after another, they cried out to Moses: "Was it because there were no graves in Egypt that you brought us here to die? It would have been better to serve the Egyptians than to die in the desert!"

Moses tried his best to calm them. "Do not be afraid. Stand firm, and this day you will see the Lord deliver you. The Egyptians you now see, you will never see again. The Lord will fight for you; you need only to be still."

The Israelites were soon trapped between Pharaoh's advancing army on one side and the Red Sea on the other. Moses pleaded with God to do something.

"Why are you crying out to me?" the Lord said. "Tell the people to go toward the sea. I will divide the water and you will cross on dry ground."

Then the angel of God and the pillar of cloud moved from the front of Israel's army to the rear, coming between the Israelites and Pharaoh's army. During the night the cloud brought darkness to the Egyptians' side while it sent light to the Israelites.

The people stared as Moses raised his staff. All night long, the Lord used a strong east wind to drive back the sea, until it left a path of dry ground. Everyone cheered as they crossed the sea. No sooner had they reached the other side, when they saw the Egyptians pursuing them.

The dry ground now turned to mud as the wall of water collapsed. Pharaoh's soldiers struggled to force their chariots forward, but the muddy wheels fell off. So they dismounted and ran on foot, but it was too late—the waters swept over them. The Israelites were free at last!

TBC 38

A Nation Tested

TBC Book One, Chapter 39
Exodus 15:22-27; 16:1-36; 17:1-7

As the Israelites looked back at the Red Sea, they could see the waters now crashing down on Pharaoh's chariots, sweeping away his entire army. Shouts of joy rose from the Israelites. But their ecstasy gradually waned. Three days into their journey, they grumbled and blamed Moses for their new plight: Where would a million people find fresh water in the desert?

Even Moses wondered how he would move a nation of people through the desert all the way to Canaan. So he slipped away from the masses, dropped to his knees, and cried out to God.

The Lord told Moses to throw a piece of wood into the bitter waters of Marah. Then Moses knelt down and tasted the cold, sweet water. So they drank from the pool and filled their flasks. Then they camped at Elim, which had twelve springs and seventy palm trees.

Finding Elim was like reaching an oasis. But the Israelites knew they could not stay. They must reach the land of their forefathers. So they set out again, traveling until they reached the Desert of Sin. They all grew tense as they realized what lay ahead—another desert.

Once again, they grumbled against Moses and Aaron: "If only we had died in Egypt! There we had all the food we wanted. But you have brought us into the desert to starve to death."

Before Moses uttered a prayer, the Lord was answering the cry of his heart. "I will rain down bread from heaven," he said. "Each day the people are to gather just enough for that day. On the sixth day of each week, they may gather twice as much, so they will have food for the Sabbath. In this way I will test them to see whether they indeed follow my instructions."

Moses spoke to Aaron, who gathered their tribal leaders. While Aaron relayed God's message, the Lord's glory cloud moved near. Then Moses called out, "The Lord says, 'In the morning you will be filled with bread, and you will know I am the Lord your God.' "

The next morning, a layer of dew surrounded their camp. When it disappeared, thin frost-like flakes appeared on the ground.

"What is it?" they asked.

"It is the bread the Lord has given you," Moses said. "Take one omer per person." An omer was about two quarts or two liters.

The Israelites did as they were told, gathering just enough for that day. And every family found that they had enough. But some people hoarded it and kept leftovers, for they feared they might starve in the desert. The next morning, those extra portions turned to maggots.

Each morning they were to gather only as much food as they needed. When the hot sun rose, it melted away what was left. On the sixth day, they gathered enough for two days, so they could rest on the Sabbath day, and the extra portions never spoiled.

Now some of people did not gather twice as much on the sixth day. And on the Sabbath, when they went out to gather their food, no bread appeared. Moses saw their surprise, and he called out, "How long will you disobey God's commands? He has given you the Sabbath to rest."

The Israelites called the bread from heaven "manna." That was the Hebrew pronunciation for the phrase, "What is it?" Its white flakes tasted like honey wafers. The first time it rained down, the Lord commanded Moses to have Aaron gather some and place it in a jar. That manna never spoiled. God preserved it so that years later it would remind them of how he had fed them.

When the Israelites moved on to Rephidim, they realized once again there was no water.

"Give us water to drink!" they demanded. Their anger flared against Moses.

"Oh, Lord," Moses cried out. "What should I do? The people are ready to stone me!"

"Walk ahead of them with your staff," the Lord said, "and take some of the elders with you. I will stand before you at the rock of Horeb. Strike the rock, and water will come out."

So Moses did as the Lord commanded. The elders stared in dismay as water gushed out from the rock. They all shouted for joy. Then they raised their hands and praised God.

TBC 39

God's Ten Commandments

TBC Book One, Chapter 40
Exodus 19:1-20:26

Three months after all the Israelites fled from Egypt, they began to realize that their greatest enemy had never been left behind. Their pursuers were destroyed, their stomachs were full, but their souls were always craving more. Outwardly, they were one people aiming for the same destination. But inwardly, they were restless wanderers, unruly children destined for self-destruction. The Lord could see where they were heading. Like a wise father, he knew it was time to set boundaries for their protection.

The Israelites now camped at the base of Mt. Sinai. Moses went up the mountain and listened to the Lord's instructions: "Tell the people, 'If you obey me and keep my covenant, out of all nations you will be my treasured possession.' " Then Moses returned to the people and delivered God's message to the elders. One after another, they responded, "We will do everything the Lord has commanded."

Once more, Moses climbed the mountain. He delivered the people's reply. Then he listened carefully as the Lord explained his plans. "I am going to come to you in a dense cloud, so that the people will hear me speaking and will always put their trust in you."

After receiving the Lord's instructions, Moses returned to the people and relayed what God had said. For the next two days the people were to consecrate themselves and wash their clothing. On the third day, the Lord would make his presence known.

That day, the people were commanded to approach the mountain, but they were warned not to touch it or they would die. Suddenly, smoke billowed like a furnace and the whole mountain itself trembled, for the Lord descended on it in fire.

Moses spoke, and the voice of God answered. He commanded Moses to come up the mountain with Aaron.

"These are my commandments," the Lord said, and his voice boomed like thunder. "You shall have no other gods than me. You shall not make any idols nor worship anything else in heaven or on earth. Nor shall you misuse the Lord's name.

"Remember the Sabbath day by keeping it holy. Do your work the first six days of the week, but not on the seventh. For in six days the Lord made the heavens and the earth, but he rested on the seventh day. The Lord has blessed that day and made it holy.

"Honor your father and your mother. This command carries a promise with it. If you do indeed honor your father and mother, you will live a long life in the land the Lord your God is giving you." Moses and Aaron listened earnestly as the Lord continued.

"You shall not take someone's life by murder. Nor shall you take someone's wife or husband, for it is wrong to commit adultery. You shall not steal. Neither shall you pervert justice by giving false reports; remember, it is wrong to follow the crowd in wicked plans.

"And finally, you shall not covet someone's house, nor shall you covet someone's husband or wife. Likewise, you shall not covet anyone's servant nor any of their possessions. For it is wrong to make comparisons of others and then envy them for what they have."

The people trembled with fear at the lightning and thunder and at the trumpet and smoke. "Speak to us yourself, Moses!" one man shouted. "If God speaks to us any longer, we will die."

"The Lord has done this to test you," Moses replied, "so that the fear of God will keep you from sinning."

The people watched as Moses turned and walked back up the mountain. This time the Lord spoke only to Moses: "Now the people have seen for themselves that I have spoken. So do not make any gods to be alongside me. Sacrifice your offerings on an altar of earth. Tell the people, 'Wherever I cause my name to be honored, I will come to you and bless you.'"

TBC 40

The Golden Calf

TBC Book One, Chapter 41
Exodus 32:1-35

Something must have happened to Moses. Many days had passed since he climbed up Mt. Sinai to receive the rest of God's commandments. The people began to wonder: What if he does not return? What if Moses himself has been consumed by God's wrath?

A large group gathered around Aaron. Someone in the crowd shouted out: "If Moses were coming back, he would have been here by now. I say we should continue our journey. "

"How would we know where to go?" Aaron said. "It is the Lord who has led us so far."

"Then let us make new gods who will go before us!" someone cried out.

So Aaron called a meeting of the elders. "Have the people remove their gold earrings," he said, "and bring them to me. We will make a god to go before us on our journey."

Aaron took all their jewelry, melted it down, and shaped it into a golden calf. When he presented it to the people, someone shouted, "This is your God, O Israel, who brought you out of Egypt!" Soon all of the people began shouting the same chant.

Seeing how the people responded, Aaron built an altar in front of the golden calf. When it was finished, he announced, "Tomorrow we will hold a festival to the Lord." Early the next day, they sacrificed offerings to the golden calf. Then they ate and drank and held a wild party.

Meanwhile, the Lord's voice changed to anger as he spoke to Moses. "You must leave. Go back down the mountain, for your people have become corrupt. Already they have turned away from me and bowed down to idols they have made. Now leave me alone so I may destroy them. But I will spare you and make you into a great nation."

Moses dropped to the ground with his face down. "O Lord," he pleaded, "why let the Egyptians say, 'He rescued them only to destroy them completely.' Remember what you swore to our forefathers, to be their inheritance forever." So the Lord listened to Moses and relented.

Moses left at once with his assistant, Joshua. They carried two stone tablets down the mountain. On both sides of these stones the Lord had engraved his commandments. As they neared the camp, Joshua thought he heard sounds of war, but it was only loud singing.

When Moses and Joshua approached the camp, they saw the golden calf, and the people were dancing around it. Moses' face grew red with anger. He lifted the tablets above his head and hurled them down, breaking them into pieces at the foot of the mountain.

The people stopped dancing. Fearfully, they stared at Moses. He motioned for Joshua. Together they set the golden calf in the fire and melted it down. Moses ground it into powder and dumped it into their water. Later that night, he made all the Israelites drink it.

Moses now turned to Aaron. "What caused you to lead the people into such great sin?"

"Don't be angry, my lord. We didn't know whether you would even return. So when the people asked me for gods, I melted down their jewelry, and out came this calf!"

By now, everyone was running around wildly. Some had even stripped off their clothes to imitate the religious rites they had learned in Egypt. So Moses called out, "Whoever is for the Lord, come to me!" The men who were Levites rallied to Moses, for he, too, was a Levite.

Moses turned to his kinsmen and shouted, "This is what the God of Israel commands: Strap a sword to your side. Go throughout the camp and kill all who are still sinning, regardless of who they are." People fled in terror, but the 3,000 who continued their frenzy were all killed.

The next day, Moses fell to his knees and begged the Lord to forgive the people for their sin. "And if you cannot," he said, "then blot out my name from your book of life."

The Lord replied firmly, "Whoever has sinned against me I will blot out of my book." God remembered what they had done, and later, he punished them with a plague.

TBC 41

Show Me Your Glory

His face was so radiant that they were afraid.

TBC Book One, Chapter 42
Exodus 33:1-23; 34:1-35

A surge of fear swept through Moses as he heard the Lord's decision: "You are to leave this place and travel to the land I promised your forefathers, but I will not go with you. For you are a stubborn people, and I might destroy you." When the people heard what he had said, they were full of sorrow. They took off their gaily decorated jewelry and began to mourn.

Before this, whenever they traveled, they were accustomed to seeing Moses pitch a special tent some distance away, where he could look down over the camp. He called it the "tent of meeting," and there he would talk to the Lord. Whenever Moses entered the tent, each family stood at the entrance to their own tent, watching him go in.

As Moses entered the tent, the pillar of cloud would come down. It hovered at the entrance while the Lord spoke to Moses. And when the people saw this, they would worship. Meanwhile, the Lord would speak to Moses the way a person speaks to his friend.

But God's latest piece of news made Moses feel like he was losing his best friend. "You have told me to lead these people," Moses said. "I have some concerns about that. Since you know me by name, and you say I have found favor with you, then stay with me and teach me your ways. And please—do not send us away unless you go with us."

"Very well," the Lord said, "my Presence will go with you."

Moses pondered his next request, for it was a bold one: "Lord, show me your glory."

The Lord was pleased to see that Moses wanted a deeper relationship. "Here is what I will do," he said. "I will cause all my goodness to pass before you, and I will reveal my name to you. For I will have mercy on whomever I wish, and I will have compassion on whomever I wish. But you may not see my face, for no one can see my face and live."

Then the Lord told Moses to chisel out two more stone tablets and come to Mt. Sinai. Early the next morning Moses made his way up the mountain. Then the Lord directed him to a cleft in a rock, to shield him from seeing God's face. As the Lord passed by, he let Moses see his back, and he revealed to him the meaning of his name: "The Lord, compassionate and gracious, slow to anger, abounding in love and faithfulness." Moses bowed to the ground and worshiped.

The Lord said, "I am making a covenant with you. I will do awesome wonders and drive out those in the land I am giving you. Make no treaties with them. Destroy their idols.

"Continue to celebrate the Feast of Unleavened Bread to remind you how I delivered you out of Egypt. Remember, every firstborn male belongs to me; claim it back by sacrificing a lamb.

"There are other celebrations you must also keep: Celebrate the Feast of Harvests with the first fruits of your crops. The Feast of Ingathering will be celebrated at the turn of the year, when crops are gathered. All the men must appear before me three times a year. Do not worry about anyone coveting your land while you are gone. I will protect it. Remind the people you shall work on six days but rest on the seventh, even during the planting season and the harvest."

For the next 40 days, Moses met with the Lord. The Spirit of the Lord was so strong upon him that he had no need to eat or drink. As he came down from the mountain, his face was radiant because he had spoken with the Lord and seen his glory. But Moses did not realize this, until he saw that the people were afraid to come near him.

Moses told the people all that the Lord had said. When he finished speaking, he walked back to his tent. Then he realized that the radiance he felt was starting to fade. So he put a veil over his face. That way the people would not see that the glory was fading away. For then they might question his leadership. But whenever he spoke to the Lord, he drew back the veil. Then he walked among the people and let them see the radiance of God.

TBC 42

The Tabernacle

TBC Book One, Chapter 43
Exodus 35:1-38:20; 39:32-40:38

Sorrow turned to joy when the Israelites learned that their God had changed his mind: Not only would he travel with them, but he would make his home among them. Moses told the people that the Lord would need a special dwelling. All who desired it, both men and women, would have a part in building this great tent, this tabernacle.

Moses explained to them that various materials would be needed—cloth, animal skins, and precious stones. But more than that, they would need people who were willing to work together in using their creative skills.

God gave special ability to the artists and craftsmen. He filled them with his Holy Spirit so they could build a tabernacle fit for his presence. The "tent of meeting," as it was called, was made of linen and yarn, with pictures of cherubim (winged angels) woven in. Animal skins were used to cover the top.

God chose Bezalel as the chief craftsman. He was the grandson of Hur, one of their godliest leaders. Bezalel made a special box, called "the ark," and it was overlaid with pure gold. Two gold cherubim covered the top, as if to show they were guarding God's holiness, there where God's glory cloud would rest.

A table was made of acacia wood, and it, too, was overlaid with gold. Large rings were placed at each corner, as with the ark, so poles could be slipped through them to carry the structure. The plates, bowls, and pitchers for drink offerings were also made of gold.

A beautiful lampstand was hammered out of pure gold, as were the wick trimmers and trays. Three branches extended from each side, making seven lamps. Its cups were shaped like almond flowers with buds and blossoms. These gave light to the tent of meeting.

The altar of incense, used to give off sweet smelling aromas, was also made of acacia wood, overlaid with pure gold. It, too, had gold rings and gold poles to carry it. A skilled perfumer made the sacred anointing oil and the incense that would be used for worship.

A larger altar was made of acacia wood and overlaid with bronze. Its pots, shovels, bowls, and forks were also made of bronze. This altar would be used for burnt offerings, called holocausts.

A bronze basin was made for the priests to wash their hands before entering the tabernacle's courtyard. The courtyard walls were curtains of finely twisted linen. Like the entire tabernacle, they could be packed up for traveling, similar to tents.

Those who would serve the Lord in the tabernacle were referred to as "priests." They would lead the people in worship, in making sacrifices, and in gaining the Lord's guidance.

One man, the high priest, would wear an elegant apron-like garment called an "ephod." Over the ephod, he wore a breastpiece, near to his heart. Like the ephod, it was made of gold, with blue, purple, and scarlet yarn and fine linen. Twelve precious stones were mounted on it, engraved with the names of Israel's twelve tribes. On the high priest's turban rested a gold diadem that carried this inscription: "Holy to the Lord."

At the hem of the priest's blue robe dangled ornamental pomegranates with bells in between. Whenever the people heard the bells, they knew that the priest was walking inside—he was still alive: God's holiness had not consumed him. It meant God had accepted both the priest and their sacrifice.

After inspecting their work and blessing it, Moses chose the first day of the first month to have the people set up the tabernacle. He anointed not only the entire tabernacle, but also the priests who would serve there. Then God's cloud rested on the tent of meeting and his glory filled the tabernacle.

TBC 43

Making Peace with God

TBC Book One, Chapter 44
Leviticus 1:1-8:36; 25:1-55

From ancient days, the people of the earth knew that a heavy weight held down their souls, a feeling that they just could not shake. No matter how hard they tried, they all did things that made them feel guilty. And thoughts of the Creator left them feeling unworthy.

Their earliest ancestors had told them it was not that way in the beginning. The Creator had once been their friend. But something severed their friendship. Trust had been broken. It would not be easy to regain. A price must be paid. Until that payment could be met, people would need a peace treaty with the Lord God who had made them.

It was for this reason that God commanded the Israelites to sacrifice a bull, a lamb, or a goat. But if someone were poor, he could substitute a dove or a pigeon. After the animal's blood was shed, it would burn on the altar, and the aroma would please God.

Different types of offerings were made, and each burnt offering also required a grain offering, seasoned with salt. The Israelites knew fire could not destroy salt. So God had them add salt to their offerings, to show that his promise or covenant with them would last forever.

The fellowship offering was like a peace offering for health and well-being. A person would offer it to express thankfulness or to show devotion to God by making a promise or a vow. The family would then eat a meal from portions of the offering.

When people sinned without knowing they had done wrong, God still held them responsible. They had to sacrifice a bull, a goat, or a lamb as a guilt offering. If a person refused to tell what he knew about someone else's wrongdoing or their innocence, that, too, was sin.

When a person accidentally wronged someone, he was still held responsible. And if a person deceived or cheated someone, that showed unfaithfulness to God. The person must sacrifice a ram and pay for anything damaged or taken dishonestly, plus one-fifth more.

Because the priests served both God and the people, they received part of every fellowship offering. The worshiper would wave the right thigh from the sacrifice then give it to the priest. Then he would give the breast for other priests and their families.

God told Moses to ordain Aaron as the high priest and appoint his sons as other priests. "Because every firstborn in Israel is mine," the Lord said, "I will take the Levites in their place." So all the men from the tribe of Levi, ages 25 to 50, would serve at the tabernacle.

As the Lord had commanded, Aaron first made peace with God for himself. He slaughtered a bull calf, dipped his finger in the blood, and touched the horns of the altar. The rest he poured out at the base of the altar while he burned his offering.

Then he made offerings on behalf of the people. Finally, he lifted his hands toward the people and blessed them. Suddenly, God's glory appeared, and fire sprang out to consume the entire offering. The people shouted for joy then dropped facedown in worship.

Because Aaron had done everything as God commanded, the Lord had accepted the people's offering. But when it was time for his sons to participate as priests, they ignored God's directions. Nadab and Abihu chose to light the censers their way instead of God's way. So God's anger was kindled. In one quick moment, fire from his presence flared out and killed them.

God gave specific directions not only for worship, but also for work. They were to work six days a week but rest on the seventh to honor God. They were to grow crops for six years but let the land rest on the seventh. So every seventh year was a sabbath rest for the land.

After forty-nine years (seven sabbath years) came a Year of Jubilee. Israelites who had sold themselves as slaves would be set free, and the land would be returned to the family who first owned it. For the land belongs to the Lord, and his people, are merely tenants, blessed by God.

TBC 44

A Demanding People

TBC Book One, Chapter 45
Numbers 11:1-34

The Israelites had no idea that someone was listening in on their conversations. Now that the tabernacle was completed, their enthusiasm was dampened by a new realization—they must continue to travel through the desert. As they journeyed onward, the people started to complain among themselves about the hardships they faced.

This was the very thing the Lord feared would happen, that his presence would be taken too lightly. Already they had kindled his anger with their constant whining. So the Lord struck the edge of the camp with fire.

The people cried out in terror. When Moses saw what happened, he knew God had sent the fire. Quickly he prayed, and the fire ceased.

But some people had learned nothing from God's fiery warning.

"If only we had meat to eat!" they complained. "In Egypt we had fish, cucumbers, melons. . . . We're sick of this manna!"

Yet the people had discovered many ways to prepare it. After gathering the thin, wafer-like flakes, they would grind them up. Then they would cook the manna in a pot or bake it as small cakes. The cakes tasted like they were made with olive oil.

Their complaining began with a few families in every tribe, but it soon spread like wildfire throughout the entire camp. Moses could hear one family after another, wailing from the entrance of each tent. The Lord became angry, and Moses grew depressed.

"Why have you put the burden of all these people on me?" Moses asked. "Where can I get meat for such a large mass? They keep complaining and saying, 'Give us meat to eat!' I cannot take care of all these people. The burden is too heavy for me. If this is how you wish to treat me, Lord, put me to death right now—don't let me see failure!"

The Lord listened to Moses' plea. "Bring me 70 of Israel's elders," he said. "Make sure they are leaders who are respected by the people. Have them stand at the tent of meeting. I will take some of the Spirit I've placed on you and put it on them. From now on, they will help you carry this burden of dealing with the people.

"Then send this message to all the people: 'The Lord heard you wailing, "If only we had meat! We were better off in Egypt!" Tomorrow the Lord will give you so much meat that you will wind up hating it. For your words have revealed what is in your hearts. You have rejected the Lord, who is among you, and desired to return to Egypt.'"

So Moses relayed all that the Lord had said. Then the elders stood with him around the tent of meeting. The Lord came down in the cloud and spoke further with Moses. Then he took some of the Spirit that was on Moses and placed it on the elders. Immediately, they began to prophecy, to speak forth the messages of God.

Meanwhile, back in the camp, two of the elders who were chosen had refused to go to the tent. Eldad and Medad stayed behind, ignoring Moses' orders. Yet the very moment that the other elders began prophesying, they too received the Spirit and started to prophesy. A young man who saw them prophesying ran to tell Moses.

When Joshua heard that, he said, "Moses, my lord, stop them!" Moses just smiled.

"Are you jealous on my behalf? Don't be. I wish that all God's people were prophets."

As Moses and the elders returned to the camp, the Lord sent a mighty wind. It drove quail into their camp and kept them from flying away. The birds were no more than three feet above the ground, and people could easily catch them. Every family gathered at least 60 bushels.

All around the camp, people spread out their quail. They prepared some of the meat and started to eat it. But those who had earlier complained about the food now tasted God's judgment. As they began to chew their meat, the Lord struck them with a plague, and they died.

TBC 45

The Spies Who Brought Back Fear

'They make us look like grasshoppers!'

TBC Book One, Chapter 46
Numbers 13:1-33; 14:1-45

Twelve brave, cunning Israelites were selected for a special mission. The men had reached the Desert of Paran, not far from their promised land. Now, at God's command, they selected one man from each tribe, who stood before Moses, waiting earnestly for their instructions.

"I am sending you out ahead of us to explore the land. Find out what the land is like and what kind of people are living there."

The 12 men traveled throughout the entire region. In Hebron they saw descendants of a man named Anak, known for their great size. Never had the Israelites seen men that tall. The land was rich and lush, and they picked samples of fruit, including some pomegranates and figs. Their cluster of grapes was so big that it took two men to carry it.

At the end of 40 days, the men returned to the camp. "You were right," they told Moses. "It is a land flowing with milk and honey. Look at the size of this fruit! But we must warn you—the people living there are big and powerful. Their cities are large and well-protected."

As the men described the descendants of Anak, Caleb motioned for everyone to be quiet. "Enough about the Anakites. I say we go up and take the land. We can do it!"

But the other men shook their heads in disagreement. "Caleb," one of the men argued, "how can you say that? You saw them with your own eyes. We can't attack those people. They are too strong. They make us look like grasshoppers."

All but two of the spies were in agreement—taking this land would be too risky. They painted such a negative picture that they made the people afraid to go in and fight for the land.

So all that night the people grumbled against Moses and Aaron. One after another, people said the same thing: "We should choose another leader and go back to Egypt."

As tensions mounted, Moses and Aaron fell facedown among the people, appealing to the Lord. Not far away, Joshua and Caleb tore their own clothes as a sign of their desperation. "Listen!" Joshua said, "We saw the land too, and it is excellent. The Lord can give us that land. Don't be afraid of the people there. Their protection is gone, but we have the Lord."

Yet the people would not listen. Instead, they talked about stoning Moses and Aaron.

Just then the glory cloud appeared at the tent of meeting, and the Lord spoke to Moses. "How long will these people refuse to trust me? I will destroy them and make you into a nation."

"O Lord," Moses said, "the surrounding nations have already heard that you are with us. If you put all these people to death, those nations will say, 'The Lord was not able to bring them into the land.' Since you are a loving God, forgive the people of their sin."

The Lord replied, "For my name's sake, I will forgive them. But none of the people who saw my glory and my miracles will enter the land. Instead, they will wander in this desert for 40 years—one year for each day the spies traveled. By then, all the faithless people will have died."

So the people who refused to trust God would never enter the land. But one day, their children would. As for the spies who caused so much fear, the Lord struck them dead with a plague. Only Joshua and Caleb were spared. For their faith, they would enter the land.

When Moses told the people what God had decided, they mourned bitterly. "We have sinned," they said. "We will go into the land after all."

"No," Moses said. "It's too late. If you try to enter the land now, you will be disobeying God. Don't even attempt it, for the Lord will not go with you."

But they refused to listen. Without Moses or the ark of the covenant to lead them, they approached the hill country. Then the Amalekites and Canaanites came down and attacked them, driving them all the way back. They would not enter this land apart from the power of God.

TBC 46

Korah's Rebellion

TBC Book One, Chapter 47
Numbers 16:1-50; 17:1-11

The only thing more lonely than tending sheep was shepherding one million men, women, and children. It seemed they were traveling in circles. And indeed, they were. Though they now stood at the threshold of their promised land, no one would enter it for 40 years.

There were no happy campers. Some said Moses was to blame as much as they. Even the Levites were beginning to draw back their support, thanks to a conspiracy begun by one man.

Korah had always resented it that one of his younger relatives was appointed as tribal leader. And why should the family of Moses take the role of priest over all the tribes? That was not how their forefathers handled leadership: Each family had their own spiritual leader.

Korah built friendships with leaders from the tribe of Reuben. He reminded them that they were descendants of Israel's firstborn son. Shouldn't they have a major role in leadership?

Korah's plan was working. He and his friends criticized Moses so much that even the elders agreed. "Were there not 70 of us who had prophesied by the Spirit of God?" So the elders met with the tribal leaders, and they agreed with Korah—it was time to confront Moses.

Accompanied by 250 men, Korah made his way to the tent of Moses. "We have something to tell you," he announced. "All the people are holy—not just you and your brother!"

When Moses heard this, he fell facedown. And the Lord revealed what he should do.

Moses rose and said, "Tomorrow morning, take censers and put fire and incense in them. The Lord himself will show who is holy." Then he added, "You Levites have gone too far!"

The Levites worked at the tabernacle. But they too had grown jealous of Aaron. As for Dathan and Abiram, the two Reubenites, they blamed Moses for their long, hard journey. But when Moses called for them, they refused to come. Their arrogant attitude made Moses angry.

He thought of the challenge his accusers would face in the morning. "Lord," he prayed, "do not accept their offering of fire and incense. I've done nothing to wrong any of them."

Early the next morning, people watched as 250 men stood near the tent of meeting. Then the Lord's glory appeared. "Move away," he said, "so I can destroy all of them."

"O God," Moses pleaded, "will you be angry with everyone when one man sins?"

God listened to his plea. "Have the people move away from the tents of Korah, Dathan, and Abiram." So Moses warned them. "Now you will know that God appointed me," he added.

Immediately, the ground shook and split open. The tents of Korah, Dathan, and Abiram, as well as their families, fell into the opening. Just as suddenly, the ground closed up again, and they all lay buried beneath the surface. When the Israelites saw this, they fled in terror.

Then God's fire consumed the 250 who opposed Moses. Only their censers remained.

The next day, the people were angry over the lives lost. They blamed Moses and Aaron. "You have killed the Lord's people!" they said. Suddenly the glory cloud appeared. Once more the Lord told Moses and Aaron, "Get away from this assembly so I can put an end to them."

The two men dropped facedown, but the Lord's plague had already started. "Hurry," Moses told Aaron, "and put incense and fire in your censer. Then run to the assembly and make atonement for the people." As Aaron did this, the plague stopped—but 14,700 people had died.

The Lord would now put an end to their grumbling about who should lead. He said one man must come from each tribe. "Have each man write his name on his staff," the Lord said, "and place them at the tent of meeting. The man I choose will find his staff has budded."

Aaron was selected to represent the tribe of Levi, and the next day, all the people saw that his staff had not only budded, but it had also blossomed and produced almonds. From then on, his staff was kept by the ark of the testimony, a reminder to all that they should not rebel.

TBC 47

Everyone Loses Patience

TBC Book One, Chapter 48
Numbers 20:1-29; 21:1-9

About 40 years had passed since the exodus from Egypt, and Moses was on the verge of a painful turning point. Almost all who had left Egypt as adults were dead. But the legacy they left was more than Moses could bear: Their grown children were just like them.

In spite of all that the Lord had done, the people argued with Moses. When they reached the Desert of Zin, they found no water. One after another they cried, "Why did you take us out of Egypt and bring us to this terrible place?"

Moses and Aaron slipped away to the tent of meeting and dropped facedown. The Lord's glory appeared, and the Lord spoke: "Take the staff and gather the assembly near that rock. Then speak to the rock, and water will pour out for the people and their livestock."

Moses took the blossoming staff from its memorial site and gathered the assembly near the rock. But instead of speaking to the rock, he spoke to the people in a burst of anger.

"Listen, you rebels! Must we bring you water out of this rock?"

Then he struck the rock. Nothing happened. He struck it again. This time, water gushed out, and everyone drank from it.

But the Lord was not pleased with Moses and Aaron. Almost 40 years ago, the Lord had caused water to come from a rock after Moses struck it with the staff. But that was before the staff had budded. This time, the staff served as a reminder of God's power and his authority. He had only to speak to the rock. What's more, he had failed to give glory to God for the water.

"You did not trust in me enough to do what I commanded," the Lord said. "Your actions and words did not honor me as holy before the Israelites. So neither of you will enter the land."

As the Israelites continued, they approached Edom, the land inhabited by Esau's descendants. Like the Israelites, they were also related to Abraham. So Moses sent a friendly message to their king, asking permission to travel through their land.

More than 400 years had passed since the Israelites lived near this region. Perhaps Esau's descendants still held a grudge against Jacob's descendants because of Jacob's deceit. Perhaps they feared losing their water or their land. Whatever their reason, their king replied, "No."

So the Israelites took a different route. At Mount Hor, Moses ascended the mountain with Aaron and his son Eleazar. Then God commanded that Aaron's priestly garments be put on Eleazar. Aaron died on that mountain and rested with his forefathers.

After 30 days of mourning Aaron's death, the Israelites continued. They traveled on the road leading to Atharim—until they were caught off guard by a Canaanite army. The army was sent by a king from the Negev. They attacked the Israelites and captured some of them.

The Israelites were distraught. "O Lord," they pleaded, "if you enable us to defeat those Canaanites, we promise to destroy their cities totally." The Lord granted their request. So the Israelites freed the captives and destroyed the Canaanite cities in Arad.

As they traveled along the route to the Red Sea, going around Edom, the people grew impatient. They spoke against the Lord and against Moses: "Why have you brought us out of Egypt to die in the desert? There is no bread! There is no water! And we hate this awful food!"

The Lord answered by sending poisonous snakes. The snakes bit them, and many died. The people ran to Moses and cried out, "We have sinned against the Lord and against you! Pray that the Lord will take away these snakes!" So Moses prayed for the people.

But instead of destroying the snakes, the Lord offered them this provision: "Make a replica of a snake and put it up on a pole. If anyone who is bitten will just look at it, that person will live." So Moses made a bronze snake. And those who turned to look at it were saved from death.

TBC 48

God Speaks Through a Donkey

Only now did he see what the donkey had seen.

TBC Book One, Chapter 49
Numbers 22:1-24:25

Rumors spread that an army of people was forcefully advancing. As the Israelites approached Canaan, Moses sent a message requesting permission to pass through. King Sihon refused and sent his army to attack. But the Israelites defeated them and took residence there.

Meanwhile, in Moab, King Balak grew terrified. He heard Israel's powerful army had crushed the mighty Amorites and feared his people would be next. So he sent for a sorcerer to curse Israel, to call on spirits to bring Israel's downfall.

Some princes from Moab personally delivered the king's message to a man named Balaam. It was said he could he predict the future and even shape it by pronouncing blessings and curses.

The messengers, who were tired from their journey, rested overnight in Balaam's home. That night, God confronted Balaam and warned him not to curse Israel.

The next morning Balaam sent the group away. But the king sent back a larger group, promising money if Balaam would curse Israel.

"I can only do what God permits," Balaam said. "I will see what he says." And that night, God said, "Go with them, but do only what I say."

The next morning, the sorcerer and his two servants followed the group toward Moab. But God was angry with Balaam. Near the vineyard, Balaam's donkey suddenly stopped. Then he moved sideways and crushed Balaam's leg against the wall. Angrily, Balaam beat the donkey.

They traveled a bit farther, when they came to a narrow passageway. Once again the donkey stopped. This time she lay down, with Balaam still in the saddle. As he began to beat her, the Lord caused the donkey to speak: "Have I ever behaved this way before?" she said.

"No," he answered. The prophet's madness had dulled his ability to reason, even to recognize the miracle before him. Only now did Balaam suddenly see what the donkey had seen all along—the angel of the Lord, standing with a drawn sword. Balaam fell facedown.

"This donkey saved your life," the Lord said.

"I have sinned," Balaam replied. "Shall I go back?"

"No," the Lord said, "but say only what I tell you."

Balaam had almost arrived at his destination when King Balak went out to meet him.

"What took you so long?" he said. "Have you forgotten that I am able to make you rich?"

"Well, I am here now," Balaam replied. "But I can speak only the words God gives me." Then King Balak sacrificed cattle and sheep and held a feast.

The next morning, the king led Balaam up into the mountains. From there they could look down and see the Israelites. Balaam told King Balak to build seven altars. They sacrificed a bull and a ram on each altar. Then Balaam slipped away to a barren cliff to meet with God.

When Balaam returned, he gave a prophetic judgment: "From the rocky peaks I see them, a people separate from the other nations. They are as numerous as dust; who can count them?"

"What have you done?" the king cried. "You have blessed my enemies!"

Balaam replied, "I must speak God's words."

So the king took Balaam to another viewpoint and built seven more altars. Once again, Balaam met with the Lord. When he returned, he said, "The Lord is with Israel. No sorcery or divination can stand against them. Like a lion, Israel does not rest until he devours his prey."

King Balak simmered with anger. From another site, he tried to get Balaam to curse Israel. To his chagrin, Balaam cried out, "How beautiful is your dwelling, O Israel! Your kingdom will be exalted. May those who bless you be blessed, and those who curse you be cursed." The more he demanded curses, the greater the blessings pronounced. Finally, Balaam predicted what would happen to the Moabites—they would be destroyed, at the hands of Israel.

TBC 49

What Matters to God

TBC Book One, Chapter 50
Deuteronomy 6:1-8:20; 12:4-7; 13:1-5

The Israelites sensed that the end was near—their leader was about to die. And yet nothing indicated his health was failing. His eyesight was better than men much younger. But it was the way he spoke that hinted at his departure. He began to remind them of what they must remember long after he was gone, what was important to God.

"First and foremost," Moses said, "you are to love the Lord your God with all your heart, soul, and strength. Teach your children God's commands. Talk about them throughout each day.

"When the Lord brings you into the land he promised, you will inhabit cities and houses that you did not build. You will draw from wells you did not dig and eat from vineyards and groves that you did not plant. When that happens and you feel satisfied, do not forget the Lord.

"Remember to fear the Lord your God and serve him only. Do not follow other gods, as the peoples nearby are doing. For the Lord your God is a jealous God. If you forget him and worship other gods, he will surely destroy you, just as he has destroyed other nations."

"When your children and grandchildren ask about the meaning behind our rituals and laws, tell them, 'We were slaves in Egypt. But the Lord miraculously brought us out. He gave us this land, the land he had promised to our forefathers. And we will prosper if we obey him.'

"'The Lord will enable you to conquer the seven nations that live in the land, even though they are larger and stronger. Make no treaties with them, and do not intermarry with them. Destroy them completely. Break down their altars and smash their idols.

"God has chosen you as his special people because of the promise he made to your forefathers. If you obey his commands, he will keep his covenant of love: He will bless you with many children, abundant crops, and vast herds of livestock, and he will protect you from disease.

"When you see the nations you must fight, you might think, 'How can we possibly defeat them?' When that happens, remember what the Lord your God did against Egypt. Do not be afraid. He will drive out those nations for you. But he will do it little by little, so wild animals do not multiply quickly, before you have a chance to populate each region.

"The Lord led you in the desert 40 years to humble you and test you—to learn what was in your hearts. Your clothes never wore out. When you hungered, he fed you. The Lord did this to show you that there is a hunger bread cannot satisfy, a hunger only God can feed.

"Remember God's commands, do what pleases him, respect him as Lord. He is bringing you into a good land, with streams and springs, wheat and barley, vines, fig trees, pomegranates, olive oil, honey, and so much more. The land is rich with iron and copper. You will lack nothing.

"When you have settled in the land and found comfort, praise the Lord your God for all that he has given you and obey his commands. Otherwise you may forget the Lord and think, 'I've done pretty well for myself.' But it is the Lord who gives you the ability to grow wealthy.

"Do not use the places of worship created by other nations. Seek the place of worship that the Lord will choose. He will put his Name there for his dwelling. Offer your sacrifices there.

"If someone foretells the future by dreams or visions or shows you something miraculous to get you to follow another god, do not do it. Even if it appears to be a miracle, do not heed it. God is testing you to find out whether you really love him. Hold fast to him."

The people listened earnestly. They were now a vast people, numbering in the millions. So Moses would speak to the leaders, and they in turn would gather with their tribes and clans.

For 40 years Moses had led them. Yet now God would not permit him to enter the land. Some wondered if God might change his mind. Moses had persuaded him in the past. Perhaps he could do it again. They did not know that Moses was pondering the same thing. . . .

TBC 50

Moses Prepares to Leave

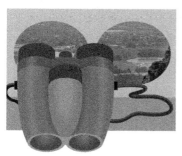

TBC Book One, Chapter 51
Deuteronomy 3:21-28; 31:1-8; 34:1-12

It was almost too good to be true: After 40 years of wandering in the wilderness like nomads, the Israelites were on the verge of crossing over and entering their land. All those who had believed the ten spies, instead of trusting God, had finally died. The only ones who were left from that generation were Caleb, Joshua, and Moses. But Moses would not be going with them.

Still, Moses could not bear the thought of not entering the land. He hoped that the Lord would change his mind. "Please, Lord," he pleaded, "let me go in with them to see the land."

But the Lord remained firm. "No, and do not ask me again. You will not cross the Jordan with them. But if you climb to the top of Pisgah and look out from there, you will see this land.

"Now go and prepare Joshua to take your place. Encourage him, for he is the one I have now chosen to lead the people into the land."

All the Israelites now assembled, and they grew silent as Moses appeared. "I am now 120 years old," he said, "and no longer able to lead you. I cannot cross the Jordan, but you shall. Joshua will lead you, and you will indeed possess the land.

"The Lord will defeat your enemies, just as he did the Amorites. He will deliver them into your hands. But remember to do all that I have commanded you. Do not be afraid, for the Lord your God is going with you."

Then Moses turned to Joshua. With all the Israelites watching, he said, "Be strong and courageous. God has chosen you to lead these people into the promised land. Divide the land among them as their inheritance. Do not be afraid, for the Lord himself will go with you."

For some time now, Moses had recorded details concerning their journey. He had also written down the fuller commands that the Lord gave to him on Mt. Sinai. Calling these scrolls the "Book of the Law," he now gave them to the priests and the elders. It was their responsibility to teach them to the people and to their descendants.

"At the end of every seven years," Moses said, "when the people cancel the debts they are owed, have all the men, women, and children meet at the place of worship. Then read aloud these words of the Law."

While the words of Moses were being relayed to the people, Moses slipped away to the tent of meeting, and Joshua went with him. There the Lord appeared in the glory cloud.

"Moses, you are about to die, and you will rest with your fathers. But first I want you to teach the people a song. I will give you the words. This song reveals what will happen to them."

Once more Moses gathered the assembly. "The Lord has given me a song to teach you. It reveals what will happen one day. You will indeed turn away from him. When this happens, and your descendants hear this song, they will realize God that predicted this long before it happened."

Then Moses climbed Mount Nebo to the top of Pisgah, across from Jericho, and the Lord showed him the whole land. "This is it," the Lord said, "the land I promised on oath to Abraham, Isaac, and Jacob, the land I promised to give to their descendants. Now you have seen it."

On that mountain, Moses died, just as God had predicted. At age 120, his eyes were not weak, and he still had a great deal of strength. Had he not disobeyed God, he could have lived longer. The Lord himself buried Moses, and no one had ever learned exactly where he was buried.

The Israelites knew why Moses had climbed the mountain. And they knew that he would not return. For 30 days they grieved over his death. Never has there arisen another prophet like Moses, someone who knew God face to face and could perform such awesome miracles.

Before he climbed the mountain, Moses met with Joshua, his faithful assistant. There were tears in both men's eyes as he rested his hands on Joshua's shoulders. This was more than a gesture of farewell. Moses had imparted the power of God's Spirit. From that moment on, Joshua was filled with a spirit of wisdom. God anointed him as Israel's new leader.

TBC 51

A Strange Battle Plan

TBC Book One, Chapter 52
Joshua 2:1-6:27

God had promised he would give the Israelites the land beyond the Jordan, but now they must do their part to claim it. The people who lived there would fight to keep it, but that was part of God's plan. Israel would bring God's judgment on these pagan nations.

Joshua sent two spies to search throughout the land and bring back information about Jericho. The men slipped into the city without drawing attention to themselves—or so they thought. When they saw they were being followed, they went into the home of a prostitute named Rahab.

"Don't ask any questions," they said. "Just hide us, and we will pay you well."

Moments later, soldiers appeared at Rahab's door. "The king says you are to send those two men out of your house immediately," the spokesman said. "We are certain they are spies."

"I wish you would have come sooner," she replied. "Two men did come here. But they left already. I can show you which way they went. If you hurry, you might catch them."

Rahab watched as the soldiers hurried away. Then she walked inside. Later, when all was dark, she went upstairs to the roof. "You can come out now," she whispered. "It is safe.

"Listen—I know you are spies sent from the Israelites and that God is giving you this land. Everyone knows it, and they are scared to death. We have heard of the miracles God has done. So please, since I saved your lives, spare me and my family, just as I spared you."

"It's a deal," one of them replied, "our lives for yours. But you must be careful to do all that we say. Otherwise we can't guarantee your safety. When we attack, keep your family inside your home. Tie this red cord here and let it dangle from your window to mark your house."

"I will," she said. "May God be our witness."

Rahab's home was built against the city wall. So the spies climbed out the window and slipped away in the dark of night. They hurried into the hills and hid there for three days, until the guards gave up searching for them. Then they crossed the Jordan and returned to their camp.

"The Lord has surely given us the land," they said. "All the people are melting in fear."

Then the Lord said to Joshua, "I am about to do something so miraculous the people will never forget it. In this way, they will know I have chosen you just as I had chosen Moses."

The priests carried the ark to the edge of the Jordan River. No one suspected that the Israelites would attack so soon, for the river was at flood stage. But as the priests stepped into the river, with the ark on their shoulders, the water parted and the people followed on dry ground.

After they crossed, Joshua called for 12 men, one from each tribe. He told each of them to pick up one large stone from the riverbed. At Gilgal, they set up camp and piled the stones as a memorial. This would remind their descendants of what God had done for them.

Word spread that the Israelites crossed the Jordan and were steadily advancing. When people learned that God had parted the river for them, the surrounding nations were terrified.

The Israelites remained at Gilgal. Then Joshua gave the orders God had given to him. They were to march around Jericho's walls silently, with no sound but that of trumpets.

Following the ark, they marched around Jericho once a day for six days. On the seventh day, they circled it seven times. Joshua said, "When I give the signal, shout loudly, for the Lord has given you the city."

"Now!" he yelled.

They all shouted, and Jericho's walls collapsed.

The two spies were waiting near Rahab's house. She and her family were unharmed, though parts of the wall had collapsed. The spies led them to a safe place. Then Israel attacked the city and burned everything in it, just as God had commanded. Joshua pronounced a curse on anyone who would rebuild Jericho. The only survivors were Rahab and her family.

"From now on," Rahab said, "we will live among the Israelites and worship the Lord."

TBC 52

Enemies in Disguise

TBC Book One, Chapter 53
Joshua 8:1-35; 9:1-27

Jericho's defeat marked the beginning of a brilliant military campaign, and led by God's Spirit, Joshua emerged as a cunning leader. At Ai he kept most of his men hidden while he advanced with a small group. Then they retreated, luring the men of Ai to chase them. Suddenly, the hidden soldiers appeared. With great swiftness the Israelites defeated the people of Ai.

When the nations west of the Jordan River heard about Joshua's military feats, their fears mounted. The kings of six different nations met together and decided they would all join forces to attack Israel—that is, all but one. After the Hivites of Gibeon heard about Jericho and Ai, they met with the other kings. But later, they met among themselves and made a plan of their own.

"No army can stand against the God of the Israelites," said one of the leaders, "not even a team of allies. They took no captives at Jericho or Ai. So how can we possibly bargain with them?"

"I know!" said another. "Let's dress up a few men in tattered clothes and send them to the Israelites as if they are from a distant land. Then we can trick them into signing a treaty."

So a group from Gibeon loaded up donkeys with worn-out sacks, carrying cracked wineskins and bread that was dry and moldy. Wearing ragged clothes, they approached Gilgal. Their spokesman called out, "We have come from a distant country to make a treaty with you!"

"Who are you?" Joshua asked. "Where do you come from?"

"We have come from a very distant country," the man replied. "We heard of all the Lord your God did to the Egyptians and the Amorites." The man said nothing about Jericho and Ai, pretending not to know about their destruction. He wanted the Israelites to think the group had only old information, for news traveled slowly to far-away regions.

Joshua turned to consult with some of his other leaders. Seeing that they were hesitant, one of the Gibeonites said, "Could we trouble you for some supplies? We will pay whatever you like. We have been traveling for so long that our food is stale and our clothes are worn out."

"Yes," said another Gibeonite, "it's hard to believe this bread was still warm when we left. But look at it now!" He held it up for all to see. "It's dry and moldy."

Skeptically, one of the Israelites picked up the loaf of bread. It was hard as a rock. Then they examined the cracked wineskins and their food. They were convinced. Without seeking God's guidance, Joshua made a peace treaty and both leaders confirmed it with an oath.

After receiving provisions from the Israelites, the Gibeonites left. By the time they reached Gibeon, the Israelites learned the truth—they had made a treaty with one of the nations they should have driven out. So Joshua and other leaders traveled to Gibeon to confront them.

Meanwhile, the Israelites were angry with their leaders for making the peace agreement. They had sworn their pledge to God. So Israel could not break the treaty by attacking them.

When they arrived in Gibeon, Joshua confronted the men who had fooled him. "Why did you deceive us like this? Because you have done this, your people will now live under this curse: You will always serve as woodcutters and water carriers for Israel and for the house of our God."

The Gibeonites were relieved just to save their lives. "We knew what the Lord your God had commanded Moses," explained one of the leaders. "We had heard that you were commanded to wipe out all the inhabitants in this land, including us. And we were afraid. That's why we did this. We accept your demands. We are now your servants. Do as you wish."

If it were not for Joshua, the people of Israel would have attacked them despite the treaty. But Joshua knew that breaking their oath would only bring God's judgment. So from that day on, the Gibeonites became woodcutters and water carriers for the Israelites. And one day, when God would reveal Israel's place of worship, they would help the Israelites build a house for the Lord.

TBC 53

The Day the Sun Stood Still

TBC Book One, Chapter 54
Joshua 10:1-43

The king of Jerusalem could hardly believe this news—Gibeon had made a peace treaty with Israel. Gibeon was a large, important city, with many good fighters. It was even larger than the city of Ai. If Gibeon had indeed made a treaty with Israel, then there was no stopping them.

Jerusalem's leader summoned four other kings and made plans to battle Gibeon. "Let's attack," the king urged, "before the Israelites can come to their rescue. We must act quickly and decisively, before they have a chance to strengthen their forces."

He had made a compelling argument. So the five kings joined forces to attack Gibeon.

Because of their treaty, the Israelites were required to rescue the Gibeonites if they were invaded. When they realized the Amorites were planning to attack, a messenger from Gibeon ran to Joshua's camp: "Come quickly!" he shouted. "The Amorites are about to attack us!"

Joshua left Gilgal with his entire army. He knew this would be one of the largest battles they had ever faced. As he prayed in his spirit, he could hear the Lord's reply: "Do not be afraid. I have given them all into your hands."

By traveling all night, Joshua surprised the Amorites. The Lord added to their panic by causing great confusion when they awoke, and Israel easily defeated them. As the Amorites fled, the Lord hurled down large hailstones and more died from the hail than from the battle.

Joshua wanted to finish all that the Lord commanded him to do, but he was afraid he would run out of time. Once it grew dark, the rest of the Amorites would get away.

In one of his greatest acts of faith, Joshua stood before the Israelites and cried out so that all could hear: "O sun, I command you to stand still until we have destroyed our enemies!"

For a full day and night, light prevailed, as if the sun were standing still. With great intensity, Israel pursued its enemies. The five kings refused to surrender, knowing it would mean certain death. So they kept running until they found a cave and hid. But Joshua's men were not far behind. When they reached the cave, they covered the entrance with a stone.

After destroying the armies completely, the Israelites returned to the cave. As was the custom among Eastern peoples, Joshua made the kings lie on the ground. He told his officers, "Place your feet on their necks." Then he said, "This is what God will do to all your enemies."

Joshua himself killed all five of the kings. He ordered that their bodies be hung on trees until evening, a sign that they were under God's curse. That night Joshua's soldiers threw the bodies into the cave and sealed it again with stones.

Meanwhile, Joshua and all Israel continued their campaign to the south, where they defeated Makkedah. From Makkedah, Joshua's forces traveled to Libnah and began attacking the cities of the five kings. After defeating Libnah, they attacked Lachish. The Lord gave the people into Israel's hands. As God had commanded, they put everyone to the sword. No one survived.

Israel then moved on to Eglon. They captured the city in a single day and killed all its people. From there they went on to conquer Hebron. God warned the Israelites to have no pity on these peoples, for if they were left alive, they would draw Israel into worshiping their idols.

The Israelites now turned farther south and headed for Debir. They defeated that city as well as the surrounding villages, putting everyone to the sword. Both Hebron and Debir were walled cities. Their destruction showed what great power God had given to Israel.

After conquering the entire southern region, including the hill country and the Negev, Israel returned to Gilgal. From Kadesh Barnea to Gaza, from Palestine's Goshen toward the land of Gibeon, they destroyed all the inhabitants. In every battle, they proved successful, for the Lord God had fought for them.

TBC 54

Israel's Lottery—Pick Twelve

TBC Book One, Chapter 55
Joshua 10:40-43; 11:1-23; 13:1-24:33;
Judges 1:1-36; 2:1-9

In the northern parts of Canaan, tribal leaders refused to believe the stories they had heard. How could a nomadic people with primitive weapons stand against a trained army that boasted horses and chariots? They did not know that God was using their pride and arrogance against them. Thousands of troops joined forces to attack Israel. But Joshua caught them off guard by striking them first. His maneuver proved so successful that he destroyed them completely.

Under the leadership of Moses, Israel had captured land east of the Jordan. That territory went to the Israelite tribes of Reuben, Gad, and half of Manasseh. But those tribes knew that they must now help their Israelite brothers fight to gain all the land God had promised them.

By now Israel had also conquered land west of the Jordan. Yet there was still more to be taken. So Caleb approached Joshua with a bold request.

"Remember when the Lord promised me the hill country where the Anakites live? I am now 85 and strong as ever. Let me take that land."

With Joshua's permission, Caleb's family conquered the territory that became known as Hebron.

The Israelites drew lots (like drawing straws) to decide which tribes should take each piece of land. The large tribes of Ephraim and Manasseh were given territory just west of the Jordan. But they complained that their land was not large enough. So Joshua challenged them to conquer the Canaanites and take their land. But they were afraid of the Canaanites' iron chariots.

In spite of their past success, many of the tribal commanders had lost their ambition. So Joshua called a meeting and confronted them: "How long will you wait to take the land? Appoint men to map out the territory so we can divide it among the seven remaining tribes."

Joshua did not want to repeat the mistake they had made with their large tribes of Ephraim and Manasseh. From now on they would survey the land ahead of time, and they would fight until they had acquired enough territory to support their people.

This time the first lot fell to Benjamin, then Simeon, Zebulon, Issachar, Asher, Naphtali, and Dan. Then the Israelites gave Joshua an inheritance of land in the hill country of Ephraim. As for the Levites, the Lord was their inheritance. When God spared Israel's firstborn from death in Egypt, he claimed the Levites as his own. So instead of receiving a region of land, they were given pastureland in 48 cities throughout the region, to serve God among all the tribes.

Then the Lord told Israel to set apart six "cities of refuge." If a person accidentally killed someone, he could run to one of them for safety until he stood trial. No one could kill him.

After the land divisions were settled, the three tribes east of the Jordan built an altar. When Phinehas, the high priest, heard about it, he and other leaders traveled there to confront them. They were relieved to learn it was only a monument, not an idol. It was a way to remind future generations that they, too, belonged to Israel.

As Joshua neared the end of his life, he charged the Israelites to drive out the other nations from their land. "Make no alliances with them," he warned, "and never bow down to their idols. For if you do, they will become a snare, and you will perish from this good land. Remember all that the Lord has done for Israel. If you own any idols, throw them away. Decide today whom you will serve. As for me and my house, we will serve the Lord."

Then the people shouted, "We will serve the Lord!" And they set up a stone monument to remind them of their vow.

At age 110, Joshua died. The Israelites heeded his command and waged war against their enemies. But they failed to drive them out completely. So God sent an angel with this message: "Because you disobeyed me, the inhabitants of this land will always be a thorn in your side."

When the people heard that, they wept. If only they had chosen to obey. . . .

TBC 55

Broken Promises

TBC Book One, Chapter 56
Judges 2:1-23; 3:1-30; 4:1-24; 5:1-31

If Joshua had known what his grandchildren and their children would do with their freedom, he would have gone to his grave with tears. And it was not just them—it was all the Israelites. As long as Joshua was alive, they obeyed the Lord. But after his generation died, they started worshiping the gods of the nations they had not driven out. They even arranged marriages with people from the pagan nations, which led to more idolatry and evil behavior.

The Israelites had broken their covenant with God. So the Lord decided he would not drive out those pagan nations. Instead, he would use those very nations to test Israel.

When the Israelites began to worship the gods of Baal and the Canaanite goddess Ashtoreth, the Lord grew angry. He allowed Israel's enemies to raid their villages and plunder their crops. But sometimes a leader would rise up from among them and save them by turning them back to God. That leader would then be recognized as their judge.

Unlike their forefathers, these Israelites quickly turned away from obeying God's commands. Their actions often led to their own suffering. From time to time, God would feel compassion for them and would raise up a judge to save them. But as soon as the judge died, they would go back to worshiping idols.

For eight years Israel slaved to pay tribute money to the king of Aram, who had conquered them. Then they cried out to the Lord. So God raised up Othniel, Caleb's nephew. The Spirit of God came upon him, giving him both power and wisdom. He led Israel to defeat Aram. Then Israel enjoyed peace for 40 years.

When Othniel died, the people again turned to evil. So God allowed King Eglon of Moab to conquer them. After 18 years, they cried out to the Lord, and he raised up a man named Ehud.

One day Ehud delivered the tribute money, and he whispered, "I have a secret message for you, O King." King Eglon dismissed everyone from the room. Ehud stepped closer. "I have a message from God," Ehud said. As the king stood, Ehud, who was left-handed, drew his sword and killed Eglon. Meanwhile, Eglon's servants waited impatiently behind the door. They wondered what was taking so long. Ehud dashed out the porch and escaped before they knew what had happened.

From the hills of Ephraim, he blew a trumpet to summon the men of Israel. "Follow me," he yelled, "for the Lord has given you Moab!"

The Israelites killed almost 10,000 Moabites, and Moab served Israel for 80 years.

After Ehud died, Israel returned to its idolatry and evil practices. So God let them be conquered by Jabin, a Canaanite king who owned 900 iron chariots. After 20 years of cruel oppression, Israel cried out to God. So the Lord raised up a prophetess named Deborah.

As Israel's new leader, Deborah sent for an officer named Barak. "The Lord commands you to lead 10,000 men to Mount Tabor. He will lure Jabin's forces into your hand." But Barak refused to go without Deborah. So she went, and Israel routed them, despite the chariots.

The Canaanite commander, Sisera, fled to save his life. When he came to the tent of Jael, a Kenite woman, he accepted her offer to come in and rest. He did not know her husband was a descendant of Moses' brother-in-law. As Sisera lay sleeping, she killed him with a tent peg.

Before the battle, it was clear that Barak was afraid to fight without Deborah's presence. His lack of faith cost him the honor that would have been his. Deborah had predicted that the credit for capturing Sisera would go to a woman. With the battle now over, she and Barak sang about their victory. Their song praised the Lord, and it also pronounced a blessing on the greatest hero among them, the woman Jael.

TBC 56

A Cowardly Hero

TBC Book One, Chapter 57
Judges 6:1-7:25

After 40 years of peace during Deborah's leadership, Israel again turned to evil. So God let the Midianites and other tribes invade their land like swarms of locusts. They ruined the crops with their livestock. Meanwhile, the Israelites hid inside caves. Finally, they cried out to God.

The Lord heard them, and he sent a prophet with this reply: "I snatched you from Egypt and brought you out of slavery. Then I drove out these nations who now oppress you, and I gave you their land. I said, 'Do not worship their gods.' But you have not listened to me."

Later, a man named Gideon was fearfully threshing his wheat in a winepress, when the angel of the Lord appeared with a message: "The Lord is with you, mighty warrior! Save Israel from Midian."

At first the man was startled. Then he thought about the stranger's words. "If God is with us," he said, "why is this happening to us? And how could I save Israel? My clan is the weakest one in Manasseh, and my family would tell you there is nothing special about me."

"I will be with you," the Lord replied, "and you will defeat the Midianites."

Gideon asked the stranger for a sign to know this message really was from the Lord. So the Lord waited as Gideon ran to prepare an offering. When Gideon finished, fire flared from the rock to consume the meat and the bread. Immediately, the angel of the Lord disappeared.

Gideon realized he had seen the Lord! Yet he did not die. So his heart was moved, and he built an altar to the Lord.

Then the Lord returned and told him to destroy his father's Baal altar and Ashterah pole. Fearfully, he did it during the night. Then he sacrificed a bull, as commanded.

The next morning, everyone was angry, for the idols were shared by the community. When they learned who had destroyed them, they went to Joash and demanded his son Gideon.

Joash, too, was upset by Gideon's actions, but he refused to send his son to an angry mob.

"Listen," he said, "if Baal really is a god, he can defend himself. He doesn't need you to do it." So the men left.

Meanwhile, some Eastern tribes joined forces to raid Israel again. Then God's Spirit came upon Gideon. He blew a trumpet and summoned his relatives and the other tribes.

Fearfully, he prayed, "If you will indeed save Israel by my hand, show me by letting me find dew on this fleece but not on the ground." The next morning Gideon wrung out the dew. Then he asked God for another sign—to make the fleece dry and the ground wet. And God did.

At the spring of Harod, the Lord said, "You have too many men. They will think they defeated Midian themselves. Send away those who are fearful." Two-thirds left and 10,000 remained. "That is still too many," said the Lord. "Take them to the spring." Gideon obeyed.

Then the Lord said, "Watch the men drink. Keep only those who kneel on one leg and cup the water with their hands." Now only 300 remained, and God was satisfied. He told Gideon, "If you are afraid to attack, take your servant and sneak up to the Midianite camp to listen."

That night, Gideon and his servant crept to the edge of their enemy's camp and heard a man recounting his dream: "It was the strangest thing. A huge barley loaf crushed our tent!"

The man listening to him grew alarmed, "That can only mean one thing—God has given us into the hands of Gideon." When Gideon heard that, he worshiped the Lord.

Quickly they ran to their camp. "Get up!" he shouted. "The Lord has given us Midian!"

Gideon divided them into three groups. They all carried torches, but as they neared the camp, Gideon made them hold clay jars over each flame. Then he gave his final orders.

The Israelites quietly surrounded the camp. At Gideon's signal, some blew trumpets, others broke their pots. Then they shouted, "For the Lord and for Gideon!" The Midianites were so shocked that they attacked one other. When they realized what was happening, they fled.

The Israelites had won far more than a battle. For 40 years their land enjoyed peace.

TBC 57

The Strong-Willed Child

TBC Book One, Chapter 58
Judges 13:1-25; 14:1-20

Once again, the Israelites drifted away from the Lord, so he allowed the Philistines to dominate them for 40 years. Eventually, his people cried out for help. But this time, instead of raising up a godly judge, God sent someone who was just like them—always lusting over things that would only bring their downfall.

God's plan began with a woman who was unable to get pregnant. The angel of the Lord appeared to her and said, "You will have a son. And from his birth he must be set apart for God."

When the stranger disappeared, the woman immediately raced to tell her husband. She told Manoah everything: She was not to drink wine during her pregnancy nor to eat foods considered unclean. The boy's hair must never be cut; he must keep the vows of a Nazarite, set apart to serve God.

Manoah wanted to hear these words for himself. So he prayed. Again the angel appeared to the woman. She ran for her husband. Manoah came quickly and invited the stranger to a meal.

"No," he said, "but you may prepare an offering to the Lord."

"What is your name?" Manoah asked.

"Why do you ask my name? It is too wonderful for you to understand."

Manoah left to prepare the offering, a goat and some grain placed on a rock. No sooner had he set them down when fire blazed from the rock. There in the flame appeared the stranger, ascending toward heaven. Only then did the couple realize they had seen the angel of the Lord.

The woman did give birth to a son. She named him Samson, for he was the sunshine of her life. As he grew up, the Lord blessed him, and God's Spirit began to stir in his life.

One day Samson came from Timnah and told his parents he wanted to marry a Philistine. They tried to persuade him to change his mind, but Samson would not be dissuaded.

"Get her for me!" he demanded.

His parents did not know God was using his demanding nature to fulfill God's plans. He was also using their weak will, for they gave in and traveled to Timnah to arrange the marriage.

Samson took a different route, and on the way, he was attacked by a young lion. But he was so strong and so quick that he killed it with his bare hands. Yet he said nothing about it.

When the family traveled to Timnah for the marriage, he again took the vineyard route. The lion's dead carcass now contained a beehive. As a Nazarite, he should not have touched it. Ignoring his vows, he scooped out honey and ate it. Then he took some for his parents.

In Timnah, Samson held a feast for 30 Philistine men invited by the bride's family. He taunted them with a challenge. "I'll bet you 30 sets of clothes that you can't solve my riddle."

"All right," one of them replied. "Tell us your riddle."

Samson smiled. "Out of the eater, something to eat; out of the strong, something sweet."

Three days later, the men cornered Samson's bride: "Did you invite us here just to rob us with this riddle? Find out the answer for us. Otherwise, you and your father will be killed."

For the rest of the week, Samson's wife threw herself on him, crying and saying, "You don't really love me. You gave my people a riddle, and you didn't even tell me the answer." She nagged him so often that finally, on the seventh day, he told her.

Later that day, the men came to Samson. This time they were the ones to smile. The spokesman said, "What is sweeter than honey? What is stronger than a lion?"

Samson was furious. Without a word he left them. He now owed a set of new clothes to each of the 30 guests. *I know what I'll do,* thought Samson. He made his way toward Ashkelon, and God's Spirit came upon him mightily. He entered the city and struck down 30 Philistines. Then he ripped off their clothes and used them to pay his debt.

With his anger still surging, Samson left his wife and returned to his parents' house.

TBC 58

Samson's Revenge

In a fit of rage he vowed to get even.

TBC Book One, Chapter 59
Judges 15:1-20; 16:1-31

Many months passed before Samson decided to return to Timnah, and when he arrived, his wife was gone. Her father thought Samson would never return. So he gave his daughter to another man.

In a fit of rage, Samson vowed revenge. He caught 300 foxes, tied them in pairs, and set their tails on fire. As they struggled to escape, they raced through the fields and burned the crops.

When the Philistines learned what had happened, they blamed Samson's wife and father-in-law. To retaliate, they seized them both and burned them to death.

Samson heard what they had done. In a fit of rage, he slaughtered many of the Philistines. Then he hid in a cave in Etam. Meanwhile, the Philistines demanded that the men of Judah hand over Samson. With 3,000 men, Judah's leaders found Samson's cave and surrounded it.

"If you promise not to kill me," Samson said, "I'll let you tie me and take me to the Philistines." Surely that would pacify the Philistines. So the men agreed.

When the Philistines saw Samson tied up, they shouted for joy. Then God's Spirit came upon Samson powerfully. He snapped the ropes, grabbed a donkey's jawbone from the ground, and struck down a thousand Philistines. The rest fled, and Samson became Israel's new leader.

Years later, Samson fell in love with a woman named Delilah. When the Philistines realized this, their leaders offered her money to learn the secret to Samson's strength.

So Delilah asked Samson, and he replied, "If I were tied with seven fresh bow strings, I could not break free."

As Samson lay sleeping one day, Delilah tied his arms with seven fresh bow strings. With the Philistine leaders hiding nearby, she called, "Samson, the Philistines are upon you!" He snapped the cords as if they were burned strings. The men did not dare come out from hiding.

"Samson," she said, "you made a fool of me. Tell me the truth—how can you be tied?"

Pretending to be sincere, Samson said, "Only with new ropes."

As he slept again, she tied him with ropes and shouted. He snapped them like thread.

"Samson," she pleaded, "why make a fool of me? You lied. Now tell me the truth."

"All right. If you tie my seven braids into the fabric on that loom, I'll become weak."

Again he slept, again she shouted, and again he broke loose, pulling up the entire loom.

"How can you say you love me," she chided, "when you won't even confide in me?"

Delilah nagged him so much that he finally said: "If my hair were shaved I would lose my strength." Quickly she sent for the Philistines. While he slept, she had someone cut his hair.

"Samson!" she yelled. "The Philistines are upon you!"

And they were. Samson woke up, not knowing that the Lord had left him. Immediately, the Philistines seized him. They gouged out his eyes and led him to Gaza in shackles.

Years passed, and one day the Philistines held a huge celebration. They boasted about their god Dagon, that he had allowed them to capture Samson. As the day wore on, they grew drunk, and one of them said, "Let's have Samson brought out of the prison to entertain us." Before a crowd of thousands, they made him perform.

By this time, Samson's hair had grown out. He looked pathetic, groping about blindly while the crowd mocked him. At one point, Samson whispered to the servant who stood nearby. "Lead me between the center columns," he said, "and place my hands on each pillar."

As the Philistines roared with laughter, Samson uttered a prayer to God. "Oh Lord," he prayed, "let me die with the Philistines!" Pushing with all his might, Samson shoved the pillars apart. All around the arena, the terraced balconies caved in. At that moment, in his final show of strength, Samson killed more Philistines than he had during his entire lifetime.

TBC 59

Naomi's Devoted Daughter

TBC Book One, Chapter 60
Ruth 1:1-2:23

In the days when judges still ruled Israel, a famine swept over the land, and families grew desperate. One man, named Elimelech, decided to take his family to Moab. There they would make a new life for themselves, but their dreams were cut short when Elimelech died.

Elimelech's wife, Naomi, decided to stay in Moab with her two sons. In time she found them wives, Moabite women. But within a few years, both of her sons died.

After ten years in Moab, Naomi learned that in her homeland, the famine was over. So she and her daughters-in-law packed their belongings and set out on for Judah. But Naomi's heart felt heavy. How could she ask these fine women to leave their own people? And for what?

Naomi stopped and said, "You have been wonderful daughters. I will never forget you. But you must return to your families. I have nothing to offer you. I would only be a burden."

Orpah and Ruth wept to hear her speak like this. They refused to leave her.

"No, my daughters," Naomi insisted, "you must return home. I have no more sons to offer you. Go back and find husbands from among your own people. And may God bless you."

The three women cried and hugged one another. Finally, Orpah kissed her mother-in-law and waved goodbye. But Ruth clung to Naomi. "Don't try to make me leave you," Ruth said. "Wherever you go, I will go. Your people will be my people, and your God my God."

Naomi saw that Ruth would not be dissuaded. So they traveled on together. When they entered Bethlehem, people stared in surprise. One woman exclaimed, "Can that be Naomi?"

"Don't call me Naomi. Call me Mara, for God has made my life bitter." Her response troubled them. They remembered a warm, friendly Naomi. Even her name meant "pleasant."

After reaching Naomi's house, Naomi started teaching Ruth about Judea's customs, how she could go out to the fields and pick up leftovers that the harvesters dropped. So the next day, Ruth gleaned barley from the fields of Boaz, a man highly respected in the community.

When Boaz arrived in the field, he greeted his harvesters as usual. "The Lord be with you!" he called out.

"The Lord bless you," they replied.

Then he noticed Naomi. "Who is she?"

"She's the Moabitess who came back with Naomi. She has worked steadily all morning."

Boaz walked near her and said, "My daughter, keep gleaning in this field. Follow my servant girls as the men harvest and help yourself to whatever grains they drop. You will be safe here; no one will touch you. Whenever you are thirsty, come drink from our water jars."

Ruth bowed low. "My lord, why do you offer such great kindness to me—a foreigner?"

"I have heard a great deal about you, all that you have done for Naomi since your husband died, leaving your own people to remain with her. May the Lord richly reward you."

At mealtime, Boaz called Ruth to join them. "Have some bread," he said. As she sat down among his harvesters, Boaz offered her roasted grain, and she saved some of it for Naomi.

Boaz watched as Ruth returned to the fields. Then he whispered to his men, "Drop extra stalks so Ruth can gather them."

That evening, Ruth threshed all the barley she had gathered. It amounted to almost 22 liters. When Naomi saw all the grain, she knew someone had purposely dropped extra stalks.

"Where were you gleaning?" she asked, Ruth told her all about Boaz. "The Lord bless him!" Naomi exclaimed. "He is one of our kinsman-redeemers." Naomi explained Israel's law of the kinsman-redeemer. If a man died leaving no children, his closest relative, (his kinsman) must marry the widow. Then she could have children to continue (or "redeem") the family line.

The next day, Ruth thought about the law of the kinsman-redeemer. The more she gleaned, the more she wondered. . . .

TBC 60

The Rewards of Love

TBC Book One, Chapter 61
Ruth 3:1-4:22

The barley and wheat harvests were now coming to a close, but instead of worrying, Naomi was bursting with excitement. She had an idea. "My daughter," she said to Ruth, "it is time that I find you a husband. What about Boaz? After all, he is a kinsman of ours.

"Listen. He will spend this evening winnowing barley on the threshing floor. So wash yourself, put on perfume, and dress up in your best clothes. After Boaz falls asleep, go in and uncover his feet. Then lie down near them. When he wakes up, he will tell you what to do."

So that evening, Ruth slipped in and uncovered his feet. In the dark of the night, he woke up. He was startled to see a woman lying at his feet. "Who are you?" he asked.

"Your servant, Ruth." Then she remembered what Naomi had told her. "Spread the corner of your blanket over me," she explained, "since you are my kinsman-redeemer."

Ruth was asking Boaz to marry her. The covering symbolized a husband's protection.

"Bless you, my daughter," he replied. "The whole town knows you are a noble woman. I would be honored to redeem you. But Naomi has a closer relative. If he does not wish to act as redeemer, I will surely do it. Now lay down and go to sleep. We will talk more tomorrow."

Early the next morning, Boaz woke up and called Ruth. "Bring me your shawl," he said. "Hold it out." Boaz filled it with barley and tied it so she could carry it on her back. Then he left.

It was early when Ruth entered their house. "How did it go, my daughter?" asked Naomi.

Ruth told her everything, adding, "He gave me this so I wouldn't come home empty-handed."

Naomi smiled with approval. "The man won't rest until he settles the matter today."

And she was right. Boaz had already walked to town. There he waited at the city gate.

Now a kinsman would do more than take a widow as his wife. He would also acquire the land that belonged to his relative. Boaz realized that Naomi's other relative might be eager just to gain her property. But if that were his motive, Boaz knew how to expose that.

By the time the kinsman arrived, the town's elders were all sitting nearby as witnesses.

"Naomi is selling her property," Boaz began. "You are her nearest kinsman. Do you care to buy it?"

The man thought, *Naomi is old. She doesn't need a husband, just someone to take care of her. Her sons are dead, and she has no daughters. The land is as good as mine!*

"Yes," the man replied, "I have thought it over, and I do wish to act as her redeemer."

"Very well," Boaz said. "Did you know you must also marry Ruth, the Moabitess?"

That news surprised him. If he married Ruth, Naomi's property would go to a son that she would bear. The man sighed. "I cannot redeem it," he said. "Buy it yourself." He pulled off one of his sandals and handed it to Boaz. All that Naomi owned was now deeded over to Boaz.

When a kinsman-redeemer failed to fulfill his duties, the woman could shame him by taking one of his sandals and spitting in his face. But since Naomi was not there, the man just gave his sandal to Boaz: That settled the matter. Boaz would redeem Elimelech's family.

The elders all smiled and blessed Boaz. "May your wife be like Rachel and Leah," said one man. "May your family become famous in Bethlehem, and may your offspring be blessed."

So Boaz married Ruth, and the Lord enabled her to bear a son. When they later traveled to Bethlehem as a family, women rushed to see Naomi and the baby. One woman cried out, "Praise the Lord, who has given you this grandchild! May he become famous throughout Israel!" As Naomi held the child on her lap, one of the women smiled and said, "Naomi has a son."

They named the baby Obed, and he did make that family famous. For Obed became the father of Jesse, Jesse became the father of David, and David became the king of Israel.

TBC 61

And God Remembered

TBC Book One, Chapter 62
1 Samuel 1:1-2:11

In the days when judges ruled Israel, it was not uncommon for a man to have several wives. And though that was permitted by law, it often led to conflicts. No one knew that more clearly than Elkanah, who lived in the hill country of Ephraim, with his wives Hannah and Peninnah. Peninnah had children, but Hannah had none. And that posed a thorny problem.

Each year Elkanah took his wives and children to Shiloh to worship and offer sacrifices. Then he served the meat to his family. Always he gave twice as much to Hannah, because he loved her dearly, and he knew she was sad that she had borne no children. But as always, Hannah's large portion went untouched.

Year after year, during this festive occasion, Peninnah would make Hannah feel bad. She knew Elkanah loved Hannah deeply—far more than he loved her. So she would say cruel things, reminding Hannah that God had kept her from having children.

When Elkanah came home, he would go to Hannah to comfort her. "Why are you weeping? Come now and have something to eat. Why be so downhearted? Listen—am I not better to you than ten sons?" But Hannah felt so grieved that all she could do was cry.

Every year it went like that, until one day when Hannah stood up and quietly walked away. She headed toward the temple. Then she entered the courtyard, crying softly as she went. In fact, she felt so troubled that she couldn't stop crying.

"O Lord," she whispered, "remember me. If you will give me a son, I will give him back to you to serve you always."

Meanwhile, Eli, the high priest, sat and watched from a distance. He could not hear Hannah. But when he saw her lips move and her body sway, he shook his head in disgust. "How long will you people keep on getting drunk?" he shouted. "Get rid of your wine!"

Hannah's heart pounded in fear. "Oh no, my lord," she replied, "do not mistake your servant for a wicked woman. I have not been drinking wine or liquor. I have been praying, for I am deeply troubled. This whole time I have been pouring out my heart to the Lord."

As Eli approached, he saw her tears and realized the truth of her words. With his voice softened, he said, "Go in peace, my daughter. And may the God of Israel grant your request."

Hannah bowed then returned to her family. As she ate, her face was no longer sad.

Early the next morning, Elkanah's family worshiped the Lord. Then they returned home to Ramah. And the Lord remembered Hannah.

In the course of time, she conceived and gave birth to a son. She named him Samuel, saying, "Because I asked the Lord for him."

The following year, Elkanah prepared to take his family to Shiloh to offer his annual sacrifice and to fulfill his vow to the Lord. But this time, Hannah did not go. "After the boy is weaned," she said, "I will go, and then I will present him before the Lord."

So Hannah stayed at home with Samuel and nursed him until he was weaned. That day arrived all too fast. Samuel was only three years old when Hannah took him to the temple at Shiloh. This was by far the hardest thing she had ever done. Samuel was the joy of her life.

But she must keep the vow she made. As they stood there in the tabernacle courtyard, Hannah and Elkanah sacrificed a three-year-old bull. Then they presented young Samuel to Eli.

"My lord," Hannah said, "I am the woman who stood here years ago, praying from the anguish in my heart. I prayed for a child, and the Lord has granted my request. So now I give him to the Lord, just as I had promised." With tears rolling down her cheeks and a crack in her voice, she added: "For his whole life, he will serve the Lord."

TBC 62

Samuel Meets the Lord

TBC Book One, Chapter 63
1 Samuel 2:12-36; 3:1-21

On the road to Ramah trudged a brokenhearted woman. She had given her word to the Holy One, and He had blessed her with a son. Now she had given him back. In spite of her pain, she had not withheld from him her son—her only child. Here was a true daughter of Abraham. And once again, her tears had touched the heart of God.

Each year Hannah would make Samuel a little robe and take it to him when they offered their sacrifice. Then Eli would bless them: "May the Lord give you children to take the place of the one you gave him." And he did. God gave Hannah three more sons and two daughters.

Young as he was, Samuel ministered before the Lord, a little boy wearing a linen ephod. As he grew older, Samuel developed not only in his physical appearance, but also in character. More and more, Samuel gained the Lord's favor and the people's approval.

Unfortunately, that could not be said of Eli's two sons, Hophni and Phinehas. Everyone knew that hey were wicked men. Instead of serving God, they served their appetites. They forced people to give them the raw meat from their sacrifices, even though it violated God's commands.

Eli, who was now quite old, began to hear about the many other evil things his sons were doing. One day he finally confronted them: "Listen, my sons. When you sin against another person, God may act as a peacemaker. But when you sin against the Lord himself, who can make peace for you then?"

His sons ignored his warning.

Then God sent a man to confront Eli, for he, too, was at fault: "The Lord says to you, 'Why do you honor your sons more than me by fattening yourselves on the choice meats? God honors those who honor him.

" 'I will cut off your family and raise up a priest who is faithful. All your descendants will die at a young age. And when I establish for myself a faithful priest, your descendants will beg him for priestly tasks just to get a crust of bread. Here is the sign to prove that this will happen—both your sons will die on the same day.' "

In those days a word from the Lord was rare. But one evening, as Samuel slept near the ark, the Lord called him. Samuel thought it was Eli. So he ran to Eli and said, "Here I am."

"I did not call you," Eli said. "Go back and lie down."

Again the Lord called, "Samuel!" Now Samuel did not yet know the Lord. Nor did he realize that the Lord might speak to him to convey his messages. So again he ran to Eli. "Here I am," he said. "I heard you calling me."

"No, my son," Eli said. "I did not call you. Now go back and lie down."

For the third time that night Samuel came running to Eli. Only then did Eli realize that perhaps Someone had indeed called the boy.

"Samuel," Eli said, "that voice you hear might be the Lord speaking to you. So if you hear it again, say, 'Speak, Lord, for your servant is listening.' "

Later that night, the Lord stood near the child, calling him as before, "Samuel! Samuel!"

This time he answered, "Speak, for your servant is listening."

The Lord said to him, "I am about to carry out my judgment against Eli's family. Eli has failed to control his sons, and no atonement can remove their guilt."

The next morning, Samuel was afraid to tell Eli what the Lord had said. But Eli asked, "What did the Lord tell you? Don't hide it from me: May God deal with you harshly if you do." So Samuel told him.

Eli sighed, then he said, "He is the Lord. He will do what he judges is best."

As Samuel grew, the Lord's presence remained with him. Whenever the Lord gave him a message for the people, everything he said came to pass. The Lord continued to appear to him in his adulthood. And everyone throughout Israel recognized him as a true prophet of the Lord.

TBC 63

Lost and Found

TBC Book One, Chapter 64
1 Samuel 4:1-7:1

Panic gripped Israel's elders as they heard the news from the front lines. Over many years, Israel had battled against the Philistines, for their forefathers never drove them out when God gave them the power to do it. Now they faced a grim situation—4,000 Israelites had died in battle. In desperation, the elders said, "Let's bring the ark into the battle with us."

They knew the stories their forefathers had passed down to them, how their people overcame enormous obstacles as they marched behind God's Ark of the Covenant. But they failed to realize that it was not the ark that had saved them. It was God himself.

Thinking that the ark would rescue them, the Israelite soldiers shouted for joy when it arrived. When the Philistines heard what was going on, their hearts pounded with fear. *Oh no!* they thought. *This is the god who struck Egypt!*

Fearful of being conquered, the Philistines could feel the adrenaline surging through them. They fought fiercely and killed 30,000 Israelites. The rest of Israel's soldiers fled.

Eli's two sons were killed, and the ark of God was captured. A soldier ran back to Shiloh with the news. Eli, who was now 98, sat in a chair, waiting anxiously. The soldier ran to him and said, "Israel has fled from the Philistines. We lost many soldiers. Your sons died too, and the ark has been captured."

When Eli heard that, he fell backwards, broke his neck, and died.

Eli's daughter-in-law, the wife of Phinehas, was pregnant and due to deliver soon. When she heard that the ark had been captured, and that her husband and father-in-law had died, she was so distraught that she went into labor. Later that day, she too died, giving birth to a son.

Meanwhile, the Philistines carried the ark of God into their temple in Ashdod. There they set it beside their idol Dagon.

The next morning, they found Dagon lying on the floor. The following day, he was on the floor again, but this time with his head and his hands broken off.

What could have caused this? Terrible things began to happen with no explanation. Rats began to multiply and bring deadly diseases. The people developed painful tumors that were like hemorrhoids. They soon realized that it all began when the ark arrived.

So the people of Ashdod sent the ark to Ekron, a city at the northern end of their country. But the people there refused it, for they heard what had happened and feared God's judgment.

After seven months of agonizing about what to do, the Philistine rulers finally consulted their priests and diviners. "Don't harden your hearts as Egypt did," said the spokesman. "Send the ark back to Israel with a guilt offering." So they designed ten gold bars, five shaped as rats and five as tumors. They placed the gold and the ark on a new cart, pulled by two young cows.

"These cows have recently given birth," explained the priest. "A mother never leaves its suckling. If these cows travel to Israel, we'll know it really was their God who struck us."

The Israelites of Beth Shemesh were in the fields harvesting their grain, when they looked up and saw a cart coming their way. It carried a chest and something else. When they realized it was the Ark of the Covenant, they shouted for joy. They must thank God with a sacrifice! So they chopped up the cart for firewood and sacrificed the cows as a burnt offering.

The people had placed the ark on a large rock and set the chest beside it. After opening the chest and finding the gold objects, they decided they would also look inside the ark. Seventy men now gathered closely to peek inside, ignoring what their forefathers had always told them— that the ark was holy. Immediately, God struck them dead.

Their joy now turned to mourning. "Who can stand in the presence of this holy God?" cried one woman. "What shall we do with the ark?" They decided to send messengers to the people of Kiriath Jearim, asking them to take it. So the ark remained in Kiriath Jearim.

TBC 64

Israel Wants a King

TBC Book One, Chapter 65
1 Samuel 7:2-8:22

Israel had finally regained the Ark of the Covenant, but it took 20 more years before they rekindled a heart for the Lord. With the death of Eli and his sons, Samuel emerged as Israel's spiritual leader. After years of oppression from the Philistines, their conscience was now pricked with remorse, and the Israelites pleaded with Samuel to speak to God on their behalf.

"If you really do want to return to God with your whole hearts," Samuel challenged, "get rid of your foreign gods."

So they took down the idols of Baal and the Ashtoreths. They would serve the Lord.

"Now assemble at Mizpah," Samuel said, "and I will pray for you." They fasted from eating and drinking so they could focus entirely on God. Then they confessed to him their sins.

When the Philistines heard that all the Israelites had gathered at Mizpah, they feared it meant an uprising. So they prepared to attack them. Some Israelites ran to Samuel with the news: "Don't stop praying—the Philistines are about to attack! Ask God to rescue us!"

Samuel sacrificed a young lamb as he cried out to God. And the Lord answered his plea. While Samuel offered the sacrifice, the Philistines drew closer to attack. Then suddenly, the Lord sent thunder. It was so loud that the Philistines panicked. When the Israelites saw them fleeing, they rushed out to attack them, pursuing them past Beth Car. They dealt them such a severe blow that the Philistines planned no more invasions.

Samuel set up a stone to commemorate what God had done. He named it "Ebenezer," meaning, "So far, the Lord has helped us." It reminded them they must continue to love God and obey him. And throughout Samuel's lifetime, God kept his hand against the Philistines.

Samuel made his home in Ramah, where his parents had lived. There he built an altar to the Lord. He also traveled from town to town, settling disputes and guiding the people, for he was now Israel's judge.

When Samuel grew too old to fulfill his duties, he appointed his sons to take his place as judges. But his sons did not follow his example;

they did not love the Lord as he did. And they made unfair decisions, favoring those who would bribe them with money and valuables.

Everyone knew that Samuel's sons were dishonest men—that is, everyone except Samuel. So all the elders decided to gather together to speak to him.

"Listen," they said. "Your sons are not like you; they are not good judges. We think you should appoint us a king, like all the other nations."

Their request for a king displeased Samuel so much that he turned and walked away. Then he began to pour out his heart to the Lord.

"Do not be troubled," the Lord said. "It is not you they are rejecting. It is I, for they have rejected me as their king. Listen to what they say but warn them of all that a king will do."

Samuel returned to the elders and delivered God's message. "Here is what you can expect from a king: He will take your sons and your daughters to serve him. Some will be commanded to make weapons. Others will plow his fields and reap his harvests. He will use your daughters as his perfumers, cooks, and bakers. He will take your best fields and vineyards for himself. He will also take a tenth of all your crops and your livestock for his officials and attendants. Ultimately, you will become his slaves. You will eventually cry out to God, but he will not answer you."

Even with Samuel's warnings, they still refused to listen. "No!" shouted one of their leaders. "We want a king to reign over us. Then we will be like all the other nations. He will lead us and go out before us to fight our battles."

Samuel sighed and walked away. Then he knelt down and asked, "Lord, what shall I do?"

The Lord replied, "Give them a king."

TBC 65

Humble Beginnings

TBC Book One, Chapter 66
1 Samuel 9:1-10:27

No one would have guessed what was in store for the eldest son of Kish. Saul certainly looked impressive, a head taller than his tribesmen. But while his kinsmen stared in admiration, Saul was crouching on the inside. He felt relieved when he had an excuse to slip away.

"Saul!" called his father. "Take one of the servants and see if you can find our donkeys."

The two men traveled through the hills of Ephraim, then on through the territory of Benjamin. They were about to give up, when Saul's servant had an idea.

"There's a prophet in this town," he said. "Why don't we ask him about the donkeys?"

"But what can we give him?" Saul replied. "We have no food or other gifts to offer."

"I have a quarter of a shekel of silver," the servant said. "We can use that as our gift."

Now the day before this, God had spoken to Samuel. "About this time tomorrow," the Lord said, "I will send you a man from Benjamin. You are to anoint him as Israel's leader. He will deliver my people from the Philistines, for I have heard their cry."

As the two men entered Ramah, Samuel caught sight of Saul. "That is the one," said the Lord. So Samuel walked toward him. Saul asked, "Do you know where I can find the seer?"

"I am the seer," Samuel replied. "Go up ahead of me to the high place. Today you will eat with me. In the morning I will tell you all that is in your heart. As for your donkeys, don't worry about them. They have already been found." Saul was speechless. Samuel smiled and added, "Surely the one Israel has desired is you and your family."

Saul was still puzzled by his greeting. Israel had suffered at the hands of the Philistines, and there was much talk about the new king that God would give them. Surely it was not he.

"Excuse me, sir," Saul replied. "I am from Benjamin, Israel's smallest tribe. My family is the least prominent clan. So why are you saying this to me?" But Samuel waited to answer.

After dining with Samuel, Saul and his servant rose early the next day. Saul sent the young man to prepare for their journey. That's when the man of God motioned to Saul.

Once they were alone, Samuel poured oil over Saul's head. This was a symbolic act, signifying that Saul was to lead Israel. "Now," said Samuel, "I will tell you all that you will encounter on your journey home. And you will know for certain the Lord has spoken.

"When you reach Gibeah, you will meet a group of prophets surrounded by musicians. As the music plays, they will be prophesying. Then the Spirit of God will come upon you. You, too, will prophesy, and you will be changed into a different person."

Everything Samuel predicted happened, and the people of Gibeah were shocked to hear Saul prophesying. Even Saul himself was surprised. From that day on, he was a different man.

When the two men arrived home, Saul's uncle asked them where they had been.

"Looking for the donkeys," Saul said. "We went to the seer to seek his help."

"And what did he say?" his uncle asked.

"He said the donkeys had been found." But Saul did not tell him the rest of the story.

Samuel sent word to all the Israelite tribes, summoning them to Mizpah to choose a king. The leaders of each tribe and clan stepped forward. They drew lots, first by tribes, then by clans, and finally, by families. The final lot fell to Saul—he would become the king of the Israelites. But Saul had hidden himself among the baggage.

Samuel found Saul and led him before the people. "Long live the king!" they shouted.

Then Samuel explained the rules Saul must obey as their king. All the people presented him gifts, everyone except for some troublemakers. But God was watching. He touched the hearts of some valiant men, and they showed their support by escorting Saul home.

TBC 66

Israel's New Hero

TBC Book One, Chapter 67
1 Samuel 11:1-12:25

Trouble brewed for the Israelites in the town of Jabesh Gilead. Ammonites had surrounded the city. The people were ready to surrender—until they heard the terms of the treaty.

"The only way we will let you live is if we gouge out the right eye of every person."

Quickly, some messengers slipped away and raced to Gibeah, the home of their new king. They arrived just as Saul was returning from the fields with his yoke of oxen.

When Saul heard the news, God's Spirit came upon him mightily, and he burned with anger. He cut up his oxen and sent the pieces throughout Israel, with this message: "Here is what will happen to the oxen of any Israelite who fails to follow Saul and Samuel."

Saul's message put the fear of God into Israel, and their men turned out by the thousands.

Meanwhile, the men of Jabesh cheered when they learned Saul would rescue them. To catch the Ammonites off guard, they sent them this message: "We will surrender tomorrow."

With 330,000 men volunteering from throughout Israel, Saul marched his forces all night. He divided them into three groups, and just before dawn, they were ready to attack. Taking them by surprise, Saul's army slaughtered the Ammonites. The few who did survive scattered in terror.

When the Israelites returned home, a hero's welcome greeted Saul. Those who supported Saul from the beginning now called for vengeance on those who had doubted his ability.

"No," Saul told them. "No one shall be killed today, for the Lord has rescued Israel."

The support for Saul was now so great that Samuel seized it as an opportunity. He urged the people to go to Gilgal and reaffirm Saul's appointment as king. The Israelites would hold a great celebration and sacrifice offerings to the Lord.

With Saul confirmed as king, Samuel stepped down as Israel's leader. At their celebration in Gilgal, Samuel gave the people his final counsel.

"Now that I am old and gray," he said, "I must ask you something, and I want you to answer me. Have I ever cheated anyone? Have I ever taken any bribes?"

"No," the people answered, "you have not."

"The Lord and the king are my witnesses; they have heard you say that I wronged no one.

"Now it is my turn. I do have evidence, and it points against you and your fathers. When your forefathers were in Egypt, God rescued them and settled them in this land. But they forgot the Lord their God. So God gave them over to the Philistines and the Moabites. Then they cried out, 'We have sinned; we have turned away from God and have worshiped idols. Deliver us, and we will serve you.' So God sent them judges to deliver them from their enemies.

"When you obeyed the judges God gave you, you lived securely, without any nations attacking you. But then you heard that the king of the Ammonites made plans to overrun Israel. So you came to me and said, 'We want a king to rule over us,' even though God was your king.

"Now here is the king you have chosen. God has given you what you desired. If both you and your king fear God and obey his commands, good! But if you do not obey him, if you rebel, his hand will surely be against you, just as it was against your forefathers who disobeyed.

"Now then, stand and see what the Lord is about to do. You know that this is the season you harvest wheat; it never rains this time of year. So I will now call upon the Lord to send thunder and rain. He will do this as a sign to show you how evil it was to ask for a king."

That same day, the Lord sent thunder and rain. The people now cowered in awe. One after another, they cried out: "Pray to the Lord so we won't die!" "We know we have sinned."

"Don't be afraid," Samuel said. "The Lord will not reject his people.

"So I charge you, serve him faithfully, with all your heart."

TBC 67

A Daring Prince

Though outnumbered they attacked.

TBC Book One, Chapter 68
1 Samuel 13:23-14:45

The longer Saul reigned as king, the greater his confidence grew, and the shy young man from Gibeah had transformed into a bold leader. As the years progressed, his eldest son, Jonathan, also acquired a reputation for valor.

Jonathan and his armor bearer were alone when they spied Philistine soldiers on a mountain. "Let's go to that outpost and let the Philistines see us," he said. "Perhaps the Lord will act on our behalf. If they tell us to come, that's our sign; God will allow us to conquer them."

Meanwhile, back at Israel's camp, Saul gave strict orders to his men: "No one is to eat any food today. We are taking an oath before the Lord. May a curse fall on any man who eats before I have gotten even with my enemies." So none of the troops ate any food.

Back near the Philistine outpost, Jonathan and his armor bearer crossed the ravine. The Philistines began to mock them: "Look! The Hebrews are crawling out of their holes."

The Israelites had indeed been hiding in caves, for they had no weapons nor any blacksmiths—thanks to the Philistines. So the Israelites were unable to create any swords or armor. Only Saul and Jonathan carried weapons. Jonathan knew he had a golden opportunity.

"Come right up," shouted the Philistine guards, "and we'll teach you a lesson."

"Follow me," Jonathan said. "The Lord has indeed given them to Israel." The two young men climbed up the steep ravine then attacked the Philistines. They were badly outnumbered, but by the time they were finished, 20 Philistines lay dead. Then God caused the ground to shake, and panic gripped the Philistine army. All their outposts and raiding parties began to scatter.

From a distance, Saul and his men saw the Philistines fleeing, and they wondered who could be chasing them. Then they realized Jonathan was missing.

Saul rallied his men and led them to the battle. When they arrived they found the Philistines striking each other, in total confusion. And the

Israelites who had hidden themselves now ran to join Saul's forces.

The Israelites chased them through a wooded area and saw honey oozing on the ground. Yet no one stopped to eat it, for everyone remembered the vow Saul had made—everyone except Jonathan. He knew nothing about his father's oath, for he was absent when it was made.

Reaching out with his staff, Jonathan dipped it into the honeycomb. When he tasted the honey, his eyes brightened. Then a soldier came up and told him about his father's vow.

"He should not have done that," Jonathan replied. "Had we eaten, we could have conquered more."

Jonathan was right. The men were tired before the battle, and by the day's end they were exhausted. They were so famished that they butchered the livestock they captured and ate the meat raw, even though that violated God's commandments.

Saul wanted to continue pursuing the Philistines throughout the night. But when he asked the Lord whether they should do that, no answer came. "Someone must have sinned today," Saul said. "When I find out who it was, even if it's Jonathan, that person will die."

Saul had all the soldiers cast lots to find out who had sinned. The lot fell to Jonathan.

"I merely tasted some honey," Jonathan said. "Must I die for that?"

But Saul was still angry that his own son had broken his vow. "May God deal with me ever so severely if you don't die, Jonathan!"

Immediately, some soldiers stepped forward, and one of them confronted Saul: "Should Jonathan, who brought this great deliverance, be killed? Never! As surely as the Lord lives, not a hair of his head shall fall to the ground. For his achievements were done by the power of God."

No one could argue with that. Jonathan breathed a sigh of relief as they returned home.

TBC 68

King Saul Disobeys

TBC Book One, Chapter 69
1 Samuel 13:1-14; 15:1-35

Long before Israel had routed the Philistines, Saul's son Jonathan ventured into some daring exploits. King Saul had appointed him to command one-third of his army, and in one military campaign, Jonathan led a surprise raid on an outpost at Geba. The Philistines now wanted revenge.

With thousands of soldiers and chariots, they prepared to counterattack. The Israelites were no match for them. They were badly outnumbered, and they had no swords or spears. When the Israelites who lived in that region saw how hopeless it was, they ran away and hid in caves.

Whenever a nation threatened to invade Israel, Saul was to wait for Samuel in Gilgal for seven days to give the tribes time to send soldiers while Samuel interceded and made offerings.

Saul remained at Gilgal according to their plan, but by the end of those seven days, his soldiers got restless and began to leave. When he saw his army dwindling, Saul began to panic. *I can't wait any longer,* he thought. *Since Samuel isn't here, I'll offer the sacrifices myself.*

Just as Saul finished the offering, Samuel arrived. "What have you done?" he asked.

"My men were scattering. I was afraid we would be attacked. So I offered the sacrifices."

"You did a very foolish thing," Samuel said, "You could have had a kingdom that endured for all time. But since you have disobeyed God's command, your kingdom will be taken from you and given to someone else. For the Lord has sought a man after his own heart."

Now that was not the only time Saul disobeyed the Lord. Some time later, after Jonathan had routed the Philistines, Samuel had come to Saul with a mission. "The Lord would have you attack the Amalekites," he said. "Destroy them totally, as well as everything they own."

Using the weapons gained from battling the Philistines, Saul's forces destroyed the Amalekites, except for Agag their king. They also spared the best of the Amalekites' sheep and their cattle.

Meanwhile, the Lord told Samuel, "I am grieved that I made Saul king. He has turned away from me and disobeyed." When Samuel heard that, he too was grieved. After praying all night, he went to meet Saul. But Saul went to Carmel to put up a monument honoring himself.

When Samuel arrived, Saul said, "The Lord bless you! I've finished my mission."

"Then what's that sound? Why do I hear sheep bleating and cattle lowing?"

"We spared only the best animals," Saul said, "to sacrifice them to the Lord your God."

"Stop!" Samuel said. "I don't want to hear any more. Now you listen! You were once a humble man, when God anointed you king over Israel. But now, when he told you to destroy the Amalekites completely, you pounced on the plunder and disobeyed him."

"But I did obey," Saul insisted. "We kept the animals to make sacrifices."

Samuel looked exasperated. "What pleases God more, to offer sacrifices or to obey the voice of the Lord? To obey is better than sacrifice. Rebellion is a terrible sin, and arrogance is as evil as idolatry. You rejected the word of the Lord. Now he has rejected you as king."

"You are right," Saul admitted. "I have sinned. Forgive me so I may worship the Lord."

Samuel walked away, so Saul grabbed his robe to stop him, and it tore. Then Samuel said to Saul, "So also has God torn Israel from your hands and given it to a better man than you."

Again Saul begged Samuel to appear with him before the people. This time Samuel went with him, and Saul and the elders worshiped the Lord.

Then Samuel called for Agag. He came with an air of confidence, thinking his life had been spared.

"Your sword has made women childless," Samuel said, "so now your mother will be childless." And Samuel did what Saul had failed to do—he obeyed the Lord and killed Agag.

Samuel returned home to Ramah, while Saul returned to Gibeah. Saul hoped Samuel would forget their conflict. But Samuel knew he would never again see the face of Saul.

TBC 69

God Looks at the Heart

TBC Book One, Chapter 70
1 Samuel 16:1-23

Samuel left Gilgal, knowing that he would never return, for the Lord had rejected Saul. He remembered how shy and humble Saul had been. Now, he mourned and prayed the way a father does for a wayward son. Finally, the Lord said to Samuel, "That's enough. Stop mourning for Saul. I have rejected him, and nothing will change my mind. Fill your horn with oil, for I am sending you to anoint a new king. I have chosen one of the sons of Jesse of Bethlehem."

"How can I do that?" Samuel asked. "When Saul learns of this, he will have me killed."

"Take a heifer with you," the Lord replied, "and say you have come to sacrifice an offering. Invite Jesse's family to join you. Then I will show you which son to anoint."

When the elders of Bethlehem saw Samuel, they trembled in fear. *What would bring him to our little town?* Everyone knew that he and Saul were at odds.

"Do you come in peace?" asked one of the elders cautiously.

"Yes. I've come to sacrifice an offering." Then he invited Jesse's family to join him.

When Jesse's family arrived, Samuel stared at the oldest son, Eliab. *Surely here stands the Lord's anointed,* he thought. But then the Lord whispered, "Do not judge by a man's stature; he is not the one. People look at outward appearances, but God looks at the heart."

Jesse soon realized that Samuel had more than a casual interest in his family. One of his sons was about to be chosen by the Lord for a special purpose. So he had each one walk before Samuel, one at a time. And one by one Samuel said, "No, this is not the one."

Finally, Samuel said to Jesse, "The Lord has chosen none of them. Have you other sons?"

"There is one more," Jesse explained, "my youngest son, but he's tending our sheep."

"Send for him," Samuel said. "We will not begin until he arrives."

Before long, a good-looking young fellow with handsome features came running up.

"That's the one," the Lord said. "Rise and anoint him."

So Samuel anointed David while all seven of his older brothers stood watching. And from that day, the Lord's Spirit came upon David in power.

Meanwhile, back in Gilgal, the Spirit of God had left King Saul, and an evil spirit now controlled him. It affected his behavior so much that his servants knew this was a spiritual problem. They also knew what would help—soothing music to drive away the evil spirit.

Saul listened to their advice and ordered them to find a skilled musician. One servant replied, "I know of one in Bethlehem who plays the harp. He's a brave young man, a warrior. He is a fine-looking fellow, and he has a way with words. What's more, the Lord is with him."

"Send for him," the king said.

Saul's messengers traveled to Bethlehem and spoke to Jesse. "The king asks you to send him your son David, who tends sheep." So Jesse called for David and told him of the king's request. Then he prepared bread, wine, and a young goat as gifts for him to take to the king.

From the very beginning, Saul liked David a great deal. In time, he even made him one of the king's armor bearers. But that's getting ahead of the story. . . .

Saul continued to have mood swings prompted by the evil spirit. But whenever that spirit overcame him, servants would send for David. Then David would come and play his harp. Immediately, Saul would feel better, for David's music caused the evil spirit to leave him.

When Saul requested David's service, he had no idea this was the very one Samuel had described, "a man after God's own heart." From that day on, David faithfully served both the king and his father. When he was not playing the harp for Saul, he was doing what he enjoyed most—singing praises to the Lord while he watched his father's sheep.

TBC 70

A Psalm: The Lord Is My Shepherd

TBC Book One, Chapter 71
Psalm 23

Like others who loved God deeply, David would put his thoughts and feelings to music. The Hebrew people collected these songs that praised God and used them in their worship. They were "psalms," songs meant to be sung with stringed instruments.

The psalms were like poems put to music, expressing one's feelings, whether joy, pain, gratitude, or sorrow. Each one was personal, like talking with a close friend.

David began writing psalms when he was a young boy, tending his father's sheep. He had no idea that his psalms would one day be sung by millions of others who love God. Even today we sing his psalms. One psalm that drives away fear and worry is this one:

The Lord is my shepherd, I shall not want.

The kings of the East were like shepherds in protecting and providing for their people. With God as his shepherd-king, David knew that all his needs would be met.

He makes me lie down in green pastures,
   he leads me beside still waters, he restores my soul.

Just as a shepherd daily leads his flock to fresh pastureland and cool, still waters, so also does God refresh his people. No matter where we are, he can give us peace within. He feeds our souls, the place inside us that holds our feelings, and makes us strong again.

He guides me in paths of righteousness for his name's sake.

Sheep do not know what paths give them safe travel. As God's sheep, we can find out from him what is the right thing to do and what would please God most. He promises to guide his people, and he never breaks his word, for his reputation is at stake.

Even though I walk through the valley of the shadow of death,
   I will fear no evil,

David recalled the place he feared most as a shepherd boy, a ravine with cliffs hanging overhead and dense forests—perfect for a wild animal to attack. But then he would remember something that took away the fear. And when we are afraid, we can remember this too:

For you are with me; your rod and your staff, they comfort me.
David remembered that no matter where he was, God was walking right beside him. Obviously, sheep cannot defend themselves. But a shepherd could use his staff to beat off small predators; he also used it to count the sheep. The Shepherd who protected David also protects us.

You prepare a table before me, in the presence of my enemies.
The shepherd-king honored special guests at his banquet table. To understand David's imagery, think back to how God delivered the Israelites from Egypt and gave them their enemies' land. To David's forefathers, that was like enjoying a banquet while their enemies watched helplessly. And David himself enjoyed similar favor from God.

You anoint my head with oil; my cup overflows.
When a person hosted a banquet, he would sometimes offer a perfumed ointment made from olive oil. It served as a welcome relief after a long, hot journey. But oil also symbolized joy and gladness. David's heart overflowed with love and gratitude for his generous Shepherd-King.

Surely goodness and mercy will follow me all the days of my life,
Just as a wedding banquet celebrates a special relationship between two people, so also does David's banquet imagery celebrate a special relationship—the covenant between the Shepherd-King and his people. God vows his never-ending goodness and mercy.

And I will dwell in the house of the Lord forever.
When David wrote this, he looked forward to returning to the tabernacle, where he would worship the Lord, his Shepherd-King. He would have loved to worship God there the rest of his life. The psalm ends as it began: I have the Lord—what more do I need?

A Giant Problem

TBC Book One, Chapter 72
1 Samuel 17:1-54; 21:9

Philistines covered the hillside as a giant of a man stepped forward. All across the valley, the Israelite soldiers stared at Goliath, who stood more than nine feet tall. His armor alone weighed 125 pounds. His shield bearer stood in front of him as he spoke.

Every day for the past 40 days, Goliath paraded in front of Israel's soldiers and taunted them. "Why line up for battle?" he shouted. "Send out one man to fight me. If he can kill me, we will serve you. But if I kill him, you will serve us. I defy you, Israel! Now send out a man!"

Jesse's oldest sons were among the soldiers posted on Israel's hillside. So Jesse called David from tending the sheep and sent him to his brothers with bread and grain.

When David arrived at the valley, both sides were drawing up battle lines, and soldiers were talking about the news: "The king will richly reward anyone who can kill Goliath." "I heard he will give his daughter in marriage and his father's family won't have to pay taxes!"

Then Goliath stepped forward. Suddenly everyone stopped talking. He began ridiculing the Israelites. And once again he challenged them to send out a man who would fight him.

David turned to one of the soldiers. "What did you say would be done for the man who kills this Philistine? Who is this uncircumcised Philistine to defy the armies of the living God?"

David's brother Eliab overheard and he was furious. "What are you doing here anyway?" he shouted. "I know how conceited you are. You brought supplies just to watch the battle."

"What have I done now?" David said. "Can't I even speak?"

So David asked someone else about the king's offer. Meanwhile, another soldier ran to the king's officers and said, "We have someone willing to fight Goliath!" So Saul sent for him.

Saul was surprised to see the same young man who played the harp for him. "David, you're only a boy. How could you fight such an experienced warrior?"

"Once I killed a lion that attacked my sheep," David said. "Another time I killed a bear. Surely God will help me kill this Philistine, too."

Saul thought, *Perhaps God is in this. How else could he have killed those predators if not by the power of God?*

Saul sighed. "All right," he said, "I will send you, and the Lord be with you."

Then Saul ordered his attendants to dress David in his own tunic and armor. But the young man felt awkward in them. Finally, said, "I can't go in these. I'm not used to them. Tell the king I will be ready shortly."

David ran to the stream. There he carefully selected five smooth stones.

Holding only a sling, David stepped out and faced Goliath. When Goliath saw the handsome young man, he shouted, "Am I a dog that you should come after me with sticks?" Then he cursed David. "Come here," he bellowed, "and I'll give your flesh to the birds and the beasts!"

David shouted, "You come at me with sword, spear, and javelin. But I come in the name of the Lord Almighty, the God of Israel. It is you and all your army who will become carcasses this day! Then the whole world will know that the living God is in Israel. For it's not by sword or spear that the Lord saves. The battle is the Lord's, and he will give us all of you!"

As Goliath walked forward, David ran toward him. Then he stopped, put a stone into his sling and whirled it above his head. The stone shot out so forcefully that it lodged itself in the giant's forehead. Goliath put his hand to his head and fell facedown. David raced toward him. Then he reached for Goliath's scabbard, drew forth the giant's sword, and killed him.

When the Philistines saw that their hero was dead, they panicked and fled. The men of Israel shouted with joy. With the Philistines fleeing, they surged forward to pursue them.

A great victory was won that day by the Israelite army. As David took Goliath's huge sword, he thought, *I will take this to the priest as a memorial. You are the living God who saves Israel.*

TBC 72

Saul's Jealous Eye

TBC Book One, Chapter 73
1 Samuel 17:55-58; 18:1-30

From the moment David ran toward Goliath, King Saul was impressed. Though David had appeared before him at times to play music, Saul had never taken a personal interest in him. As he watched David advance toward Goliath, he asked his chief commander, "Whose son did you say he was?"

Abner stared intently at the young man as he replied, "As surely as you live, O king, I have no idea."

After David hurled his sling, the Israelites routed the Philistines and confiscated weapons and possessions left behind. Abner brought David to King Saul, and Jonathan listened as David answered the king's questions. While David spoke, Jonathan knew he had found a kindred spirit.

Saul had arranged to keep David with him as one of his personal bodyguards. With David now living in the king's household, David and Jonathan became close friends.

One day Jonathan had a surprise for David. He vowed that for the rest of his life, he would regard David as own brother. To seal his pledge, Jonathan gave David his own robe and tunic as well as his most precious possessions—his sword, his bow, and his belt.

Saul, too, felt a kinship with David, and he sent him out on special missions. David fulfilled those duties so successfully that Saul promoted him to an officer. David became so popular that women would sing, "Saul has slain his thousands, David his tens of thousands."

When Saul heard that, he was furious. He thought, *They have credited David with tens of thousands but me with only thousands.* From then on, Saul kept a jealous eye on David.

The next day, an evil spirit came upon Saul. He was prophesying in his house, but he uttered such a frenzied message that the servants knew it was the prompting of an evil spirit. David came immediately and began to play his harp.

Before David's music could achieve its impact, the evil spirit stirred up Saul's dark side. Suddenly, he grabbed his spear and hurled it at David. Two times that day, David eluded him.

Now Saul became afraid of David. It was evident God was with the young warrior. So the king sent him to lead his soldiers into battle, hoping he would die in an act of bravery. But each time, he returned victorious. And Saul grew even more afraid. Everyone in Israel loved David.

One day, Saul called him into his presence and said, "David, I wish to give you my oldest daughter in marriage. Just continue to serve me bravely and fight the Lord's battles." *Surely the Philistines will kill him,* thought Saul. *How they would love to take revenge for Goliath.*

But David was humble and said, "Who am I, my lord, to marry the king's daughter?"

So King Saul gave his daughter to another man. In time, however, Saul learned that his other daughter, Michal, was in love with David. That gave the king another idea.

Once again he sent for David. "You now have another chance to become my son-in-law," said Saul. "I wish to give you my daughter Michal. Don't answer me yet. Take time to think about it."

After David left, Saul told his servants to persuade David. "Tell him I am pleased with him," Saul said, "and that I would very much like to have him as my son-in-law."

So the king's servants said to David, "Why not become the king's son-in-law?"

David replied, "Because I am only a poor man, that's why. What do I have to offer?"

When Saul heard what David said, he thought to himself, *This is even better than I had imagined.* And he sent the servant to David with another message.

"You are right," he told David, "the king's daughter is worth a great deal. That is why the king is asking for the foreskins of 100 Philistines." When David heard that, he was pleased.

Then David led his men in an attack and presented Saul with not 100 foreskins, but with 200.

Saul's anxiety mounted. Watching his daughter Michal pledge herself to David, he grew even more afraid. Not only was the Lord with David—but so was the heart of his daughter.

TBC 73

A Step Away from Death

TBC Book One, Chapter 74
1 Samuel 19:1-20:42

Saul's attendants huddled in hushed silence. The king ordered them to look for a chance to kill David. This came as a shock to everyone, including his son Jonathan. But no one dared to argue with the king, especially now. He had that wild, glassy-eyed look.

Jonathan slipped away to warn David. "My brother, you must leave at once and hide. My father wants you killed. I will speak to him privately and try to reason with him. But for now let's plan where you will hide. I'll find you there tomorrow and tell you how it turns out."

The next day, Jonathan brought up David's name. "He's done a lot for Israel, Father. He risked his own life when he killed the Philistine. So why kill an innocent man?"

Saul listened to his son. Right then and there, he vowed not to kill David. When the king returned home, Jonathan called David and re-assured him. Then David returned to Saul.

Some time later, war broke out again with the Philistines, but David's soldiers struck them so forcefully they turned and fled. The Israelites rejoiced, and everyone was talking about David. As King Saul pondered this, an evil spirit gained hold in his thoughts. So servants called for David to play his music. But while David was playing, Saul hurled his spear at him.

David lunged as the spear drove into the wall. Then he ran out and fled to his home.

That night, Saul sent men to watch David's house so they could kill him in the morning. But Michal learned of this and warned David. With her help, he climbed out their window and escaped. Then Michal put an idol in David's bed to make it look like he was sleeping there.

The next morning, Saul's men came, but Michal pretended David lay sleeping and ill. The men brushed past her into the bedroom. They pulled back the sheets—he wasn't there!

Meanwhile, David traveled through the night to Ramah. There he met with Samuel and told him everything. Then together they left for

Naioth, but someone reported seeing them. So David fled and went to find Jonathan.

"Why is your father trying to kill me?" he asked.

"No, David, my father isn't trying to kill you! He would have told me if he were."

"Jonathan, as surely as God lives, I swear, I am only a step away from death! Look, tomorrow is the New Moon Festival. Tell your father that you gave me permission to offer sacrifices in Bethlehem. If he loses his temper, you will know he's determined to harm me."

"All right," Jonathan said. "Now I have a favor to ask you. Swear you will show kindness to me and my family, even when the Lord has destroyed your enemies." So David made a vow.

"Now about your father," David said, "how will I know if he has answered harshly?"

Jonathan motioned David to follow him. "Hide in this field till the day after tomorrow. Then I'll come to target practice. If the arrows go beyond my servant boy, you are in danger."

The first day of the festival, Saul noticed David's place at the table was empty but he said nothing about it. When David failed to appear the next day as well, Saul questioned Jonathan.

"He went to Bethlehem. I permitted him to offer sacrifices with his brothers."

"You did what? As long as he is alive, your kingdom will never be established!"

When Jonathan tried to reason with him, Saul hurled his javelin at his own son.

Jonathan stood up and left in anger. The next day he took his young servant and went target practicing.

"Keep going," Jonathan yelled to the boy, "the arrow is way beyond you." After the boy retrieved the arrow, Jonathan dismissed him and sent him home.

Then David emerged. As he came near Jonathan, he dropped to his knees and bowed to the ground three times. He would forever be grateful to his friend, the prince of Israel. Jonathan lifted him to his feet. Then they hugged each other and wept, but David wept more.

"Go in peace, my friend," said Jonathan, "for we have vowed our friendship forever."

TBC 74

The Fugitive

TBC Book One, Chapter 75
1 Samuel 21:1-23:18

News traveled slowly in Israel, yet the minute Ahimelech saw David, he trembled with fear. He put to David the questions raised by his presence. "Where are your soldiers, David? Why have you come to Nob by yourself?"

If Ahimelech knew the truth, he might report David to Saul. Even if he did not report him, he would be risking his own life to help David. *The less he knows, the better,* thought David.

So David said, "The king sent me on a secret mission. I'm about to meet my men. But we left in such a hurry that we have run out of bread. Do you have any loaves you could spare?"

"I have no ordinary bread," said Ahimelech. "But we are about to replace the consecrated bread with fresh loaves. I can give you these." Then Ahimelech gathered all the leftover bread.

As David waited in the tabernacle, he noticed someone who looked familiar. It was Doeg, the Edomite, Saul's chief shepherd. David turned away quickly as the man stepped outside.

When the priest returned with the bread, David asked, "Do you happen to have a spear or a sword on hand? The king's business was so urgent that I left without my weapons."

Ahimelech just stared at David. Finally, he said, "The only sword here is the one you brought years ago that belonged to Goliath. If you want it, it's in that cloth behind the ephod."

"There's none like it," said David. "I'll take it."

David left hastily and made his way to Gath, the home of Saul's enemy, King Achish. It had also been the home of Goliath. David hoped that Achish might agree to keep him there.

As soon as he reached the city gate, David asked to see the king. But as he was being led to Achish, he overheard one of the servants talking: "Isn't that David, the one they sing about?"

Suddenly, David grew afraid. What if King Achish decided to capture him? There was only one thing to do. . . . David started acting as if he were crazy. He made strange faces and drooled so saliva ran down his beard. Then he started making wild marks all over the doors of the gate.

When King Achish arrived, he raised his hands in disgust. "Why did you bring him here?" he yelled. "I don't care who he is! Am I so short of madmen that you had to bring one?"

The plan worked: David was thrown out of the king's presence.

From Gath, he escaped to the cave of Adullam. His family met him there, fearful for their own lives. David took his parents to Mizpah and asked Moab's king to keep them safe. He thought surely he could trust him, for David's great-grandmother, Ruth, was a Moabite.

As news of David spread, many who were troubled or in debt or restless joined him. Even the prophet Gad came and warned him when he should leave the stronghold and return to Judah.

Meanwhile, Saul found out that his shepherd, Doeg, had seen David at Nob. Saul then traveled to confront the high priest. Ahimelech replied, "I didn't know David was fleeing."

Saul didn't believe him. He turned to his guards and said, "Kill him." But no one dared to strike the Lord's priests. Angrily, Saul turned to Doeg and ordered him to do it. Doeg killed not only Ahimelech, but all of Nob's 85 priests and their wives and children. Only one man escaped.

Abiathar, Ahimelech's son, fled to join David. He brought with him the ephod, which the priests used to help people make decisions. Sometimes God would work through the ephod to reveal what they should do. David would use the ephod to gain guidance from the Lord.

During this time, David's men stayed in the hills of the desert. Day after day, Saul and his men searched for them, yet God did not let Saul capture them.

At Horesh, David learned that Saul was on his way there. But Jonathan got there first, and he encouraged David. "Don't worry," he said, "my father won't be able to touch you. One day God will make you king over Israel. And I will be at your right hand."

Then Jonathan prepared to leave, and the two friends reaffirmed their covenant.

TBC 75

Songs from the Heart

TBC Book One, Chapter 76
Psalm 139

David wrote and sang many songs that remind us what God is like. Psalms like this one not only encouraged David, but they also touched the heart of God:

O Lord, you watch me closely, and no one knows me like you do.
You always know what I am doing.
You always know what I am thinking—even before I do!
You even know what I plan to do, because you know me so well.
Each time I speak, before a single word comes out,
    you know what I will say.

You have surrounded me; I am trapped by your presence;
    You have done this so you could bless me.
It seems too good to be true; it's too amazing to understand.
No matter where I might go, your Spirit would be there.
If I could fly across the world, your presence would be there too,
    ready to guide me and guard me.
If I think to myself, *Surely darkness will hide me from you,*
    then I remember:
    Darkness isn't dark to you; even then you would see me.

For you are the one who created me.
You formed me in my mother's womb,
    and what you made is wonderful!
You knew me before I was born;
    you watched me even in the womb.
You had plans for my life, since before I was born.
Just as you shaped my body,
    so also you shaped the days of my life,
    before my life on earth even began.

How special are your plans, O God!
How many details you carefully arrange.
To try to count them all would be like counting grains of sand;
    it would take an eternity.

When David wrote this psalm, he faced a dangerous situation. Certain men were trying to kill him. In this psalm, David not only praises God, but he also uses that praise to try to persuade the Lord, to convince God to deal with his enemies. So he goes on to say this:

O Lord, slay those who would kill me.
The way they talk about you shows that they are your enemies.
Because they are enemies of God,
I regard them as my enemies too.

O God, search my mind and my heart.
Test me by watching my responses,
    and look at what causes my worry.
See if I am bringing you pain,
    and if not, then lead me to safety.

TBC 76

Beauty and the Beast

TBC Book One, Chapter 77
1 Samuel 24:1-25:44

David found a golden opportunity in the Desert of En Gedi. King Saul stepped into one of the caves, looking for a place that offered privacy. He had no idea that David and his men were hiding in that very cave. When his back was turned, David slipped up behind him.

His men had urged him to kill his enemy. But David could not bring himself to do that. Instead, he cut off a piece of Saul's robe, and the king didn't even notice. Leaving his men behind him, David slipped out of the cave behind Saul.

"My lord, the king!" he shouted. When Saul turned around, there was David, bowing down in homage.

"My father," David said, "why would I harm you? See this piece of your robe? Had I wanted to kill you, I could have. But I will not lift my hand against God's anointed."

Then Saul began to cry as he spoke. "You are more righteous than I. May God reward you for how you treated me this day." And the Lord did reward David—in more ways than one.

Saul could change his mind in an instant. So David and his men stayed in the wilderness of Carmel, near the property of Nabal, who was wealthy. Nabal's wife, Abigail, was beautiful and intelligent. But Nabal was mean-spirited; he dealt with people in an arrogant, selfish way.

David heard that Nabal's sheep were now being sheared. So David sent some of his young men to ask Nabal what he could spare for them. "Tell him our men always treated his shepherds well," David said. "His own servants can vouch for us."

The men delivered David's message, but they were surprised by Nabal's response.

"Who is this David?" Nabal said. "Lots of servants are breaking away from their masters these days. Why should I take my bread, my water, and my meat and give them to men from who knows where?"

When David's men reported Nabal's words, David was livid. "Put on your swords!" he yelled. "The whole time we have been here, we have protected his shepherds from marauders. And what do we get? He's paid back evil for good. I swear he and his men will die!"

Meanwhile, one of Nabal's servants ran to tell Abigail what had happened. "David sent messengers to request food, but our master only insulted them. But they have never taken anything from us; they even protected us. Surely harm will come to us unless you do something."

Abigail had her servants pack up some food. Without telling her husband, she sent it ahead with her servants and followed behind them. They entered the ravine just as David's men were descending toward them. Quickly Abigail dismounted and knelt facedown at David's feet.

"My lord," she said, "pay no attention to Nabal; his name means fool. Please, accept these gifts and forgive your servant's offense. The Lord will make a lasting dynasty for you, because you fight the Lord's battles. When he gives you the kingdom, you will not want your conscience stained by needless bloodshed. In that day, master, remember me, your servant."

David's anger had suddenly dissipated. "Praise be to the Lord for sending you," he replied. "May God bless you for your good judgment and keeping me from bloodshed. By daybreak every male in your household would have been killed. Go in peace."

When Abigail returned, Nabal was holding a banquet. He was so drunk she didn't say a word until the next morning. Then she told him what David had intended to do and how she stopped him. Nabal was so shocked by her news that he got a heart attack. Ten days later he died.

When David heard about Nabal's death, he realized the man's behavior brought God's judgment. He felt relieved that God had kept him from taking the matter into his own hands.

Then he thought of Abigail. She was a widow now. . . . He called one of his men and sent him with a message to Abigail. Quickly she packed her belongings. Taking five maidservants with her, she traveled back with the young man. The Lord had given David another wife.

TBC 77

The Forbidden Witch of Endor

TBC Book One, Chapter 78
1 Samuel 26:1-25; 27:1-12; 28:1-25

Many years had now passed since David first fled from Saul, and a spirit of paranoia still controlled the king. With 3,000 soldiers, Saul again pursued David and his 600 men. At night, David and his nephew Abishai slipped into Saul's camp. Then they took Saul's spear and his water jug—proof that David could have killed Saul if he wanted to.

The next morning, when Saul realized what David had done, he wept in shame. From a distance he called out to David: "I have sinned. May God bless you, David, my son. I have acted like a fool. I promise I will not try to harm you anymore." But David knew Saul would change his mind.

For that reason, David took his men and their families and traveled to Gath. By now everyone knew that Saul wanted to kill David. The people in Gath still respected David, but now they were not afraid of him. So David offered to serve King Achish in exchange for a city where he and his people could live. Achish was Saul's chief enemy, and he readily agreed. He gave them the city of Ziklag for their loyalty and service.

Over the next 16 months, David made Achish think he was raiding the Israelites. Instead, he was raiding neighboring tribes, the enemies of Israel. His men would take their livestock and clothes. Then they would kill all the people so no one would be left to tell Achish the truth.

Achish was pleased, for he thought, *David's raids have surely made his people hate him.* During this time, the Philistine tribes united to wage war against Israel. Achish sent word to David that he and his men must join them. David replied with such eagerness that the king promoted him: David would become his bodyguard for life.

Meanwhile, as the Israelites prepared for battle, Saul looked down on the Philistine forces and was terrified. He inquired of the Lord, but God gave him no answer. How he wished that he could speak to his spiritual father, Samuel! But Samuel had died some time ago.

In desperation, Saul told his servants to locate a medium who calls forth spirits from the dead. This would not be easy. Years earlier, when

Saul was obeying God, he had expelled all the mediums. But his servants knew of one woman. So the king disguised himself and went to her.

"Whom shall I bring up?" she asked.

"The prophet Samuel," he said.

When the woman saw Samuel's image, she let out a sharp cry. "Why have you deceived me? You are Saul!"

"Don't be afraid," Saul reassured her. "Tell me—what do you see?"

"I see the spirit of an old man, wearing a robe."

Saul knew it was Samuel. He bowed down with his face to the ground.

A man's voice called out, "Why have you disturbed me by bringing me up?"

"The Philistines are fighting us and God has turned away from me. What should I do?"

"Why do you consult me now? You disobeyed the Lord, and God has done what I said he would do, torn the kingdom from you and given it to David. He will hand over you and Israel's army to the Philistines. By tomorrow you and your sons will be here with me, for you will die."

When Saul heard all of Samuel's words, he fell full length to the ground, overcome by fear. His strength had totally left him, for he had eaten nothing all that day or night.

The woman came closer to Saul and saw that he was greatly shaken. "Look," she said, "your servant has obeyed you. I took my life in my hands to do what you wanted. Now please, listen to me. Let me give you some food so that you may regain your strength."

Saul refused to eat, but then his men joined the woman in coaxing him. Finally, he listened and sat up on the bed. The woman butchered a calf and cooked it. Then she baked some bread without yeast. The men ate in silence. Then they thanked her and left. They traveled through the night. All the while, Saul thought to himself, *Oh, God, let this be only a dream. . . .*

TBC 78

Israel's New King

TBC Book One, Chapter 79
1 Samuel 29:1-31:13; 2 Samuel 1:1-5:5

David looked disappointed when King Achish told him the news: "You cannot come with us into battle. As surely as the Lord lives, I wish you could join me. But the other rulers are afraid you will turn against us and help Saul's army. So I must send you back."

"What have I done to deserve this?" David protested. "Haven't I served you faithfully? Why can't I fight against the enemies of my lord, the king?"

Achish gave him a smile of approval. "You have been as pleasing to me as an angel of God. But the other commanders have made up their minds. Return to Ziklag in the morning."

David had given such a convincing performance that even his own men were not sure how he really felt. As for them, they were relieved. It took them three full days to reach their home in Ziklag. But when they arrived, they were horrified by what they saw.

The entire city had been burned to the ground. The Amalekites knew this was their chance to take revenge on David for his raids. All the women and children were taken hostage.

David and his men tore their clothes in grief and wept aloud. When they could cry no longer, some talked of stoning David.

David's grief now turned to fear. *Oh, Lord,* he thought. *Help me! Show me what to do.* He made his way to Abiathar and got the special ephod. It indicated they should pursue the raiders.

By dusk they had caught up with them. The Amalekites were celebrating, for they had taken great plunder from the Philistines and from Judah. As darkness approached, David's men attacked. They fought them all night long and all the next day. They defeated them and rescued every captive. The plunder was now theirs, and David sent some as a gift to the elders of Judah.

Meanwhile, the Philistines warred powerfully, and many Israelites fled. The fighting grew fierce. Jonathan, Abinadab, and Malki-Shua, Saul's three oldest sons, were all killed.

Then archers shot King Saul. Saul called out to his armor-bearer, "Draw your sword and kill me, for the Philistines will torture me." But the young man could not bring himself to do that. So Saul set up his own sword and thrust himself upon it. Then his armor-bearer did the same.

While the Israelites were retreating, David's people returned to Ziklag. Three days after they got back, an Amalekite prisoner escaped and told David about Saul and his sons.

"How do you know they were killed?" David asked.

"The king had been wounded," he said, "and he was near death. He told me to kill him. So I did. Here is the king's crown, my lord." David did not know he was lying about killing Saul.

When David and his men saw the crown, they all began to weep, but none more than David. They tore their clothes and mourned until evening. Then David called for the Amalekite.

"Why were you not afraid to kill the Lord's anointed?" he asked. The man looked surprised. He had thought David would reward him. But instead, David had him killed.

Some time later, David asked the Lord if he should go to Judah. "Yes," the Lord answered, "to Hebron." And there the people of Judah anointed him as their king. In the north, however, Saul's son Ish-boseth governed the ten tribes known as Israel.

In the years that followed, the men of Israel and Judah battled to gain control of the nation. David's forces grew stronger, and the elders of Israel wanted David as their king.

Abner met with David and agreed to help him. But when he left, David's commander, Joab, murdered him, for Abner had killed his brother in battle. Men also murdered Ish-boseth, thinking David would be pleased. Instead, David had them killed and mourned those they had murdered. When the Israelites saw he was as sad as they were, they loved him even more. So all the tribes of Israel came to Hebron and anointed him as king over both Judah and Israel.

TBC 79

City of David, City of God

TBC Book One, Chapter 80
2 Samuel 5:6-25; 6:1-23; 1 Chronicles 13-15

In his first military exploit as Israel's new king, David led their army to a city fit for royalty, called "Jerusalem." The Jebusites boasted their walled city was so well-protected even their blind and lame could ward off David. Since it rested on a hill, few armies could penetrate its walls. But David's military commander, Joab, had a cunning plan. Using a tunnel that brought fresh spring water into the city, David's forces slipped inside and caught the Jebusites off guard.

After reigning over Judah in Hebron for seven years, David now established his throne in Jerusalem, and it became known as the City of David. At age 37, he had become king over both Israel and Judah, and Jerusalem served as the perfect place from which to govern both nations

Capturing Jerusalem was such a stunning military feat it won the attention and approval of Hiram, king of Tyre. He sent cedar logs with his craftsmen to build a palace for David.

When the Philistine kings learned that David now ruled both Judah and Israel, they joined forces to attack him before he could strengthen his kingdom. They began by raiding the Valley of Rephaim, just four miles southwest of Jerusalem.

David wondered whether he could win a battle against the united Philistine forces. "Shall I attack them?" he asked the Lord.

"Yes," he replied.

True to his word, the Lord allowed David to defeat them. The Philistines fled, abandoning their idols. So David's men carried them off, and David ordered that the idols be burned. But Israel's enemies had not given up.

The Philistines returned to the valley. This time, the Lord said, "Do not attack them head-on; circle around behind them. When you hear the sound of marching in the balsam trees, move quickly, for I will have gone out in front of you." David obeyed, and his army drove them out.

After he finished building his palace, David chose 30,000 men to accompany him in bringing the Ark of the Covenant to Jerusalem. They set the ark on a new cart, pulled by oxen, and some Levites walked nearby. All of Israel celebrated joyfully with songs and musical instruments.

The oxen, however, stumbled and a Levite named Uzzah reached out to steady the ark. But the Lord's anger burned against him, and God struck him dead, for the ark of the Lord was holy. David became angry, then frightened. He wondered, *How will the ark ever come to me?*

Afraid to take the ark with him into Jerusalem, David decided to leave it at the house of Obed-Edom, a person living in Gath. For three months the ark remained there. During that whole time, God blessed Obed-Edom's entire household so much that King David heard about it.

So once again, David arranged to bring the ark to Jerusalem, but this time he did it the right way. After consulting the books of God's Law, David learned that it was to be carried on poles by Levites, and not even they could touch the ark.

David was so excited about finally bringing the ark into Jerusalem that he took off his king's robe and put on an ephod, similar to what priests wear. With the people shouting joyfully and trumpets blaring, David danced and leaped for joy. His wife Michal watched him from a window.

The men set the ark in the tent David had pitched for it. Then David sacrificed burnt offerings and fellowship offerings. He blessed the people in the name of the Lord. Before they went home, he gave each one a loaf of bread, a cake of raisins, and a cake of dates.

When David finally returned home to bless his own household, Michal came to meet him. But David knew something was wrong. "That was a fine thing to do," she said, "disrobing like a vulgar peasant! You looked ridiculous, leaping and dancing in front of the slave girls."

"I was celebrating before the Lord, who chose me rather than your father as king." Their relationship was never the same after that, and Michal never bore David any children.

TBC 80

The House that God Built

TBC Book One, Chapter 81
2 Samuel 7:1-10:19; 1 Chronicles 17-19

Nathan the prophet recognized that gleam in the eyes of his friend, King David. It had taken David years to complete his palace in Jerusalem, and his kingdom was finally enjoying a time of peace. Now he found himself dreaming about the one thing he would most like to accomplish.

"Nathan," he said to the prophet, "do you realize that here I am, living in a palace of cedar, while the ark of God remains in a tent? Somehow, that just doesn't seem right. . . ."

If ever there were a man on whom God's favor rested, it was David. The king was leading up to something. "Whatever you have in mind, O King, do it, for God is with you."

But Nathan had spoken too freely. So that night, the Lord spoke to Nathan. And early the next day Nathan returned to David. "The Lord spoke to me last night after I left the palace. He gave me a message for you. The Lord says, 'Are you the one to build me a house? I have never dwelt in a house. When have I ever asked anyone to build me a house of cedar?

" 'I took you from the pasture, tending the flocks, and set you as the ruler of Israel to shepherd my people. I have stayed near you and cut off your enemies. Now I will make you one of the greatest men on earth. And I will provide a place for my people, a home for them.

" 'It is I who will establish a house for you. When your life on earth is over, your offspring will rule Israel, and he is the one who will build a house for my Name. When he does wrong, I will discipline him, but I will never take away my love, as I did with Saul.' "

After Nathan delivered God's message, he left, and David sat alone before the Lord. He spoke to him as one speaks to a friend. "Who am I, O Sovereign Lord, that you have brought me this far? You have even revealed future blessings. Is this the way you usually deal with man?

"What more can I say? For I know that you know me. How great you are, O Sovereign Lord! There is no one like you, no God but you. And what other nation is like Israel? You have performed miracles for us, driving out other peoples and their gods to reveal yourself as God.

"Lord God, please keep forever the promise you made to me, your servant, and to my family so that your name will be great forever. You have revealed you will build a house for me—not a building, but a lasting kingdom. Bless this dynasty you have promised."

In time, David conquered the Philistines and took control of their land. He also defeated the Moabites. Then he made them lie down by a measuring cord. Every two-thirds of them were killed, for they had murdered David's family. Those left alive paid tribute to Israel.

God blessed David's military campaigns with victory over the Ammonites, Amalekites, and Edomites. He captured thousands of chariots and soldiers from Zobah. All the gold, silver, and bronze he dedicated to the Lord. The nations paid tribute, and King David became famous.

Then David remembered his promise to Jonathan. He asked Ziba, Saul's servant, if Saul had any grandchildren. Jonathan's son, Meribbaal, was five when his father died. He became crippled when his nurse dropped him, as she ran to save his life. Now an adult, Meribbaal lived in hiding, fearful King David would kill him. When David learned that, he called for him and reassured him: "Don't be afraid. I will show you kindness for your father's sake and give you the land that belonged to your grandfather, Saul. You will eat at my table, like a prince."

Some time later, King Nahash of Ammon died. David sent some of his officials to tell his son Hanun how sorry he was. But Hanun's advisors pulled him aside and said, "Do you really think David is sending you sympathy? Why these men are surely sent here as spies!"

When he heard that, Hanun ordered that the men's beards be shaved in half and their clothes be cut off at the waist. So the men returned to David in humiliation. Fearful that David would get even, Hanun hired Arameans to fight Israel. But David defeated them, and they served as his vassals.

TBC 81

A Bathing Beauty

TBC Book One, Chapter 82
2 Samuel 11:1-27

If only David had gone out to battle, he might have avoided the biggest temptation of his life. After defeating the Arameans and turning back the Ammonites, Israel's forces returned to Jerusalem—but not for long. As spring approached, David sent out Joab with Israel's entire army. They destroyed the Ammonites then surrounded their capital city, Rabbah. The fighting grew fierce as the Israelites prepared to attack the city.

While the battle at Rabbah continued, King David chose to remain in Jerusalem. One evening, as he walked around on the top of his palace, he looked down at the rooftops below and saw a beautiful woman bathing. He sent a servant to find out who she was. "She's Bathsheba, Eliam's daughter, the wife of Uriah the Hittite."

She was also the granddaughter of Ahithophel, David's wisest advisor. Although she was Uriah's wife, David went ahead and sent for her. He thought, *No one will find out.*

He was wrong. Soon everyone would know. Bathsheba had come, just as King David had requested. She stayed at the palace a number of days. After she returned to her home, she sent a secret message to David: She was pregnant. David knew the baby in her womb was his. Soon everyone would find out he had taken another man's wife as his own.

David thought, *If only Uriah would come home right away. . . .* By the time Bathsheba would start to look pregnant, Uriah would assume that he had fathered the baby. No one would find out the truth. So he summoned Uriah from the battle at Rabbah.

Pretending to want information about the battle, David asked Uriah some questions. Then he said, "You may go home now and refresh yourself." So Uriah left, but instead of going home, he slept at the entrance to the palace, near David's servants.

The next morning, David was surprised to learn Uriah had stayed near the palace. When questioned why, he said, "With the ark and Israel staying in temporary shelters, and our soldiers camped in the fields, how could I indulge myself by eating and drinking and enjoying my wife?"

This was going to be harder than he thought. Another idea came to mind. David kept Uriah in Jerusalem one more day and invited him to dine with him. How could he refuse the king? After dinner, David managed to get him drunk. Then he sent him home. But once again, Uriah slept as one of the servants and refused the comforts of his home.

David was growing desperate. What could he do to cover his sin? He did have one more idea. . . . The next morning, he wrote a letter to Joab, sealed it, and sent it with Uriah. The note read: "Put Uriah at the front of the battle line, then draw your soldiers back so he will be killed."

Uriah had no idea what David had written. After he delivered the letter, Joab turned aside so he could read it privately. He sighed when he realized what David wanted him to do.

Joab sent Uriah to the front, to advance against the city's strongest defenders. A number of Joab's soldiers died, including Uriah. Then Joab sent a messenger to give David a report.

"When you give this report to the king," Joab said, "he might get angry when he learns how many soldiers we lost. He might say, 'Why did you get so close to the wall, where their arrows could reach you?' If he says that, tell him, 'Your servant Uriah has also died.' "

The messenger traveled to Jerusalem and gave Joab's full report: "The men came out from the city and attacked us in the open. As we drove them back to the city gate, archers shot arrows at us from atop the wall. Some of our soldiers died, including your servant Uriah."

When Bathsheba learned that her husband was dead, she mourned for him. After her time of mourning, David sent for her and married her. Months later she bore him a son. But David had done an evil thing to cover up his sin, and the Lord was displeased.

TBC 82

The Deadly Price of Sin

TBC Book One, Chapter 83
2 Samuel 12:1-25

This was one visit that Nathan dreaded. He knew he must confront the king. Not only had David committed adultery, but he had also arranged for an innocent man to be killed, a man more noble than he. The question was: How could he go to the king of Israel and persuade him to see his sin from God's perspective? As he prayed, a thought came to mind. . . .

Nathan rose and made his way to the palace. Nathan was always a welcomed guest. But as he waited to be called into the king's chambers, Nathan wondered whether David would see him. Finally he heard someone say, "The king says you may enter."

"I need for you to render judgment on a matter," Nathan said. David sat on his throne, listening as Nathan began the account: "Two men lived in a certain town. One man was rich and owned large herds of sheep and cattle. The other was poor and owned only one ewe lamb. It grew up with his children as a pet. It even slept in his arms.

"Now a weary traveler happened to come to the rich man. So the rich man arranged a meal for him. But instead of going out to his herds to select one of his sheep or cattle, he took the poor man's ewe lamb, even though it was like the man's own child."

When David heard that, his eyes flashed with anger. He pounded his fist on the arm of his throne.

"As surely as the Lord lives," he said, "that rich man deserves to die! He must pay four times the lamb's price, for he had no pity!"

His response went far beyond the judgment required by God's Laws. He was still seething with anger when Nathan stepped closer.

The prophet raised his arm and pointed at David. "You are the man! The Lord says, 'I anointed you king over Israel. I protected you from Saul and gave you his inheritance. If that had been too little, I would have given you more. Why have you despised me by doing such an evil thing? You used the Ammonites to strike down Uriah, and you took his wife.

" 'Because you have shown disregard for me by doing these things, violence by sword will plague your family. Out of your own family, I the

Lord will bring disaster on you. Before your own eyes, one of your close relatives will lie with your wives. You slept with someone's wife in secret. But I will allow this to happen in broad daylight, and everyone will witness it.' "

David put his face into his hands. Then he said, "I have sinned against the Lord."

"The Lord has taken away your sin," Nathan replied. "You will not be killed. But your actions have caused the Lord's enemies to sneer at God. So the son born to you will die."

As soon as Nathan had left, the Lord caused Bathsheba's baby to become ill. David begged God to spare their child. He refused to eat anything, and he spent the nights lying on the floor. The older people in his household tried to coax him to get up and eat, but he refused all of them.

Seven days later, the infant died. David's servants were so worried about him that they were afraid to tell him. They thought he might do something desperate, like take his own life.

David heard them whispering, and he asked, "Is the child dead?"

"Yes," they replied, "he has died." So David got up from the ground, washed himself, and changed his clothes. Then he went to worship the Lord. When he returned he asked for food.

His servants were perplexed. One of them finally asked, "Why are you acting like this?"

"When my child was still alive," David said, "I fasted and wept in hopes that God would change his mind and let the baby live. Now that he has died, why should I fast? It won't bring him back from the dead. But one day, when I die, I will go to him."

David went to his wife Bathsheba and comforted her. In time she became pregnant and gave birth to another son. They named the baby Solomon, meaning "peaceable." The Lord loved him, and he told Nathan to call him Jedidiah, meaning "loved by God."

TBC 83

Charm Is Deceitful

TBC Book One, Chapter 84
2 Samuel 13:1-16:23

Nathan was right—when David's children grew up, the sword did bring bloodshed to his family. It began when his son Amnon was attracted to his beautiful half-sister, Tamar. One day Amnon pretended he was sick, and when his father came to visit, he requested Tamar to prepare him a meal and keep him company. But when she came, he forced her into his bed.

When David learned what Amnon had done to his half-sister, he was furious. Yet he said nothing to him. After his own sin with Bathsheba, how could he possibly judge Amnon?

Disgraced by what had happened, Tamar went to live with her brother Absalom. And Absalom made a vow—someday, he would get even for what Amnon had done to his sister.

That day came two years later. Absalom invited all his brothers, David's sons, to a feast at his house. Then he said to his servants, "When Amnon gets drunk, I want you to kill him."

As soon as they struck Amnon, all of Absalom's brothers fled in terror. Word of his death was sent to David, and now Absalom fled for his own life. He stayed in Geshur, where his grandfather, his mother's father, ruled as king of Aram.

Three years later Absalom was finally permitted to return to Judah. But his father ordered that he must go to his own house. For two more years, David punished him by refusing to see him. Finally, Joab persuaded David to change his mind, for he knew David missed him.

David was not the only one who missed him. People said he was the most handsome young man in all Israel. He had three sons and one beautiful daughter, whom he named Tamar.

Early each morning Absalom rode in his chariot, led by 50 guards, then stood near the city gate. He greeted those who waited there for legal judgments. And when King David did not appear, Absalom would say, "If only I were judge! Everyone would get justice."

Whenever anyone paid homage to the prince by bowing down to him, Absalom would reach out his hand, draw him to his feet, and kiss him, a sign of affection and brotherhood between men in the East. Absalom was so charming that everyone loved him.

Four years after returning to Jerusalem, Absalom went to Hebron, pretending to fulfill a vow. He invited 200 men to join him. They had no idea Absalom had sent messengers throughout Israel to announce, "Absalom is king in Hebron!"

When David heard about it, he told his advisors, "We must flee quickly or none of us will escape!" Gathering his household, David left only ten concubines, women who were like wives, to care for the palace. The priests, Zadok and Abiathar, along with the Levites brought the ark and followed David. But David said to them, "Take back the ark; perhaps I will find God's favor and return to see it. You can serve me best by staying there and sending me messages through your sons."

David's household and followers wept as they hurried away. Then David learned that Ahithophel, Bathsheba's grandfather, had joined Absalom. So he prayed God would thwart Ahithophel's counsel and sent his friend Hushai back to Jerusalem to pretend to serve Absalom.

Absalom led his own followers to the royal city and moved into the palace. Hushai appeared before him and said, "Long live the king!"

"Why didn't you go with your friend?" Absalom asked.

"I will serve the one chosen by the Lord and by Israel," he replied.

Absalom then turned to Ahithophel for advice on what to do next. Now Ahithophel was gifted with wisdom and regarded as highly as a prophet or seer. Ahithophel said, "Lie with your father's concubines so everyone will know you have broken ties with your father."

When a man overpowered a king, he would take everything that king owned, including his harem of wives. So Absalom pitched a tent on top of the palace, where everyone could see it. Then he lay with each of his father's concubines. What Nathan predicted had now come true.

TBC 84

Son of My Sorrows

TBC Book One, Chapter 85
2 Samuel 16:23-19:8

In a single day, Absalom had ascended to power as Israel's king. Sitting on his father's throne in Jerusalem, Absalom summoned his chief advisor, Ahithophel. He was one of the wisest men in Israel, and Absalom knew he could trust him: As Bathsheba's grandfather, he had a score to settle with David. Everyone in the room now listened as the older man began to speak.

"I would take 12,000 men and pursue your father now while he is weak and tired," said Ahithophel. "Strike down only the king and bring back his people unharmed."

Absalom pondered his words. Then he asked Hushai. "And what is your counsel?"

"You know your father and his men," Hushai said. "They are all experienced fighters. If they attack your troops first, rumor would spread that your troops got slaughtered. Then even the bravest soldiers you have would melt with fear. So I would advise you to be better prepared. Gather soldiers from throughout Israel; lead them into battle. We could attack, leaving no men alive."

Absalom now looked to the elders. He knew what they thought of his father: How could a king rule justly when he himself skirted justice? David had offended many of them by being such an independent leader. Absalom knew he must show the elders that he valued their opinion.

Seldom did the elders reach a unanimous decision about anything. But this time they all agreed. They took Hushai's advice, for God was thwarting Ahithophel's counsel.

Immediately, Hushai slipped outside. He met secretly with Zadok and Abiathar, the priests loyal to David. "Tell David I stopped Absalom from attacking now while David and his men are exhausted. He must cross the Jordan right away. Absalom is gathering his forces."

A servant girl took the message to the priests' sons in En Rogel. But someone saw them and ran to tell Absalom. So the young men now hurried to a friend's home in Bahurim. There they hid themselves in his well.

Then his wife spread a covering over it and scattered grain all over the top of it.

Absalom's men soon arrived and asked, "Where are Ahimaaz and Jonathan?"

"They crossed the brook," she said. So the men crossed the stream. Finally, they gave up searching and returned to Jerusalem. The two men climbed out of the well and raced to David.

David's group now crossed the Jordan River and headed for Mahanaim, one of the Levites' cities. Then they received supplies from nearby kingdoms that remained loyal as David's vassals.

Meanwhile, in Jerusalem, Ahithophel knew Absalom would be defeated. *Better to die now,* he thought, *than to be killed by David's men.* So Ahithophel took his own life.

While Absalom prepared for battle, David listened to the advice of his commanders and decided to stay in the city. But before his men left, David commanded, "Be gentle with Absalom for my sake."

David's army marched out and fought Israel in the forest of Ephraim. They defeated Absalom's army, and 20,000 Israelites died, most trapped by the forest's thick growth. Absalom himself rode under an oak tree that caught his hair. He hung from the tree helplessly while his mule kept going.

One of Joab's soldiers reported seeing Absalom hanging in a tree. "What!" Joab said, "You saw him and you didn't kill him?"

"I heard what the king told us; I will not kill his son." So Joab himself killed Absalom. Then he halted his soldiers from pursuing Israel.

When David heard that Absalom was dead, he was badly shaken. He went to a room over the city's gate and wept. Then he cried out: "O Absalom, my son! If only I had died instead of you—O Absalom, my son, my son!" When his men heard him mourning, they mourned, too.

Then Joab said to David. "Do you realize what you are doing? Those men risked their lives to save yours! They shouldn't be mourning. You love those who hate you and don't care about those who love you." So David listened and sat in the gateway to encourage them.

TBC 85

A Senseless Census

TBC Book One, Chapter 86
1 Chronicles 21:1-30; 2 Samuel 24:1-25

Joab turned around in astonishment. For a full moment he just stared at David in disbelief. Then he said to the king, "You want me to do what?" He studied David's expression, looking for a way to broach his concern.

David stared back with his unflinching, penetrating look. "I said, go throughout all the tribes of Israel and find out how many men are old enough to be enlisted in our army. I want a detailed list, naming every man in Israel whose age qualifies him as a soldier."

Joab's mind raced as David waited for him to respond. He feared David's motives. And he knew David would not tolerate a challenge. Somehow he must find a way to reason with him.

"My lord, may the Lord your God multiply your troops a hundred times over, and may it happen in your lifetime. But why do this?" Even Joab knew this was against God's will.

David's other officers listened anxiously. They feared this edict just as much as Joab did. The people would also be suspicious—either David was about to set up a permanent system of taxing them, or, more likely than that, he was planning an enormous military campaign.

But David gave them no explanation. By yielding to his own pride, the thrill of planning one more major conquest, he was opening up himself to a spiritual attack. That voice he heard within, inspiring him to do this, was not God's Spirit, but an evil, satanic spirit.

So Joab and his commanders went throughout Israel, listing all men who could handle a sword. But Joab refused to count the priestly tribe of Levi and the small tribe of Benjamin.

By the time Joab and his men returned, David's conscience began to bother him. He realized he had made a foolish decision.

"Lord," he prayed, "I have sinned greatly. Please take away my guilt."

Early the next morning, God answered him through his friend, the prophet Gad.

"I have a word for you, my lord. The Lord says, 'Choose one of these three disciplines for me to carry out against you—three years of famine, three months of running from your enemies with them overtaking you, or three days of a deadly plague.' "

David was deeply distressed. What should he choose? He sighed heavily. Finally he said, "Let me fall into the hands of the Lord, for his mercy is very great, but do not let me fall into the hands of men." So the Lord sent a plague upon Israel, and it began that very morning.

By the third day, the angel of the Lord had killed 70,000. He was about to destroy the people of Jerusalem, when the Lord himself called out in grief. "Enough!" he said.

David could see the angel, sword drawn, now hovering above Jerusalem, ready to strike.

Israel's elders joined David in pleading for God's mercy. "O Lord," David prayed, "I am the one who sinned. I am the one who ordered that the fighting men be counted. These people are like innocent sheep. Please—let the discipline fall on me and my family, not on your people."

At that moment, the angel of the Lord sent Gad to deliver God's reply: "Tell David to go to the threshing floor of Araunah the Jebusite to build an altar to the Lord." A few moments later, Araunah and his four sons looked up from threshing wheat, and suddenly they saw the angel.

When David and his servants approached, Araunah bowed down in respect.

"I'd like to buy your threshing floor to offer sacrifices," David said. "Take it," Araunah replied, "it's yours."

"No," David said, "I will not give to the Lord that which cost me nothing."

So David bought the property for its full price and built an altar to the Lord. Then he sacrificed burnt offerings and fellowship offerings and declared that the Lord is God. The Lord answered by sending fire from heaven to light the sacrifice.

Then the Lord commanded the angel to put away his sword. So David offered more sacrifices. Instead of making plans to expand his kingdom, he now made plans for God's temple. He announced that it would rest on that very spot—the mountain where God had spared Isaac.

TBC 86

Out of the Heart

TBC Book One, Chapter 87
1 Chronicles 22; 28:1-29:20

The last time David stood in this spot, a flame of fire suddenly appeared on the altar, the Lord's way of showing he accepted his offering. Their broken relationship was restored. But why did God select this spot? Could this be the special place of worship that he would reveal to his people? As he closed his eyes, David imagined a magnificent temple. . . .

The more he thought about it, the more ideas that came to his mind. It was as if God himself were inspiring David, giving him a detailed picture of a majestic house of worship. Yet God had clearly told him he was not the one to build a "house for the Lord." That honor would fall to one of his sons. *Why then,* David wondered, *is my mind so full of these ideas?*

Toward the end of his life, David thought, *My son Solomon is the man of peace who will build God's temple. But he is still young and lacks experience, and God's temple must be magnificent. So I will help him by making preparations for it.*

One day, David sent for Solomon and said, "My son, I had it in my heart to build a house for the Lord. But God revealed I would have a son who is a man of peace, and he is the one to build it. I believe you are that son, and I have made preparations to help you."

Then David met with the leaders of Israel, and he commanded them to help his son build the temple: "God has given you rest from all your enemies, so devote your heart and soul to seeking the Lord. Begin building a sanctuary for the Ark of the Covenant."

In time David summoned all of Israel's officials to gather at Jerusalem. Then he said, "My brothers, the Lord who chose me as king of Israel has chosen my son Solomon to succeed me. I had desired to build a house for the Lord, but it is Solomon who will do that.

"Now I charge you, my people, to follow the commands of the Lord your God.

"My son, Solomon, I charge you to serve God wholeheartedly. For the Lord searches every heart and motive. If you seek him, you will find him. If you turn from him, he will turn from you."

Then David handed Solomon some drawings that pictured what the temple should look like. David said, "The Lord inspired me and gave me these details for the design of the temple." David also gave him instructions for organizing the priests and Levites who would serve there.

Turning once again to the large assembly, David said, "I have provided gold, silver, and bronze, iron and wood, and precious stones. I have also given my personal treasures of silver and gold. Now I ask all of you, who else is willing to give to the Lord's house?"

A great many leaders stepped forward, leaders of families, leaders of the tribes, and military commanders. They gave money, silver, gold, bronze, iron, and precious stones. The people got excited when they saw their leaders giving to the Lord so wholeheartedly.

David got excited too, and he gave glory to God: "Praise you, O Lord, God of our father Israel! You are great and mighty. All splendor and majesty belong to you. Yours is the kingdom, and you are the head over all. We thank you and praise your name."

Then David bowed down and said, "Who are we to be able to give so generously? We have only given back what you gave to us. Like our forefathers, we are just tenants. Our days on earth are like a shadow; without you we have no hope. All these things, Lord, belong to you.

"I know, my God, you test the heart, and you are pleased when you find integrity, a heart with pure motives. We give all this willingly and with an honest intent to please you. Keep this desire forever in the hearts of your people; keep them loyal to you. "Give my son a wholehearted devotion to you, to keep your commandments and to build this magnificent structure." Then David directed the people to praise God. They all bowed and prostrated themselves before the Lord and the king. With a full heart, everyone praised the Lord.

TBC 87

On David's Throne

TBC Book One, Chapter 88
1 Kings 1:1-53

This was the moment Adonijah was waiting for. His aging father, King David, no longer appeared in public, and people wondered who would take his place. At one time, David had told his officials that Solomon would be Israel's next king. But that was years ago. People now wondered if David had changed his mind, especially when they saw Adonijah.

If ever a young man looked like a king, it was he. Since Absalom had died, Adonijah was now David's oldest son and every bit as handsome as Absalom. He drew attention by arranging for chariots and horses and 50 men proceed him on his travels. Yet his father never questioned his actions. And now, nearing the end of his life, David did not realize what his son had in mind.

King David was now bed-ridden, and he could no longer keep himself warm, even when wrapped in many blankets. So his servants found a beautiful young woman, named Abishag, to keep him warm as his concubine. But David refused. He only wanted her to wait on him.

As David's health continued to decline, Adonijah began meeting with his father's chief officials. He reasoned that the rights of the firstborn belonged to him, including his father's throne. So he discussed the idea with Joab, David's chief commander, and Abiathar the priest. Both men now agreed with him that David could no longer rule Israel, and they gave Adonijah their support.

They decided to make him king at a great celebration feast at En Rogel. There Adonijah offered sacrifices. He invited Judah's royal officials and all of his brothers—except for Solomon.

Officials like Nathan, who were loyal to David, were not invited. That's when Nathan knew Adonijah did not have his father's consent. So he rushed to Bathsheba and told her what was happening. Then he said, "Now here is how you can save both your life and Solomon's. . . ."

Obeying Nathan's advice, Bathsheba hurried to speak to David. "My lord," she said, "you promised that my son would be king. But Adonijah has just appointed himself. Unless you do something, Solomon and I will be treated as criminals as soon as you die."

Then a messenger interrupted them: "My lord, Nathan is here." Bathsheba stepped out as Nathan entered. "My lord, have you declared that Adonijah would sit on your throne? Right now he is at En Rogel, celebrating with Joab, Abiathar, and all your sons except Solomon."

David looked alarmed. "Call back Bathsheba," he said. When she stood before him, David pledged: "As surely as the Lord lives, today I will carry out what I swore to do. Your son Solomon shall sit on my throne as king." Bathsheba bowed low and left the chamber.

David then summoned the officials who remained loyal to him, Zadok the priest, Nathan the prophet, and Benaiah, his chief bodyguard. "Set Solomon on my mule," he said. "Take him to Gihon and anoint him as king. Then blow the trumpet and shout, 'Long live King Solomon!' "

Many people fell into line behind the three officials who escorted Solomon to Gihon. There Zadok and Nathan anointed him king, and the people shouted, "Long live King Solomon!" Everyone returned to Jerusalem, rejoicing so loudly that the ground shook.

Meanwhile, Adonijah and his guests were finishing their feast, when Joab heard a trumpet sound in the distance. A young man came running in with the news: "David has made Solomon king! He's sitting on the throne and royal officials are congratulating him!"

Hearing this news, all the guests fled, afraid that they would be punished for acting against the king's wishes. Adonijah ran to the altar and clung to its horns, which symbolized God's salvation. From there he sent messengers to ask for Solomon's mercy.

Solomon replied, "If he proves himself worthy, not a hair of his head will be touched. But if he takes any more steps that are evil, he will die." Then Solomon sent men to bring him in. As Adonijah bowed before King Solomon, the king commanded, "Go to your home."

TBC 88

Dealing with His Enemies

TBC Book One, Chapter 89
1 Chronicles 29:21-28; 1 Kings 2:1-46

Everyone rejoiced as the royal family held another celebration. This time they honored young Solomon, their newly appointed king. All the royal officials as well as all of David's sons pledged their loyalty to King Solomon—all except Joab and Abiathar, for they were replaced by Benaiah and Zadok. David made sure that his son would be supported by faithful advisors. There were men in the kingdom who would seek revenge after David's death and others who would try to overthrow him as king. Somehow, he must prepare his young son to deal with them. . . .

Not long after their celebration, David called Solomon to his bedside. "My son, I am about to die. So be strong, prove yourself as a man, and obey the Lord's commands. If you and your descendants walk faithfully before the Lord, your descendants will always reign as king.

"After I die, I want you to punish all those who challenged my authority. Remember those also who remained faithful, and reward them for their faithfulness. Punish Joab and Shimei. During a time of peace, Joab killed two innocent military leaders—deal with him. Deal also with Shimei, for he cursed me and threw stones when I fled from Absalom."

Not long after that, David died, and all the people mourned for him. Just as David had feared, certain men tested Solomon's authority, and it began in his own household.

Adonijah approached Bathsheba, the Queen Mother. "May I have a word with you?" he asked.

"As you know," he said, "all Israel looked to me as king before the Lord gave my brother the throne. I have only one request. Ask King Solomon to give me Abishag as my wife."

Now Abishag was the beautiful young woman who was meant to be David's concubine in old age. Bathsheba saw no harm in his request. After all, the woman was very attractive. She didn't stop to think that Adonijah could have other reasons for wanting Abishag.

"Your request is granted," she said. "I will ask the king."

As soon as Bathsheba entered the room, Solomon stood up and bowed. When they were seated, she said, "I have a small request. Give Abishag in marriage to your brother Adonijah."

Solomon's expression turned hard. "Why not request the whole kingdom for him and for Abiathar and Joab who gave him this idea! I swear, Adonijah will pay for this with his life!"

King Solomon ordered that Adonijah be killed. Then he sent for Abiathar. "You deserve to die. But because you were faithful to my father during his hardships, I won't kill you. Go back to your fields." So Abiathar lost the priesthood, fulfilling God's word against Eli's family.

When Joab heard what had happened, he fled to the tent of the Lord and took hold of the horns of the altar, hoping for mercy. Benaiah soon arrived and commanded him to come out.

"No," Joab said, "I will die here."

Benaiah then sent word to Solomon, for this was a holy place.

The king replied, "Do as he says—strike him down right there. Joab killed two innocent men during my father's reign, Abner and Amasa. Both of them were better men than he. My father had no part in those killings. May the guilt of their bloodshed now rest on Joab."

Solomon remembered what his father had commanded him. Now was the time to deal with Shimei, who had cursed David. So he sent for Shimei and said, "Build yourself a house in Jerusalem. But should you leave it to cross the Kidron Valley, you will pay for it with your life."

"What you say is good," Shimei said. He was grateful to save his life. For a long time he remained in Jerusalem. But three years later, two of his slaves escaped to Gath. So he saddled his donkey and traveled to Gath to bring them back. When he returned, Solomon sent for him.

The king said to him, "Did you not swear to me you would stay in Jerusalem or risk losing your life? You even told me, 'What you said is good.' Now the Lord will repay you for what you did to my father."

So the enemies of his kingdom were put to death, and young King Solomon reigned securely.

TBC 89

Solomon's Wise Response

TBC Book One, Chapter 90
1 Kings 3:1-28; 2 Chronicles 1:1-12

Thanks to his father, a golden opportunity now lay before young King Solomon. Israel was now enjoying one of its greatest times of peace. One of the first things King Solomon did was to build upon that peace by making a treaty with Pharaoh, the king of Egypt.

As a sign of their bond, he married the Pharaoh's daughter and brought her to Jerusalem while his palace was being built. With no fear of war from neighboring countries, Solomon also arranged to build the temple and Jerusalem's city wall. Yet he knew the real test of his power lay not in what he could build, but in how he would lead. And all of Israel watched to see what kind of leadership this young king would offer them.

In the early years of his reign, Solomon showed his love for the Lord by obeying him and by following the example of his father, David. But there was one thing he did that David would not have done—he offered his sacrifices at the high places, as did the people. One day he went to Gibeon and there he sacrificed 1,000 burnt offerings to the Lord.

Soon after that, the Lord appeared to Solomon in a dream and said, "Ask for whatever you want, and I will give it to you."

"Please—give me a wise, discerning heart to govern your people."

His response pleased the Lord so much that the Lord gave him this reply: "Since you asked for wisdom to govern your people justly and did not ask for riches, or long life, or the death of your enemies, I will give you both riches and honor, as well as the wisdom you desire." When Solomon awoke, he realized he was dreaming. But it seemed so real. He knew the Lord had spoken to him through that dream. So when he returned to Jerusalem, he stood before the ark of the Lord and sacrificed offerings. Then he held a celebration feast for his royal court.

One day when Solomon took his place at the gate of the city, two women appeared before him requesting a judgment. One of them said, "My lord, this woman and I live together. Not long ago, I had a baby. Three days later, she too had a baby. But during the night, she accidentally lay on her baby and smothered him. When she realized what had happened, she switched our babies. The next morning I found the dead baby at my side, and I saw it was not my baby."

"No!" shouted the other woman. "The dead baby is your child! The living one is mine."

"That's not true!" the first woman said. "The dead son is yours and the living one is mine!" Back and forth they argued, as the king looked on and pondered the issue.

Finally, King Solomon spoke up: "This woman says, 'My son is alive, your son is dead.' That one says, 'No. Your son is dead and mine is alive.' There is only one way to solve this."

They watched in astonishment as the king continued to speak: "Now cut the living child in two and give half to each woman."

Immediately, the first woman cried out, "Please, my lord, don't kill him! Go ahead and let her have him, just don't kill him."

But the other woman said, "All right—neither of us shall have the baby. Cut him in two!" It was obvious that only the first woman had spoken with a mother's compassion.

"Stop!" the king ordered his servant. "Do not kill the baby. Give him to the first woman. She is the baby's mother."

Of course, the king had never really intended to have the baby killed. He knew this test would reveal which woman was the mother.

Those who witnessed the case said, "Who would have thought to test the women in this way?" So the story of these women and Solomon's wise judgment soon spread throughout Israel. And from that time one, people held the king in awe, for they knew his wisdom came from God.

TBC 90

A Temple for My Name

TBC Book One, Chapter 91
1 Kings 5:1-8:21; Chronicles 2:1-5:14

Everyone throughout Israel and the surrounding nations now took great interest in the plans of young King Solomon. He had recently married an Egyptian princess, the daughter of Pharaoh himself. Who would have guessed that almost 500 years after their escape from Egypt, the Israelites would grow into a nation that could rival the greatness of Egypt?

Surrounding nations were eager to gain a treaty with Israel. But it wasn't simply fear that drove them toward peace. King Solomon, who was now in the fourth year of his reign, was about to embark on a massive building project, and that signaled good news to neighboring countries.

Even King Hiram of Tyre sent a friendly message to Solomon. He had always been on good terms with Solomon's father, David. Hiram responded to Solomon's request, to send some cedar logs from the forests of Lebanon. Hiram was pleased to do this, for the trade would surely profit him and his country. So the two kings signed a trade treaty. Then Hiram shipped thousands of cedar and cypress logs, floating them on rafts, and Solomon supplied food for Hiram's royal household.

At this time, more than 153,000 immigrants lived in Israel, inhabitants of the surrounding region before the Israelites came from Egypt. Their forefathers were the same people Israel had failed to drive from the land. Now, hundreds of years later, Solomon decided to use them as slave laborers. They would work under Adoniram, one of his officials.

The slave laborers removed blocks of stone from quarries and transported them to the temple site. No hammers, chisels, or other iron tools were used at the temple site, for that was a holy place. Solomon himself oversaw the work, following the plans drawn up by his father.

As the temple neared completion, the Lord sent Solomon this message: "As for this temple you are building, if you carry out my regulations and obey my commands, I will fulfill through you my promise to your father. I will live among the Israelites and not abandon my people."

Encouraged by the Lord's blessing, Solomon then built another magnificent structure—his palace. In the meantime, he and the queen,

Pharaoh's daughter, lived in David's palace. Solomon also drew up plans for the Hall of Justice, where he would judge legal matters for his people.

Solomon's palace would be situated behind the Hall of Justice and built with a similar design. There he would sit on his throne. He also built a second palace, one for the queen. It took 13 years to build them. But their construction did not begin until the temple was completed.

From the very beginning, Solomon hired craftsmen who were renowned for their artistic abilities. He brought in Huram, from Tyre, who was highly skilled in all kinds of bronze work, the trade his father had taught him. Huram's mother was an Israelite, who was from the tribe of Naphtali.

Solomon also recreated the tabernacle furnishings that the Israelites had made during the time of Moses. After seven years, the entire temple was completed. Solomon then took the silver and gold his father had dedicated to the Lord and placed them in the temple treasury.

The king planned a special ceremony to dedicate the temple. He set the date eleven months after the temple was built, so that it would occur during the Feast of Tabernacles. All of Israel's elders and officials joined in bringing the ark to the temple.

After the priests set down the ark and stepped out of the Holy Place, the Lord's glory cloud appeared, and it filled the temple. His glory was so great that the priests could not fulfill their duties. Now the people saw for themselves the same glory that their forefathers had seen.

As the people bowed in worship, King Solomon turned toward them and blessed them: "My father had it in his heart to build a temple for the Name of the Lord. But the Lord said, 'It is your who son will build a temple for my Name.' Now the Lord has kept his promise."

TBC 91

Near to God's Heart

TBC Book One, Chapter 92
2 Chronicles 6:12-7:22; 1 Kings 8:22-9:9

Hundreds of thousands gathered before young King Solomon. Both they and the king himself were in awe. But it was not the magnificent temple that captivated their attention. It was God's glory, filling the temple with his presence. So great was his glory that even the priests could not continue working. There was only one thing any of them could do—bow in worship.

When they finally rose, they were still deeply moved, not only by God's glorious presence, but also by the humble prayer of their king. Solomon's heartfelt plea surely touched the heart of the Lord. They and their children must never forget the petition King Solomon had made on their behalf. They could almost hear his voice as they recalled his words. . . .

"O Lord, God of Israel, there is no one like you in heaven or on earth. You keep your covenant of love with those who walk in your ways wholeheartedly.

"But will God really dwell on earth? Why even the highest heavens cannot contain you; how much less this temple. Yet may you watch this temple day and night. From your dwelling place in heaven, hear our prayers toward this place where you have put your Name.

"When a person wrongs someone then takes an oath in your name, promising to tell the truth, hear him from heaven and judge between them. May you see that the guilty one is punished according to what he has done. And may you clear the innocent person of any guilt.

"When your people to go to war and pray toward this this temple, hear their plea and uphold their cause. When they are defeated because of sinning against you, and they finally turn back to you, hear their prayer. Forgive their sin and bring them back to their land.

"When your people sin against you and you discipline them by preventing rain, may they pray toward this place. When they finally turn from their sin and confess you are Lord, then hear from heaven and forgive them. Teach them the right way to live and reward them with rain.

"In times of famine or of plague, whatever the disaster or disease, hear your people who spread out their hands toward this temple and pray.

Hear them, O Lord, and forgive them of their sin. Deal with each person according to his actions so they will respect you and obey you.

"When someone who is not an Israelite prays toward this temple, hear that prayer and grant that request. May you do this so that all the peoples of the earth will know you and respect you, just as your people Israel do. May they, too, know that this temple bears your Name.

"When your people sin against you, and you allow their enemies to take them captive to another land, may they have a change of heart. May they plead with you and admit to you that they have sinned. And when they turn back to you wholeheartedly, help them and forgive them.

"So now, O Lord, may your eyes and ears be attentive to the prayers offered in this place. We ask you to come, O Lord God, to this resting place, you and the ark of your might. We rejoice in your goodness. Remember the great love you promised to your servant David."

As soon as Solomon finished praying, a great ball of fire suddenly descended on the altar and burned up the sacrifices. The people gasped in amazement. The Lord was showing them that he was pleased to accept their offering. Suddenly his glory appeared, and it filled the temple. The people dropped facedown and worshiped. They thanked the Lord for his goodness and his love.

Years later, the Lord appeared to Solomon and said, "I heard your prayer when you dedicated the temple, and I have indeed chosen this temple for my Name. Now if my people will humble themselves, pray, and turn from their sin to seek me, I will hear and forgive them. My eyes and my heart will always be here. And if you do all that I command, you will always have a son as king. But if you turn away from me and worship other gods, I will uproot Israel from this land and reject this temple. Other nations will know I sent the disaster as my judgment."

TBC 92

A Kingdom Beyond Belief

TBC Book One, Chapter 93
1 Kings 10:1-29; 2 Chronicles 9:1-28;
Deuteronomy 17:14-17

King Solomon smiled with pleasure: The queen of Sheba had requested to visit him. Many came to Jerusalem from great distances because of stories about the king of Israel. They had heard of his remarkable wisdom, his magnificent buildings, and his great wealth. And just like the queen of Sheba, they traveled great distances to find out if the stories were true.

The queen arrived at Jerusalem with a great caravan. Her camels carried spices, large amounts of gold, and precious stones. After all, a visitor must not come empty-handed. She was eager to see not only Jerusalem's majestic structures, but also the king who built them. As the ruling leader in her royal family, she was very well-educated, and more than anything, she wanted to talk to King Solomon himself. She had questions that no wise men in her kingdom could answer. Perhaps she could stump even King Solomon.

As she was escorted into the palace, the queen of Sheba could hardly believe what lay before her. She saw an enormous table of food with a large host of officials seated around it. She noticed that even the servants were dressed in robes. Then she turned and saw the stairway leading to the house of the Lord. Already she was overwhelmed.

Yet one question still lingered: Was King Solomon as wise as people said? Over many days, the queen asked every difficult question she could pose. Yet he answered them all. From the first time they met, she knew he possessed extraordinary wisdom.

"Everything I heard about you is true," she said. "I would not have believed it had I not seen it with my own eyes. In fact, I was not told the half of it. Your wisdom and wealth far exceed the report I heard. How happy your people must be!

"May the Lord your God be praised for placing you on Israel's throne. Surely he delights in you. The Lord has made you king because of his never-ending love for Israel. With you as king, surely Israel will be governed by justice and righteousness."

The queen then presented her gifts to King Solomon, four-and-a-half tons of gold, large amounts of rare spices, and many precious stones. Though Solomon sent out ships to other lands, never again did he receive as many spices as those given that day.

Just as the queen brought gifts for King Solomon, so also did he bestow gifts upon her, treasures from his royal collections. Then he told her to ask for anything else she desired. When the queen returned to her own country, she left with far more than she had brought.

Soon people from all over the world journeyed to Israel to hear Solomon for themselves, each one bringing gifts—silver and gold, robes, weapons, horses. . . . Solomon became greater in wealth and wisdom than any other king, just as God had promised.

Every year Solomon received 25 tons of gold, besides what he received from merchants, traders, and vassal kingdoms. He imported goods, kept them in his storage cities, and then sold them to other countries. He also made caravan trade routes safer against attacks.

No other king owned a throne as ornate as Solomon's. Six steps led up to a throne inlaid with ivory and overlaid with gold. At the side of each armrest stood a lion statue, with others on each side of each step. Even the goblets were made of pure gold.

Silver became so plentiful in Solomon's kingdom that it was no longer valuable to him. So Solomon had nothing made of silver. Every three years his fleet of ships returned with riches like gold and ivory and unusual animals like apes and baboons.

Solomon also acquired thousands of chariots and horses from lands like Egypt and Kue (now called Turkey). He kept them in cities throughout Israel so other nations would be afraid to attack. But he had forgotten one thing: Israel's kings were to trust not in chariots, but in Him.

TBC 93

Treasure Chest of Wisdom

Keep these
in your
heart.

TBC Book One, Chapter 94
Proverbs 1:1-31:31

King Solomon loved to collect wise sayings. These poetic sayings, called proverbs, were written to help people make wise decisions in their everyday lives. Most of these proverbs were written by Solomon:

May love and faithfulness never leave you; keep them ever present, tied around your neck, and written on your heart. Then you will win favor and a good reputation in the eyes of God and the people around you.
—Proverbs 3:3,4

Trust in the Lord with your whole heart; do not rely solely on your own reasoning. In everything you do, seek God's counsel, and he will show you the wisest choice. Do not think you do not need his counsel.
—Proverbs 3:5,6

To fear God is the first step toward wisdom, and knowledge of the Holy One gives understanding. Through wisdom your days will be many, and God will add years to your life. If you choose wisdom, wisdom will reward you.
—Proverbs 9:10-12

Pride leads to destruction, and a haughty attitude causes one to fail. A proud heart leads to a downfall, but humility leads to honor. So let others praise you, but do not praise yourself.
—Proverbs 16:18; 18:12 27:2

The person who hides his sin will fail, but whoever confesses his sin and turns from it will find God's mercy. Happy is the person who always fears the Lord, but the one who hardens his heart will fall into trouble.
—Proverbs 28:13,14

Whoever confronts a person about his sin gains more favor in the end than one who flatters him with compliments. And whoever accepts a just rebuke will keep company with the wise.

—Proverbs 28:23; 15:31

To take advantage of the poor is to show contempt for their Maker. But showing kindness to the needy honors God. For being kind to the poor is like lending to the Lord; God himself will reward that person.

—Proverbs 14:31; 19:17; 28:27

When words are many, it leads to sin, but whoever controls his tongue is wise. The tongue of the righteous is like silver, but the heart of the wicked is worthless. The lips of those who are righteous feed many.

—Proverbs 10:19-21

A gentle answer calms down angry people, but a harsh reply stirs up their anger. Words that bring healing are a tree of life. A person who lives to please God finds that even his enemies respond peacefully to him.

—Proverbs 15:1,4; 16:7

Listen to advice and accept instruction; in the end you will be glad you did, for the person who heeds instruction will prosper. So listen to your parents' corrections; a wise son or daughter makes parents happy.

—Proverbs 19:20; 16:20; 23:22-25

As silver is refined and as a furnace melts gold, so also God tests our hearts. A person's spirit is the lamp God uses to discover the thoughts deep in one's heart. Remember, the eyes of the Lord are everywhere.

—Proverbs 17:3; 20:27; 15:3

TBC 94

Chasing the Wind

TBC Book One, Chapter 95
Ecclesiastes

Imagine a grandfather looking back over his long life, but what he says surprises everyone who hears him. For he was a successful man, a powerful man, in fact, a world-class leader. He had everything a man could ever want. Yet something was missing. Now, as he nears the end of his life, he finds himself asking the one question that even King Solomon cannot answer: "If we all have to die someday, then why were we even born?"

In an ancient book of wisdom called Ecclesiastes, an old man sums up what he has learned in his lifetime. He drops hints about himself but never reveals his name. When you hear his words, you will understand why many think King Solomon may have written these words.

Referring to himself only as "the Teacher," he says: "I reigned as king over Israel in Jerusalem. I spent my whole life studying people and nature, trying to see what I could learn from both. But the more I learned, the more restless I felt—like I was chasing the wind.

"I thought, *I'll do fun things to make myself cheer up. I'll find things that make me laugh.* I even went out of my way to get drunk. But after I was done, I still felt empty.

"So then I set goals for myself, challenging projects. I designed magnificent buildings, and I oversaw their construction. But when they were finished, I thought to myself, *Now what?*

"As I pondered all my years of gaining wisdom, I came to this conclusion: Though it's better to be wise than a fool, the same end overtakes both—sooner or later we all die. Even our hard work does not satisfy us, for what we have earned goes to someone who never worked for it.

"God has placed within all of us a yearning to know what lies beyond this life. To the sinner, nothing brings satisfaction. To the person who pleases God, however, he grants not only wisdom and knowledge, but also the ability to enjoy happiness in this life.

"It is good for a person to find satisfaction in his work during this short life that we live. The ability to enjoy your work is a gift from God:

You become so busy enjoying what you do that you don't spend time dwelling on the past.

"God has a purpose for everything; life has its seasons. There is a time to be born and a time to die, a time to cry and a time to laugh, a time to search and a time to give up searching, a time to be silent and a time to speak, a time for war and a time for peace.

"Be careful when you go to the house of the Lord: Go there to listen rather than to speak. Be careful in what you say to the Lord God, for he is awesome. The more your words, the less their meaning. So let your words be few. And when you make a promise to him, fulfill it.

"Remember that some things are not wise for you to ponder. Do not say to yourself, 'Why were the old days better than these?' And do not take to heart everything people say. For at one time or another, we have all thought badly of others and felt like cursing them.

"When someone commits a crime, discipline should be carried out right away, or others will scheme how they too can commit crimes. But even when people get away with doing evil, it is better to fear God than to be wicked, for the life of the wicked will be cut short.

"Remember your Creator while you are still a child, before troubled times come and you find no pleasure in living. Remember him now, before old age closes in, before your body returns to the dust of the ground and your spirit returns to the Lord who gave it."

The author of Ecclesiastes ends his thoughtful writings by answering the most difficult question, the one he first posed:

"So what is our purpose in life? Simply this: To fear God and obey his commandments, for that sums up what God requires. Someday God will judge everything we have done, even the things people have tried to hide, whether they are good or evil."

TBC 95

Walking Away from God

TBC Book One, Chapter 96
1 Kings 11:1-43

If only Solomon ended his reign the way he began it, wanting to please God. He did indeed govern with wisdom, and Israel had grown powerful among the nations, possessing great wealth and military strength. In fact, Israel proved so successful that neither Solomon nor his people realized that something very important was missing.

The missing ingredient began with King Solomon himself. Throughout his reign, King Solomon obeyed the Lord—but not in everything. Even though he exercised great wisdom in governing his people, Solomon made some very foolish decisions in his personal life. He had a weakness that skewed his judgment. Solomon loved many foreign women.

Now it was not unusual for a king have a harem of wives. The number of sons born to him helped to establish him as a powerful ruler in the eyes of his people. But no one had heard of a king who boasted as many wives as Solomon. It was said that he married 700 women from royal families in other lands—some from nations that were forbidden by God.

Many of Solomon's 700 wives and 300 concubines worshiped other gods. The king took a keen interest in their forms of worship, and gradually his heart turned away from the Lord. He began to worship a goddess called Ashtoreth and another god called Molech.

On a hill east of Jerusalem, Solomon built a high place for worshiping Chemosh, the god of Moab, and Molech, the god of the Ammonites. In fact, he built places of worship for all of his foreign wives. There they would burn incense and offer sacrifices to their gods.

When the Lord saw what Solomon was doing, he warned him not to follow other gods. Twice the Lord appeared to him, yet Solomon ignored both warnings. So finally, the Lord sent him this message: "Since you have chosen to disobey me, I will tear the kingdom away from you. But for the sake of your father, I will not do it during your lifetime. When your son becomes king, I will tear away all of Israel's tribes except one.

For David's sake and the sake of Jerusalem, which I have chosen to bear my Name, I will allow him to rule one tribe."

Then the Lord allowed Solomon's enemies to rise up against him. Hadad, an Edomite prince who had fled from David's army, returned to the region and caused trouble for Israel. So did Rezon, the leader of some rebels who took control of Damascus.

Meanwhile, God was raising up yet another enemy. Solomon had appointed a highly respected young man named Jeroboam to take charge of building the wall around the city of David. He did such an excellent job that Solomon then put him in charge of a much larger work force.

One day as Jeroboam was leaving Jerusalem, the prophet Ahijah met him. When they were all alone in the countryside, Ahijah did a strange thing. He took off the new robe he was wearing and tore it into twelve pieces. Then he turned to Jeroboam and said, "Take ten pieces for yourself. For the Lord says to you, 'I am going to tear the kingdom out of Solomon's hand and give you ten tribes, for Solomon has turned away from me and worshiped other gods.

" 'But I will wait until Solomon has died. Then I will take the kingdom from his son and give it to you. One tribe, however, will go to his son so that my servant David will always have a descendant ruling from Jerusalem, the city where I have chosen to put my Name.

" 'As for you, Jeroboam, if you obey me and keep my commands, as David my servant did, I will build you a lasting dynasty, just as I did for David. You will rule over all that your heart desires as king of Israel. I will humble David's descendants, but not forever.' "

In time King Solomon began to fear that Jeroboam was plotting against him. So he tried to have him killed. But Jeroboam escaped and fled to Egypt, where he stayed with King Shishak. After reigning as king for 40 years, Solomon died, and his son Rehoboam became king.

TBC 96

A Country Divided

TBC Book One, Chapter 97
1 Kings 12:1-24; 14:21-31
2 Chronicles 11:5-23

Many people throughout Israel traveled to Shechem for a special occasion—to crown Rehoboam as the new king of Israel. During the reign of David and of Solomon, Judah and Israel were a single nation, called Israel. The clans of Judah were loyal to David, for he was from their tribe. But even Israel's elders knew that God had chosen David. So the ten tribes of Israel also followed David. When Solomon became king, they renewed that agreement. But now that Solomon's son was about to be crowned, they were hesitant to pledge their support.

The Israelites met as a large group and appeared before the soon to be crowned King Rehoboam. The tribes of Israel needed some reassurance. Their spokesman stepped forward and said, "Your father worked us very hard to build up his kingdom. Lighten the harsh labor and we will serve you."

Rehoboam answered, "Come back to me in three days and I will give you my response."

During those three days, Rehoboam consulted with a number of advisors. First he met with the elders who had served his father. They all seemed to say the same thing: "If you will rule with the heart of a servant and grant their request, they will always serve you."

But Rehoboam did not like their advice. So he turned to the younger men who had grown up with him. "Tell the people that your little finger is thicker than your father's waist," said one man, "and that you will expect even more than your father did."

Three days later the people appeared before the king. By this time, Jeroboam was with them, for he had returned to Israel after Solomon died. Rehoboam answered the people harshly, just as the young men had advised. No one realized God was allowing this to fulfill his word.

When the people of Israel heard the king's harsh reply, they shouted out in anger: "Why should we have anything to do with the house of David? Rule your own tribe, not ours!"

Then all the people from the tribes of Israel left and returned home. But it wasn't long before they gathered again. And when they did, they appointed Jeroboam as their king.

Realizing that he had lost the support of every tribe except Judah and Simeon, Rehoboam fled from Shechem and returned to Jerusalem. Immediately he began to organize an army. But a man of God warned them not to fight, for this division of their nation was from the Lord.

So Rehoboam's army turned back, and the tribes separated into two countries—Israel in the north, Judah in the south. But the Levites in Israel moved to Judah, for Jeroboam rejected them and appointed other priests who were not Levites.

When the people of Israel saw what was happening, those who set their hearts on seeking the Lord also moved to Judah, for the Temple was there in Jerusalem. And the first three years of Rehoboam's reign, the people of Judah honored the Lord.

In the early years of his reign, Rehoboam strengthened his position as king. He built up certain towns as fortified cities with shields, spears, and supplies of food. From his harem of 18 wives and 60 concubines, King Rehoboam had fathered 28 sons and 60 daughters. He provided well for his sons and arranged for wives for each of them. All 28 of them were appointed to govern the fortified cities throughout Judah. Among his wives, his favorite was Maacah, Absalom's daughter, and their son Abijah became the chief prince.

But under Rehoboam's leadership, the nation began to crumble. The people of Judah did evil things. They built high places and Asherah poles to worship other gods. In time, they brought back all the evil practices that had been done by the nations that God had driven out.

In the fifth year of Rehoboam's reign, King Shishak of Egypt attacked Jerusalem. He took all the valuable treasures from the house of the Lord and from the royal palace, even the gold shields. For both Judah and Israel, the days of peace were now over.

TBC 97

Jeroboam's Downfall

TBC Book One, Chapter 98
1 Kings 12:25-13:34

Fear gripped the heart of King Jeroboam. Israel's tribes had separated from Judah and appoint him as king. Yet Jeroboam wondered, *For how long?* Every time the people celebrated a religious festival, they would travel to Jerusalem to offer sacrifices at the temple. What if they began to question their separation from Judah? What if Judah's king should persuade them that God was on his side? If they pledged their loyalty to him, Jeroboam's life would be in danger.

The king discussed the matter with his advisors, who also feared the influences of Jerusalem. Yet the people needed a place of worship. Suddenly Jeroboam had an idea. "We will create our own place of worship!"

His officials then advised him to designate two places of worship. Then the king ordered that two golden calves be formed to serve as their gods. With eagerness, the people now gathered to hear King Jeroboam's announcement.

"My people," he said, "I am concerned that you have to travel so far to worship in Jerusalem. From now on, we will have two places of worship right here in Israel, Bethel in the north and Dan in the south. These are the gods you will worship there, the gods who brought our people out of Egypt."

Jeroboam ordered that small houses of worship be built on the high places. The king then appointed priests from tribes other than Levi. He also created new religious holidays to keep the people from traveling to feasts in Jerusalem. Then he offered sacrifices on the altar that he had built at Bethel.

During this time, a man of God journeyed from Judah to Bethel, and there he prophesied: "A son named Josiah will be born as a descendant of David. He will destroy the priests of these high places. Here is the sign to prove this message is from God: This altar will split apart."

When King Jeroboam heard the prophet speak, he stretched out his hand and yelled, "Seize him!" Immediately, God caused his hand to shrivel up so that he could not move it. Then the altar split in two and the ashes fell out, just as the man had predicted.

Humbled by the incident, Jeroboam begged the man to intercede for him. So the prophet prayed and Jeroboam's hand was healed. In gratitude, the king asked the man to dine with him.

"No," he replied, "I cannot do that, for the Lord has commanded me not to eat or drink."

Meanwhile, the sons of an old prophet from Bethel heard everything he said. Quickly they ran to their father and told him all that they had seen and heard. The old prophet got on his donkey and caught up with the man of God. "Please," he urged, "come join me for dinner."

The man replied, "I cannot do that, for the Lord has commanded me not to eat or drink here. Nor am I to return the way I came."

"But I too am a prophet," the old man said, "and an angel told me that the Lord wants you to dine with me." The old prophet, however, was lying.

The man of God believed him and went to his home for a meal. While they sat at the table, the word of the Lord came through the old prophet: "You have defied God's orders by eating and drinking here. Therefore, your body will not be buried in your fathers' tomb."

The young prophet did not know what to think. Soon after he left the old man's house, he was attacked by a lion. It killed him right away, yet it did not eat his body nor maul the donkey. As people traveled that road, they saw the body, and news of the prophet's death began to spread.

When the old prophet heard what had happened, he mounted his donkey so he could find the dead body. With tears he picked up the body and brought it to his home town. After mourning the prophet's death, he placed the body in his own family's tomb.

The old prophet told his sons, "When I die, lay my bones next to his. The word he gave against the altars and high places will certainly come true." But after hearing God's word, King Jeroboam did not change his ways. Stubbornly, he appointed more priests.

TBC 98

Judgment on Jeroboam

TBC Book One, Chapter 99
1 Kings 14:1-20; 2 Chronicles 13

King Jeroboam would pay a heavy price for refusing the Lord. After the prophet from Judah delivered God's message, one of Jeroboam's sons became very ill. The king worried about him and wondered if his illness would lead to death. There was one way he could find out. . . .

He told his wife, "Let's find out what will happen to our son. The prophet Ahijah is in Shiloh. I know his words are true; he is the man who predicted I would become king of Israel."

"Then you must see him at once!" she urged.

"No," said Jeroboam, "I cannot. He has made it clear he does not approve of my decisions. I doubt he would even talk to me, or to you. But if you were to disguise yourself, perhaps he would meet with you. Just say you were sent on behalf of the king's family."

Now the prophet Ahijah was old and could no longer see. But he could hear better than most people, and in his spirit, he heard the Lord say, "Jeroboam's wife is on her way to see you because their son is ill. She is pretending to be someone else. I will tell you how to answer her."

Before she even reached the door, Ahijah heard her footsteps, and he called out, "Come in, wife of Jeroboam. Why have you disguised yourself? The Lord says to Jeroboam: 'I tore the kingdom from David's family and gave it to you, but you have not been like my servant David.'

"Tell this to your husband: 'You have done more evil than all the other kings before you. You have made gods out of idols of metal and turned your back on me. For this reason, I will bring disaster on your family. Your household will become food for dogs and birds.'

"As for you, wife of Jeroboam, return to your home. When you arrive in your city, the boy will die, and all Israel will mourn for him. He is the only one in your entire household who will have a burial, for he is the only one in whom the Lord has found anything good.

"The Lord will raise up a new king who will cut off Jeroboam's family. Then the Lord will strike Israel and uproot them from this good land that he gave to their forefathers. Because of their idolatry, he will scatter them in a land far away, a land beyond the Euphrates River."

So Jeroboam's wife returned to her home in Tirzah. As soon as she entered the palace, the boy died. Just as the prophet Ahijah had predicted, all Israel mourned for him. He received a proper burial, and many people showed their devotion by mourning for him.

During Jeroboam's 18th year as king of Israel, Rehoboam died. His son Abijah became the new king of Judah. From the beginning of his reign, he was determined to unite Israel with Judah and to reign over both countries. So Abijah led a force of 400,000 soldiers to attack Israel. Jeroboam, however, rallied 800,000 soldiers from throughout the tribes of Israel.

Abijah knew he was badly outnumbered. But he had a bold plan. From the top of Mount Zemaraim in Israel, Abijah now called out loudly: "Jeroboam and all Israel, listen to me! You all know that the Lord's covenant belongs to David's descendants forever. You have rejected the priests of Levi; therefore, you have rejected the Lord himself.

"But we have not forsaken him. Our priests are the sons of Aaron, and the Levites assist them, just as God commanded. They present the burnt offerings and keep God's requirements for the temple. The Lord is our leader! You will never succeed against him!"

Meanwhile, Jeroboam sent some of his troops behind Abijah's army to set up an ambush. When Judah's troops saw that they were being attacked from both the front and the back, they cried out to the Lord. The priests blew their trumpets and Judah gave a shout.

At that moment, God routed Israel's large force, and they fled from Abijah's army. Israel lost more than half its soldiers—500,000 were wounded or killed. God gave the smaller army of Judah a decisive victory, for they had relied on the Lord.

TBC 99

A Bitter Ending

TBC Book One, Chapter 100
1 Kings 15:9-11; 2 Chronicles 14-16

Two years had passed since Abijah delivered his bold, persuasive speech to the army of Israel. Though Abijah honored the Lord, he had committed the same sins as his father and grandfather, worshiping other gods. But his son Asa was nothing like him or his idolatrous forefathers. From the moment Asa took the throne, he did what his forefather King David would have done.

Asa destroyed the foreign altars and places of idolatry, for his heart was drawn to the Lord. He did what was right in God's eyes, and the Lord blessed Judah with 10 years of peace.

During that time King Asa built up Judah's towns, protecting them with walls and towers. And his nation prospered—until a massive Cushite army threatened to invade their borders.

The invaders were Ethiopians from Arabia, near the land of Gerar, and they were armed with 300 chariots. Asa knew that his army was no match for this vast, powerful military.

"Lord," he prayed, "there is no one like you to help the powerless against the mighty. Help us, O Lord, for we have come here upholding your Name. Do not let man win against you."

The Lord honored Asa's prayer. He struck down the mighty Cushite army. Judah crushed them so completely that all the surrounding villages near Gerar grew fearful—and for good reason. After defeating the powerful Cushites, Asa's forces plundered them as well. So they returned to Jerusalem with many droves of sheep, goats, and camels.

A few years later, the Spirit of God came upon a man named Azariah with a message for the king of Judah. He prophesied to Asa and his kingdom, saying, "The Lord will remain with you as long as you continue to honor him. If you seek him, he will let you find him. But if you turn away from him, he will also turn away from you. So be strong and do not give up doing the right thing, for your efforts will surely be rewarded."

Encouraged by Azariah's prophetic words, Asa ordered that all the idols be removed from their land. Then he arranged to have workers repair the altar in the Lord's temple.

In the 15th year of his reign, Asa assembled the people from throughout his kingdom. A large number of people moved from Israel to Judah when they realized that the Lord was with him. King Asa and the people made a covenant to seek the Lord with all their heart and soul. Then everyone rejoiced, for they had made their oath wholeheartedly. They sought the Lord earnestly, and he responded by revealing himself to them. As for King Asa, he removed his grandmother from her position as the queen mother and destroyed her idolatrous Ashterah pole.

For the next 20 years Asa's kingdom enjoyed peace, but it came to a sudden halt when the Israelites blocked a route near Ramah. This prevented anyone from entering or leaving Judah.

After pondering the matter, King Asa devised a clever plan. He would not attack Israel. Instead, he would take the silver and gold from the temple's treasury and offer it to the king of Aram. He would pay Aram to break their treaty with Israel and attack them.

No sooner had Aram agreed, when a prophet named Hanani came to Asa. "I have a message from the Lord," he said. "One day you could have defeated the king of Aram. But now that won't happen because you relied on him instead of the Lord. Have you forgotten how the Lord gave you victory over the mighty Cushite army?

"The eyes of the Lord watch throughout the earth, constantly looking for those who love him wholeheartedly so he can strengthen them. As for you, you have done a foolish thing. From now on your country will be at war." Asa became so angry that he put the seer in prison.

Then the king began to treat his own people brutally. Four years later his feet became severely diseased. But even then he called only for his physicians. Stubbornly, he refused to seek help from the Lord. Two years later, after reigning for 41 years, King Asa died, bitter to the end.

TBC 100

The Greatest Power of All

TBC Book One, Chapter 101
1 Kings 16:1-17:24

During the 41 years that Asa reigned over Judah, their sister nation of Israel grew as wicked as the kings who governed them. Jeroboam's family lost the throne when a man named Baasha murdered them. Baasha lived in the palace at Tirzah and reigned there 24 years. But he proved just as evil as Jeroboam. His was the first of many murderous plots against Israel's kings.

Baasha's son Elah succeeded him, but two years later Elah was murdered by a man named Zimri. But treacherous Zimri reigned only seven days, for when the Israelites learned what he had done, they killed him. Then they appointed Omri, their military commander, as Israel's new king.

Omri bought the hill of Samaria and built a city there. After six years he made it his royal city. Like the previous kings of Israel, Omri was a wicked man. When he died, six years after ruling from Samaria, his son Ahab became king. But Ahab proved even more evil than Omri. Worst of all, he married Jezebel, a Sidonian princess who worshipped Baal.

Ahab built a temple for Baal and stirred up the Lord's anger more than any other Israelite king. So a prophet named Elijah appeared to Ahab with this message: "As surely as the Lord, the God of Israel, lives, there will be no rain the next few years, except at my word."

Once again the word of the Lord came to Elijah. He told the prophet to leave and hide in a ravine east of the Jordan: "You will drink from the brook, and I have ordered the ravens to feed you." Elijah obeyed, and ravens brought him bread and meat every morning and evening.

Eventually the brook dried up. Then the word of the Lord came to him again: "Go to Zarephath. I have commanded a widow there to provide you with food."

When Elijah came to the gate, he saw the widow gathering sticks.

"Could you please bring me some water?" he asked.

As she turned to get the water, he added, "And could I please have a piece of bread?"

"As surely as the Lord your God lives," she said, "I have no bread, only a handful of flour and a little oil. I'm about to make one last meal before my son and I die."

"Don't worry," Elijah said. "Go home and do what you had planned. But first make a small cake for me, and then make something for you and your son. For the Lord says, 'The jar of flour will not be used up nor will the oil run dry until the day God sends rain.' "

The woman turned toward her home and Elijah followed her. After making a meal for the three of them, she still had flour and oil left over. She offered Elijah their upstairs room. And from then on, every day she had enough flour and oil to make them a meal.

Some time later the woman's son became so ill that he stopped breathing. The mother was so distraught that she lashed out in anger against Elijah. With tears she shouted, "What do you have against me, man of God? Did you come here to remind me of my sin and kill my son?"

The woman had apparently committed some grave sin in the past, and now the guilt had returned. She reasoned that God was punishing her by taking her son's life.

"Give me your son," Elijah said.

He took the boy from her arms, carried him upstairs, and gently laid him on his bed.

"O Lord," he said, "why have you brought this woman tragedy?"

Three times he lay his body on the boy and said, "O Lord my God, let his life return."

The Lord heard Elijah's cry, and the breath of life returned to him. With a smile, Elijah picked up the child and carried him downstairs.

"Look," he said, "your son is alive!"

As the woman hugged her son, tears of joy streamed down her cheeks. Then she said to Elijah, "Now I know that you are a man of God and that your words are truly from the Lord."

TBC 101

Contest at Carmel

TBC Book One, Chapter 102
1 Kings 18:1-2, 16-46

As judgment on Israel, Elijah announced no rain would fall for three years. Now, almost three years later, no rain had fallen. During that time, Elijah kept his distance from King Ahab. Then one day, the Lord said to him, "The time of judgment has been completed. Go to Ahab and tell him I will now send rain." But judgment against the prophets of Baal was just beginning.

When King Ahab saw Elijah approaching, he called out, "Is that you, you troublemaker?"

Elijah replied, "You are the one who brought this trouble by following Baal. Now send word for all the people to meet me on Mount Carmel. Bring Baal's 450 prophets as well as the other 400 prophets of Asherah—the ones for whom Jezebel provides food."

So King Ahab assembled the people and the prophets on Mount Carmel to meet Elijah.

"How long will you people waver back and forth?" Elijah shouted. "If the Lord is God, follow him! If Baal is God, follow him! Let's have a contest to see who is the real God. Go and get two bulls. You 'prophets' call on Baal, and I will call on the Lord. The one who sends fire to light the sacrifice is indeed God."

The people liked Elijah's idea and agreed to accept his challenge.

When they returned, Elijah said, "Since there are so many of you prophets of Baal, you go first. Pick one of the bulls, cut it up, and put it on the wood. Then call on your god to light it."

From morning till noon they shouted. But nothing happened.

By noon, Elijah started taunting them. "Shout louder!" he said. "Maybe Baal is deep in thought, or else he is busy. Perhaps he is traveling. Then again, maybe he's asleep."

Shouting even louder, the prophets of Baal started to slash themselves until they drew blood. A number of them prophesied frantically, but still, no fire came.

Finally, Elijah called all the people. Taking twelve stones, for the twelve tribes of Israel, he repaired an altar of the Lord, which had been torn down. He dug a trench around it and laid the wood on top. Then he cut up the bull and laid the pieces on top of the wood.

Elijah then shouted, "Fill four large jars with water and pour it on the offering."

The king nodded and the people obeyed. Many in the crowd thought to themselves, *This man is crazy.* Not only was water scarce, but how could anyone burn wet wood? After pouring water over the altar three times, the wood was soaked and water filled the trench.

Then Elijah stepped forward and prayed: "O Lord, God of Abraham, Isaac, and Israel, show these people that you are God and that I have done this as your servant. Send fire so they will know that you are the Lord and that you are turning their hearts back to you."

Immediately the fire of the Lord came down and burned up not only the sacrifice, but also the wood, the stones, and the soil. It even consumed the water in the trench.

When the people saw this, they fell prostrate and cried out, "The Lord—he is God!"

Elijah shouted to them, "Seize the prophets of Baal! Don't let any of them escape."

At Elijah's command, they brought Baal's prophets down to the Kishon Valley, and there they slaughtered them.

Elijah turned to Ahab and said, "Get something to eat now. Rain is coming soon."

As Ahab went to eat a meal, Elijah and his servant climbed up Mount Carmel. Bending toward the ground, Elijah put his face between his knees. Then he told his servant, "Look toward the sea for clouds." After sending him to look seven times, a small cloud appeared.

"Tell Ahab to hitch up his chariot," Elijah said. "He must leave before the rain starts."

Black clouds darkened the sky, the wind rose, and heavy rain poured. Elijah ran all the way back to Jezreel and arrived before Ahab did, for the Spirit of the Lord had empowered him.

TBC 102

Running on Empty

'I've had enough, Lord.'

TBC Book One, Chapter 103
1 Kings 19:1-21

Jezebel was furious over the bloody doom of her prophets of Baal. Immediately she called one of her attendants. "Send this message to Elijah: 'May the gods deal with me ever so severely if I fail to make your life end the very same way as that of Baal's prophets.' "

When Elijah heard the queen's message, he and his servant ran for their lives. They traveled until they reached Beersheba, in the land of Judah. There Elijah left his weary servant. The prophet continued by himself another day's journey into the desert.

Feeling that he could walk no farther, Elijah slunk down under a tree. He put his head in his hands and sighed heavily. Then he began to pray.

"I've had enough, Lord," he said. "Take my life. I am no better than my ancestors."

Elijah lay down in exhaustion and fell asleep. He had no idea how long he had been sleeping when he felt something touch his shoulder. He felt it again. Someone was gently shaking him, urging him to wake up. It was an angel of the Lord.

Then the angel touched him once more and said, "Elijah! Sit up now and eat."

Elijah looked up, and there near his head he saw a cake of bread baked over hot coals and a jar of water. So he sat up and ate and drank. Then he lay down.

The angel returned and touched him again. "Get up and eat some more," he urged Elijah. "The journey has worn you out."

So Elijah sat up to eat. Strengthened by the meal, he traveled 40 days and nights, until he reached Mount Horeb. He spent the night there, resting in a cave.

Then the Lord said to him, "What are you doing here, Elijah?"

"I have been very zealous for the Lord. The Israelites have rejected your covenant, broken your altars, and killed your prophets. I'm the only one left, and they want to kill me, too."

The Lord said, "Go out and stand on the mountain, for the Lord is about to pass by."

As Elijah stood, looking outside the cave, a terribly powerful wind tore the mountains apart, shattering the rocks. But the Lord was not there. Then came an earthquake, but the Lord was not in it. Next came a fire, but the Lord was not there either.

Finally, there came a gentle whisper. When Elijah heard it, he covered his face and stood at the entrance to the cave. Then the voice said to him, "What are you doing here, Elijah?"

Elijah said, "I have been very zealous for the Lord God Almighty. The Israelites have rejected your covenant. They have broken down your altars and killed your prophets with the sword. I'm the only one left, and now they are trying to kill me, too."

The Lord said, "Go back the same way you came and return to the desert of Damascus. When you arrive, anoint Hazael king over Aram. Then anoint Jehu, son of Nimshi, as king over Israel. After you have done that, anoint Elisha, son of Shaphat, to replace you as my prophet.

"My judgment will come through Hazael, and Jehu will kill any who escape his sword. Then Elisha will put to death any who escape Jehu's sword." God was revealing what would happen in the years to come. Then he added something that surprised the prophet: "For I have reserved 7,000 people in Israel, and not one of them has bowed the knee to worship Baal."

Elijah left Mount Horeb and traveled until he found Elisha. He and his servants were plowing with twelve pairs of oxen. Elijah set his cloak on him to show he was appointing him as a prophet. Then Elisha ran after him and said, "Please, let me first kiss my parents goodbye."

So Elisha told his parents he was invited to assist Elijah. Then he slaughtered his oxen, knowing he would not return to this work. He burned his plow, cooked the oxen, and gave a feast for his family and friends. Then he waved goodbye and left with Elijah.

TBC 103

Winner Loses All

TBC Book One, Chapter 104
1 Kings 20:1-43

King Ahab looked grim as he listened to the officer's report: "My lord, King Ben-Hadad of Aram has rallied 32 other kings to join his forces in attacking us. See for yourself. They have surrounded Samaria with their horses and chariots. Unless we surrender, we will be destroyed."

"What are his terms?" Ahab asked. The officer turned and motioned to his messenger.

"My lord," said the spokesman, "King Ben-Hadad demands all of the silver and gold in your treasury. He says he will choose for himself the best of your wives and children."

Ahab pondered his choices. If he refused, his whole household might face death, and his nation would face certain defeat. But if he agreed, he could save their lives. "Agreed," he said.

After Ahab agreed, King Ben-Hadad sent him another message: "I've changed my mind. We will search your palace and your officials' homes and take everything that's valuable."

King Ahab was so alarmed by his reply that he summoned the elders for counsel. The whole group was united in their response: "Don't give in to him."

So Ahab sent word to Aram that he would not agree to their demands. When Ben-Hadad heard that, he swore by his gods that he would surely destroy Samaria.

Ahab replied: "One who puts on armor should not boast like one who takes it off."

That was all Ben-Hadad needed to hear. He shouted out his order: "Prepare to attack!"

Meanwhile, a prophet came to Ahab. "The Lord says, 'I will give this vast army into your hands. Then you will know I am the Lord.' " After getting instructions from the prophet, Ahab assembled his army. While Ben-Hadad and his allies were getting drunk, Israel attacked.

Young commanders from Israel's provinces led the attack and caught Ben-Hadad off guard. The Arameans fled with Israel pursuing them. Ben-Hadad escaped, but Israel's army overpowered their horses and chariots, inflicting heavy losses on Aram. At the battle's end, the prophet returned to Ahab and said, "Be prepared. Next spring the king of Aram will return."

Aram's officials wondered how that small nation could have routed them. *Israel must have appealed to the gods of the hills,* they thought. So they planned to fight Israel on the plains.

After rebuilding his army, Ben-Hadad returned and his soldiers covered the countryside. Since they thought the Lord was just a god of the hills, God promised to deliver their vast army to Israel. Seven days later, the battle began. Israel wounded or killed 100,000 Arameans. The rest escaped to Aphek. There the Lord caused a wall to collapse on them, and 27,000 died.

So Ben-Hadad fled and hid. Then one of his officials said, "Israel's kings are merciful. Let's surrender and plead for mercy." So the officials put sackcloth around their waists and ropes around their necks. Then they appeared before Ahab, bowing low as they made their request.

"What?" replied Ahab. "Is Ben-Hadad still alive? Why, he is my brother! Bring him."

When he appeared, King Ahab held out his hand and drew him into his own chariot. Talking as if they were old friends, the two men made a treaty, and Ahab set him free.

Then the word of the Lord came to a young prophet. "Strike me," he told his companion. But the man refused to wound him, and the Lord punished him with an attacking lion. The prophet then turned to another man and said, "Strike me, please." The man did as he was told.

The young prophet then disguised himself and waited by the roadside for King Ahab. As the king drew near, the man called out, "During the battle I was told, 'Guard this prisoner. If he escapes, you will pay with your own life.' Now what will happen to me?"

The king said, "You just stated your own punishment." Removing his disguise, the prophet replied, "The Lord says, 'You set free someone who should have died. Therefore, it's your life for his life, your people for his.'" Angrily, the king returned to his palace and pouted.

TBC 104

Naboth's Vineyard

TBC Book One, Chapter 105
1 Kings 21:1-29

Everyone knew a king could demand anything from his people—except for one thing. King Ahab should have known that not even he could take away an Israelite's most sacred possession—his land. The land could not be sold permanently to anyone, for it really belonged to the Lord. Ahab made a grave error the day he ignored that truth.

King Ahab and his wife Jezebel had committed many wicked sins, but none so wicked as when Ahab wanted the vineyard belonging to Naboth. The property bordered the edge of his own land, near the palace. He had admired this vineyard for some time, imagining what he could do with the land. So one day, he stepped down from his chariot and made an offer to Naboth.

"Sell me your vineyard," Ahab said. "I want the land for a vegetable garden."

Naboth's family had owned this land for many generations. He knew he had every right to keep it. In fact, the Lord had forbidden the Israelites from selling their land. Only if they had become poor could they sell it, and even then the land must be returned to their family at the Year of Jubilee. So Naboth refused Ahab, and the king left angrily.

When Ahab returned to Samaria, he went straight to his bedroom, lay on his bed, and began to pout. At dinner time, he remained there, refusing to eat.

So Jezebel went to his room and said, "What's wrong? Why won't you eat?"

"Because Naboth won't sell me his vineyard," he said.

The queen raised her hands in dismay. "You're pouting over that? Are you forgetting that you are the king of Israel? I'll get you the vineyard myself! Now cheer up and come eat."

Immediately, Jezebel had a scribe write letters to the leaders in Jezreel, commanding the elders and officials to proclaim a fast to make people think someone in their city sinned against God. The people would assume they must punish that person to avoid God's judgment. "When the people have gathered," she wrote, "have two men testify against Naboth." As soon as the scribe finished each letter, she signed Ahab's name and sealed each one with his signet ring.

The day soon came for the people of Jezreel to gather together, just as the proclamation had ordered. After everyone arrived, two men stood up with an accusation. Both of them were wicked men, and their officials had bribed them to lie about Naboth.

"He's the man!" shouted one of them, pointing to Naboth.

"Yes," said the other. "We heard him curse God and the king."

Naboth was speechless. He could hardly believe what he was hearing. But the people refused to wait for his reply. Instead, they seized him and stoned him.

Jezebel had a smile of approval as she went to Ahab. "Remember that vineyard Naboth refused to sell you? You can take it now. I just heard that Naboth has died."

Without asking any questions, Ahab immediately went to Jezreel to acquire the land.

Meanwhile, the word of the Lord came to Elijah: "Ahab is now in Naboth's vineyard. Go there and say, 'You have murdered a man to gain his property, haven't you?' "

When Elijah arrived, Ahab said, "So, my enemy, you have found me, have you?"

"Yes, I have found you. The Lord knows you murdered a man to gain his property. Now, because you have given yourself over to evil, dogs will lick up your blood and disaster will strike your family. The Lord says, 'Dogs will devour Jezebel by the wall of Jezreel. Your relatives who die in the city will be eaten by dogs, while birds will feast on those who die in the country.' "

When Ahab heard this prophecy, he tore his clothes in grief. Then he put on ragged clothes and fasted in sorrow. Upon seeing this, the Lord told Elijah: "Have you noticed how Ahab has humbled himself? For this reason I will wait to bring disaster until after he has died."

TBC 105

Fateful Friendship

TBC Book One, Chapter 106
2 Chronicles 17:1-18:34; 1 Kings 22:1-40

A new king now sat on Judah's throne, and he was a master at establishing peaceful ties. A year after Ahab began to reign over Israel, Jehoshaphat, Asa's son, became king of Judah. At first Jehoshaphat obeyed the Lord. He even sent priests to teach the people God's Laws. So God blessed him with wealth, power, and peace—until he joined forces with Ahab.

Jehoshaphat allied himself with Ahab by having his son marry Ahab's daughter. Years later, he traveled to Samaria, where Ahab held a grand banquet for him. King Ahab wanted to regain the land he had lost to Aram. So he asked Jehoshaphat to help him fight the Arameans.

Jehoshaphat replied, "Consider my people as your people, my horses as your horses. But first, let us seek counsel from the Lord."

Ahab responded by calling for 400 prophets, none of whom knew the Lord. Yet all of them said, "Go to battle, for the Lord will give you victory."

Jehoshaphat realized that none of them were prophets of the Lord God. So he said to Ahab, "Are there any prophets of the Lord in Samaria? If so, have them inquire for us."

"Yes," Ahab said, "there is one left that I know of. But I hate him because he never prophesies anything good about me."

"The king should not say that," Jehoshaphat replied.

To please Jehoshaphat, Ahab sent for the prophet Micaiah from the prison where he was held. Meanwhile, the other prophets insisted Ahab should attack. A man named Zedekiah declared, "The Lord says, 'With these iron horns you will gore the Arameans.' "

When Ahab's official reached the prison, he told Micaiah, "The other prophets have all predicted the king will succeed in battle. So let your word agree with theirs."

"I can say only what the Lord tells me," replied Micaiah.

But when Micaiah arrived, he too said, "Attack and be victorious."

Ahab glared at the prophet of God. Why would Micaiah say something that agreed with the others? Ahab did not trust him: "How many times do I have to make you swear that you are telling me the truth?"

Then Micaiah said to the king, "I saw Israel scattered like sheep without a shepherd. Therefore, go home in peace. Do not go to war."

Ahab turned to Jehoshaphat and said, "See what I mean?"

Micaiah continued, "I saw the Lord sitting on his throne. He was surrounded by heavenly beings, and he said, 'Who will entice Ahab to attack Ramoth Gilead so he will die there?' Then one volunteered to be a lying spirit in the mouths of Ahab's prophets. So these prophets speak by a lying spirit. The truth is, the Lord has decreed disaster."

At this, Zedekiah slapped him. Then Ahab said, "Take him back to prison until I return."

"If you ever return safely, then the Lord has not spoken through me. Mark my words!"

In spite of Micaiah's warning, Ahab waged war. But he could not shake off the words of God's prophet. So before he entered the battle, Ahab disguised himself. Meanwhile, the king of Aram ordered his chariot commanders to attack no one except King Ahab himself.

Jehoshaphat also entered the battle, wearing his royal robe. When Aram's commanders saw him, they thought he was Ahab. So they started to chase him. But Jehoshaphat cried out, and the Lord helped him. Realizing that he was not Ahab, the commanders turned away. During the battle, an Aramean drew his bow and shot it at random, without aiming at anyone. The soldier had no idea his arrow hit King Ahab right between his pieces of armor.

"I've been wounded," Ahab said to his chariot driver.

By evening, Israel's army fled. Ahab died, and dogs licked the blood from his chariot.

TBC 106

The Battle Never Fought

TBC Book One, Chapter 107
2 Chronicles 19:1-20:37

King Jehoshaphat felt shaken. Had it not been for the Lord's mercy, soldiers would have mistaken him for Ahab, and he would have been killed. Quickly he left the battle at Ramoth Gilead and returned to Jerusalem. But when he arrived, a seer named Jehu met him and spoke sternly. "Why help the wicked and love those who hate the Lord? It only brings God's anger."

Still, the prophet knew there was some good in Jehoshaphat. He had gotten rid of the Asherah poles and had set his heart on seeking God. And now, after hearing the prophet's warning, he decided to appoint judges throughout the land. Jehoshaphat commanded them to fear the Lord and to teach the people to fear him, too.

Some time later, Jehoshaphat learned the Moabites, Ammonites, and Meunites had joined forces to attack Judah. Coming from Edom, they had reached En Gedi, within Judah's borders. Alarmed by this report, the king assembled the people and urged them to seek the Lord.

Families from every town in Judah gathered in Jerusalem to fast and pray. The king himself led them in prayer.

"O God of our fathers," Jehoshaphat prayed, "you rule over every kingdom among the nations. All power is yours, and no one can withstand you. You gave this land to Abraham's descendants forever.

"Our fathers built this temple as a sanctuary for your Name. They prayed, 'Hear us when we stand here and cry out to you and save us in our distress.' Our fathers did not invade the land of Edom, yet now its people are about to attack us. We look to you for help."

As King Jehoshaphat prayed, the men of Judah, their wives, their children, and even their babies were present at the temple. Their hearts were as one as they stood before the Lord.

Then God's Spirit came upon a Levite named Jahaziel, who stood and said, "You will not have to fight this battle. Go out and face this army, for the Lord will deliver you."

Jehoshaphat bowed with his face to the ground and the people also bowed low in worship. Gradually, some of the Levites stood up and started to praise the Lord with loud, joyful voices. Soon everyone joined them in praising the Lord.

The next morning the king appointed men to sing praises to God as they marched out. "Give thanks to the Lord," they sang, "for his love endures forever."

While the people of Judah sang praises, the Lord set ambushes against their enemies. He caused the Ammonites and Moabites to turn against the Meunites and strike them. They annihilated all the men from Mount Seir. Then the Lord caused the Ammonites and Moabites to turn against each other in fierce battle.

When the men of Judah finally reached a viewpoint overlooking the desert, all they saw were dead bodies. No one had survived. The men of Judah carried off so much plunder that it took three days to gather all the equipment, clothing, and valuables left from the battle.

Then they gathered to praise the Lord and joyfully returned to Jerusalem. They entered the temple playing harps, lutes, and trumpets. When neighboring nations heard how the Lord had fought against Judah's enemies, they feared their God, and Judah enjoyed peace.

Some time later, toward the end of his reign, Jehoshaphat became a partner of Ahab's son Ahaziah, the new king of Israel. Even though Ahaziah was wicked, Jehoshaphat agreed to help him build some trading ships. So the Lord destroyed their ships and they never set sail.

Yet God allowed Jehoshaphat to reign as king of Judah for 25 years, spanning the reigns of three kings in Israel, Ahab and his sons Ahaziah and Joram. Except for his alliances with the family of King Ahab, Jehoshaphat did what was right in the eyes of the Lord.

TBC 107

What Every King Needs

TBC Book One, Chapter 108
2 Kings 1:1-18; 3:1-25

One problem after another faced the new king of Is-
rael, Ahab's son Ahaziah. As soon as his father died,
Israel's vassal kingdom of Moab decided to rebel.
Meanwhile, Ahaziah injured himself when he fell
through some weak floorboards in his upper room.
Worried about his injury, Ahaziah sent messengers to appeal to an idol
in Ekron called Baal-Zebub, who was worshiped as a god of medicine.
But the Lord sent the prophet Elijah to meet the messengers.

Elijah said, "Go back and tell Ahaziah, 'Is there no God in Israel for
you to consult?' "

Ahaziah was surprised they returned so quickly. Their spokesman
explained, "A man met us on the way and told us to bring you this message: 'Because you chose to consult the god of Ekron, the Lord says, you
will not leave the bed you are lying on. You will certainly die.' "

"What did the man look like?" the king asked.

"He wore a furry garment and a leather belt around his waist."

"That was Elijah the Tishbite," said the king. He then called for one
of his commanders.

"Take 50 soldiers with you and find the prophet Elijah. These men
will tell you where to find him. Bring him here to me at once."

The captain and his soldiers had no trouble finding the prophet. He
was perched on the top of a hill, almost as if he were waiting for them.

"Man of God," called out the captain, "the king says, 'Come down
here at once.' "

Elijah replied, "If I am indeed a man of God, may fire destroy you
and all your men."

Immediately, fire from heaven came down and consumed them.
When the king heard what had happened, he sent another commander
with 50 more soldiers.

The captain called out, "Man of God, the king says, 'Come down at
once!' "

"If I am a man of God," replied Elijah, "may fire destroy you and
your men."

And they, too, were destroyed. So the king sent a third group.

Terrified, this captain fell on his knees before Elijah and begged, "Please, have respect for the lives of your servants—don't kill us!"

At this, the angel of the Lord told Elijah, "Go with this man; do not be afraid."

So Elijah traveled with them, and he repeated the message God had given him: "Is there is no God in Israel? Is that why you have sent messengers to consult Baal-Zebub, the god of Ekron? Because you have done this, you will never leave your bed. You will surely die."

Elijah's words proved true. After reigning over Israel only two years, Ahaziah died. Since he had no sons, his brother Joram became king. Joram got rid of the stone of Baal that his father had made. But like Jeroboam, he caused Israel to sin by worshiping images that symbolized God.

Like Ahaziah, Joram also faced rebellion from Moab. After Ahab died, the Moabites refused to pay the yearly tribute. They were required to supply 100,000 lambs and wool from 100,000 rams. So King Joram mobilized Israel's army and asked King Jehoshaphat for Judah's help.

Jehoshaphat agreed and suggested they travel through Edom's desert. The king of Edom also joined them with his forces. But after seven days of travel, they found no water for their army. Joram began to despair, but Jehoshaphat said, "Let's find a prophet of the Lord."

So the three kings went to Elisha. Out of respect for Jehoshaphat, he agreed to seek the Lord for them. He requested a harpist, and while the music was playing, the Lord spoke through Elisha: "You are to dig trenches. The Lord will provide water and hand over Moab."

The next morning, the trenches were filled with water. But the sunlight made the water look like blood. So the Moabites thought Israel's armies must have killed one another. As they ran for the plunder, Israel attacked them and defeated them. As God had predicted, they were destroyed.

TBC 108

The Fool on David's Throne

Then came the physical problems as Elijah had predicted.

TBC Book One, Chapter 109
2 Chronicles 21:1-22:6; 2 Kings 8:16-29

In the name of peace, King Jehoshaphat made perhaps the worst mistake of his entire reign. For the sake of keeping peace with Israel, he had arranged to have his firstborn son marry the daughter of King Ahab. If only he had known how his plans would backfire. . . .

Jehoshaphat reigned over Judah from the time he was 35 years old until he died at age 60. For 25 years he honored the Lord, but he also made some grave mistakes. He failed to remove the high places, where people worshiped other gods. For that reason, many of the people in his kingdom did not set their hearts on God. Neither did his own son.

At age 32, Jehoshaphat's first-born son, Jehoram, became king of Judah. Jehoram was anything but a man of peace. He did much evil in the eyes of the Lord, from the very beginning of his reign. He had five brothers who lived in various parts of Judah. But as soon as he took the throne, he made arrangements to have all five of them murdered.

Instead of following Jehoshaphat's example, Jehoram followed the ways of the kings of Israel. He married Ahab's daughter and was greatly influenced by Ahab's household. The only thing that kept God from destroying his dynasty was the promise that David's descendants would always remain on the throne. So the Lord chose other ways to get Jehoram's attention.

The king's troubles began when the Edomites rebelled. They appointed a king for themselves, a ruler who refused to pay tribute to Judah. When Jehoram and his military officers traveled there to break the revolt, the Edomites surrounded their chariots.

Jehoram's forces finally overpowered them. But not long after that, the Edomites did manage to break away from Judah's control. Meanwhile, neighboring Libnah also revolted by refusing to pay tribute. God allowed this to happen because Jehoram built high places for idol worship, and he led the people of Judah to turn away from God.

Elijah the prophet sent Jehoram a letter, confronting him for his evil behavior: "The Lord says, 'You have not followed the example of your father or grandfather. Instead, you have acted just like the kings of Israel. You have led the people astray, just like Ahab.

" 'You even murdered your own brothers, men who were better than you. Therefore, the Lord will strike a terrible blow against your family—your sons, your wives, and everything you own. As for you, a terrible disease will destroy your bowels.' "

The Lord then aroused the Philistines and neighboring Arab tribes to attack Judah. These tribes invaded not only the land, but also the palace in Jerusalem. They took everything of value, as well as Jehoram's sons and wives. Only his youngest son managed to escape.

Then came the physical problems, just as Elijah had predicted. For almost two years, Jehoram suffered a terribly painful disease, and it caused his bowels to come out of his body. He died an agonizing death. And no one in Judah was sorry that he died.

Jehoram had reigned for eight years, but because he was such a wicked king, the people refused to bury him in the same tomb with the other kings of Judah. They now appointed Ahaziah, his 22-year-old son, as their new king. Ahaziah was named after his uncle, who had ruled over Israel.

Ahaziah's mother was Athaliah, the daughter of Ahab. So Ahaziah, too, had learned the wicked ways of his grandfather, Ahab. And young Ahaziah often turned to Ahab's household for advice. They counseled him to join Israel in battle, and this led to his downfall.

Ahaziah joined forces with Ahab's son Joram, the king of Israel. They were defending Ramoth Gilead from Hazael, the king of Aram, also known as Syria. But the Syrians wounded Joram. So he returned to Jezreel to recover. Ahaziah went to see him, not knowing that there he would meet his own downfall. . . .

TBC 109

On the Wings of a Chariot

TBC Book One, Chapter 110
2 Kings 2:1-25

Only one other man besides Enoch has ever left the earth without dying—the prophet Elijah. When he knew God was about to take him to heaven, he told Elisha, his assistant, "Stay here, for the Lord has sent me to Bethel." But Elisha refused to stay behind.

Elisha loved Elijah the way a son loves his father, and he knew something was about to happen. When they arrived at Bethel, a group of prophets told Elisha, "Did you know the Lord is going to take away your master today?"

"Yes," he said, "but don't talk about it."

Then Elijah told Elisha to stay while he went on to Jericho. Elisha refused to leave his side. So they journeyed together. At Jericho another group of prophets said, "Did you know the Lord is going to take away your master today?"

"Yes," Elisha said, "but don't talk about it."

Elijah then told Elisha, "Stay here, for the Lord has sent me to the Jordan." Again Elisha refused.

So they continued to travel together. Fifty men from the school of the prophets watched as Elijah struck the river with his cloak. The water divided and the two walked across.

As the two stood alone, Elijah said, "Elisha, what can I do for you before I leave?"

"Let me inherit a double portion of your spirit," he replied.

"That is a difficult request. But if you see me when I leave, the Lord has granted it."

Suddenly, a fiery chariot and blazing horses appeared in the sky. The chariot swooped down and separated them as Elijah went up in a whirlwind.

Elisha cried out, "My father! My father! The chariots and horsemen of Israel!"

Elisha watched until he could see Elijah no more. Then he tore his clothes in grief. As he was wiping the tears from his eyes, he noticed Elijah's cloak. Then he remembered how the older prophet had dropped it from the chariot as he rose up to heaven. Like a father who passes on his inheritance, Elijah's role now fell to Elisha. He picked up the cloak and clutched it tightly.

With a sigh, Elisha said, "Where now is the God of Elijah?" As he reached the edge of the Jordan River, he struck the water with the cloak. Immediately, the water parted.

Now the men from the school of prophets saw when Elisha reached the Jordan. And as the waters parted, they stared in awe. "Look! The spirit of Elijah now rests on Elisha!"

As he crossed over to their side, the prophets bowed low before him, showing him the same respect they had shown for Elijah. Then one of the prophets stood and approached Elisha.

"Let us go look for your master. Maybe the Lord has set him down somewhere."

"No," Elisha replied. He was too troubled to tell them what he had seen. He knew his master was with the Lord. Yet the men kept asking to search for him. Finally Elisha said, "Go."

After three days the men gave up and returned. "Didn't I tell you not to go?" Elisha said.

Some time later, Jericho's leaders came to Elisha for help. "Our city sits in a good location," said the spokesman, "but the water is bad, and the land won't produce crops."

So Elisha took a new bowl with salt. Then he threw the salt into the spring. The Lord healed both the water and the land.

As Elisha traveled to Bethel, a group of boys followed. Rumors had spread about what happened to Elijah, and the boys made fun of the story and of Elisha: "Let's see you go up, you baldhead!" "Baldhead" was a name used to insult someone, even someone with hair. The boys kept taunting, until he stopped and turned. Using his God-given authority, Elisha called down a curse. Suddenly two bears came out of the woods, and 42 boys were harmed. It could have been much worse, and they knew it. So Elisha continued his journey and went on to Mount Carmel.

TBC 110

The Greater Gift

TBC Book One, Chapter 111
2 Kings 4:8-37

In the town of Shunem lived a highly respected woman who wished to do a kind deed for the prophet Elisha. Whenever he came to Shunem, she invited him for dinner. One day she told her husband, "Let's prepare him a room in our house, for he is a holy man of God."

Using their upper porch chamber, the couple turned it into a bedroom so Elisha could stay there whenever he came to Shunem. Elisha was grateful for the couple's generosity. So one day he sent his servant to see if they could do something to repay the woman for her kindness.

The servant, Gehazi, returned and said, "The woman says she has everything she needs."

"What do you think we could do for her?" Elisha asked.

"Well, she has no children, and her husband is old."

So Elisha had Gehazi call her, and she stood in the doorway.

"By next year," Elisha said, "you will hold a son in your arms."

"Don't say that," she said. "Don't get my hopes up, O man of God!"

So many times before, she had hoped she was pregnant. Each time she was disappointed. But this time her hopes were fulfilled. Elisha's words came true, and she gave birth to a son.

The child grew, and years later, he went into the fields with his father almost every day. One morning, he came running to his father, holding his head and shouting "My head! It hurts!"

His father had a servant carry the boy to his mother, who held him and rocked him.

By noon, however, the boy died. His mother was heart-broken.

But she kept her grief to herself and told no one about his death. Instead, she carried him upstairs to the room set aside for Elisha. Then she laid him on the prophet's bed and left the room, shutting the door behind her.

Immediately she called for her husband. When he arrived, she said, "Send one of the servants to me with a donkey. I need to go to the man of God quickly and return with him."

"Why would you go to him today? It's not a New Moon or the Sabbath," he said.

"It will be all right," she replied. "Please—just do as I ask. I have no time to explain."

Her husband knew that look of determination. A few moments later, the servant arrived. The woman quickly mounted the donkey. Then she said to the servant, "Lead on as quickly as you can. Don't slow down for my sake."

They traveled six hours to the top of Mount Carmel. Elisha saw her in the distance.

"Run meet her," he told Gehazi, "and see if everyone is all right."

The woman told Gehazi everything was fine. Then she rushed past him. She dropped to her knees and clung to Elisha's feet. Gehazi started to push her away.

"Leave her alone," Elisha said. "She is terribly distressed about something, but the Lord has hidden it from me."

"Did I ask you for a son?" she said. "Didn't I tell you, 'Don't get my hopes up'? "

Elisha turned to Gehazi and said, "Take my staff and run to her house. Don't stop for anything. Then lay my staff on the boy's face." Gehazi raced off, but the woman clung to Elisha.

"I'm not leaving until you go with me," she said. So he left and traveled with her.

When they reached her home, they saw that Gehazi's efforts had brought no life. Elisha went into the room alone and shut the door. He knelt down and prayed to the Lord. Twice he lay on the boy's body. Slowly the body grew warm.

The boy then sneezed seven times and opened his eyes. Elisha called Gehazi and said, "Go get the Shunammite woman."

As the woman appeared in the doorway, Elisha smiled. "Take your son," he said. Seeing the boy alive, she rushed in and fell at the prophet's feet. Her faith had been rewarded.

TBC 111

Miracle upon Miracle

TBC Book One, Chapter 112
2 Kings 4:1-7, 38-44; 6:1-7

Elisha taught a school of prophets, and one day the wife of one of those men came to him in tears. "My husband has died," she said, "and you know how he served the Lord. But I have no money to pay his debts. So the creditor wants to take my sons as slaves!"

"Tell me, what do you have in your house?" Elisha asked.

"Nothing, except a little oil," she said.

"Go to your neighbors and ask them for jars," Elisha said, "as many as you can get. Then go inside your house, shut the door, and pour your oil into the jars."

After gathering the jars, she went inside with her sons and shut the door, just as the prophet Elisha had commanded. Her sons brought the jars to her one at a time, and from her little bit of oil, she filled each jar to the brim. When the last jar got filled, the oil stopped flowing.

Then she went to the man of God and told him what happened. Of course, he was not surprised.

"Now go and sell those jars of oil," Elisha said, "so you can pay off all your debts. You will have more than enough money. Then you and your sons can live off the money that is left."

On another occasion, Elisha went to Gilgal, and during this time a famine had affected all the people in that region. Elisha had traveled there to meet with his school of prophets. While he was teaching them, he called for his servant.

"Put on the large pot and cook some stew for these men," he said.

One of the men went out into the fields to gather some herbs for the stew, and he found a wild vine. *I'll use this!* he thought. So he gathered from the fruit of that vine, cut it up, and dropped the pieces into the stew. No one knew what the plant was, but they ate some anyway. Suddenly they all felt sick.

"O man of God," cried out one of the men, "something in the stew must be poisonous!"

Hungry as they were, no one dared to eat another bite.

"Get some flour," Elisha commanded. He put it in the pot, and they dished out some more. By God's power, the poisonous effect was gone.

At another time, a man came from Baal Shalishah to bring Elisha some grain and 20 loaves of barley bread, baked from the first fruits of his harvest.

Elisha turned to his servant and said, "Give this to the men."

"How can I distribute this to 100 men?" he said.

"Just give it to them," Elisha said. "For the word of the Lord predicts, 'They will eat and have some left over.' "

So the servant set that portion of food before the prophets. They all ate and even had some left over, just as God's word had predicted.

Some time later, as the school of prophets were meeting, some of the men came to Elisha with a suggestion. "Look," they said, "this place where we meet with you is too small. Let's go to the Jordan, where we can each cut down a tree. Then we can build a bigger place."

Elisha went with them as they walked to the Jordan to cut down trees. While one men was felling a tree, his ax-head flew off the handle and landed in the water.

"Oh, my lord!" he said. "It was borrowed!" The man was quite distraught because he had no money to pay back the owner.

"Where did it fall?" Elisha asked.

The man showed him the place. Then Elisha cut off a stick about the size of an ax handle and threw it in the water. The ax-head floated to the surface. Then it joined to its new handle. Once again, the power of God had worked a miracle.

TBC 112

Naaman's Greatest Battle

Naaman left angrily. 'I thought he would at least come out and wave his hand over me.'

TBC Book One, Chapter 113
2 Kings 5:1-27

Though the people of Aram were enemies of Israel, there was something special about Naaman. The king of Aram (also known as Syria) regarded Naaman highly, for the Syrians had gained a great victory through him. He was a valiant warrior, but he had a problem that not even his valor could solve. Naaman suffered from a skin disease called leprosy.

On one of Syria's raiding parties, they had captured a young Israelite girl, and she served Naaman's wife. One day the young girl said to her, "If only my master Naaman would see the prophet who lives in Samaria! Surely he would cure my master of his leprosy."

The woman told her husband what the servant girl had said. So Naaman told the king and asked for permission to go there.

"Why certainly," the king replied. And he wrote a letter to Israel's King Joram: "I'm sending you my servant Naaman so you may cure him of leprosy."

When King Joram read the letter, he tore his clothes in frustration. "Who does that king think I am? God? Why is he sending this man to me?"

When the prophet Elisha heard about Joram's dilemma, he sent one of his servants to the king with a message: "Send the man to me so he will know there's a prophet in Israel."

So Naaman took his horses and chariots and went to Elisha's house. When he arrived, Elisha sent a servant outside with a message: "Go to the Jordan River and dip your body in it seven times. Then your skin will be restored and you will be healed."

Naaman left angrily. "I thought the man would at least come out and wave his hand over me," he said. "I thought he would call on the Lord his God to heal me. Aren't the rivers of Damascus better than all the waters of Israel? Why couldn't I wash in them?"

Naaman's servants whispered among themselves, then one of them spoke up. "My father, if the prophet asked you to do something difficult, wouldn't you have done it? How much more should you do something this easy?"

The commander pondered his situation. He had come so far. Perhaps his servants were right. So he listened and dipped his body in the Jordan. After the seventh time, he was healed.

With great joy, Naaman and his servants returned to Elisha. "Now I know there is no God in all the world except the God of Israel," Naaman told Elisha. "Please accept these gifts."

Elisha replied, "As surely as the Lord lives, whom I serve, I will accept nothing."

Naaman vowed that when he returned home, he would build an altar so he could continue to worship the Lord. But then, a troubled look came over his face. "I have a request," he said to Elisha. "The king requires me to enter a temple with him. He leans on me to bow before his god. When I do that, may God forgive me."

Elisha reassured him that God would understand: "Now go in peace," he said.

After Naaman left, Elisha's servant Gehazi thought to himself, *My master was too easy on that Syrian. I'll run after him and get something.* Gehazi caught up with him and said, "Could you spare a talent of silver and two sets of clothes for two prophets who just came?"

Naaman believed him, and he urged Gehazi to take two talents of silver. He gave the clothing and the two bags of silver to his servants so they could carry them ahead of Gehazi. At the top of the hill, Gehazi took the things and sent the men away.

As he stepped into the house, Elisha asked, "Where have you been?"

"Nowhere," he answered.

Elisha said, "Was not my spirit with you when the man stepped from his chariot and you made a request in my name? Therefore, now you will become leprous."

And Gehazi left as a leper.

TBC 113

Feed Your Enemies

When the king saw the army standing before him, he was shocked. 'What should I do?'

TBC Book One, Chapter 114
2 Kings 6:8-23

The king of Aram (also called Syria) raised his voice in anger as he turned to face his military commanders. "Surely one of you is a traitor!" he shouted. Instead of engaging Israel in a major battle, the Syrian king would send raiding parties to attack the Israelites. But wherever he sent his officers, they always failed to catch the Israelites off guard.

Each time the Syrians planned an attack, the Lord would reveal it to the man of God, Elisha. Then Elisha would send a message to Joram, king of Israel: "Beware of passing that place, for the Syrians are about to attack it." So Joram was always prepared.

Finally, the king of Aram once again summoned all his officers and demanded an answer. "Tell me," he said, "which one of you has been informing the king of Israel?"

"None of us," replied one officers. "But the prophet Elisha knows every word you say."

"Then find out where he is," the king commanded, "and send men to capture him."

Quickly they learned where he was and sent word to the king: "Elisha is in Dothan."

So the king sent a large army with horses and chariots. During the night, they surrounded the entire city.

Now Elisha had a young man serving him, and when the servant went outside that morning, he saw the Syrians' vast army. Their horses and chariots surrounded them, and the young man was terrified. He ran back to Elisha and told him what was happening. Then he cried out, "Oh, my lord, what shall we do?"

"Don't be afraid," the prophet replied calmly. "Those who are with us are more than those whom you see out there."

As the servant wrung his hands in anguish, Elisha prayed, "O Lord, open his eyes so he may see what I see." When the servant looked out once more, the Lord allowed him to see that the hills behind Elisha were full of horses and chariots that looked ablaze.

But the Syrians could not see the horses and chariots of heaven. So the army advanced toward Elisha. As they came closer, Elisha prayed, "Lord, strike these men in a way that makes them unable to recognize who I am and where they are."

Then the prophet stepped forward and said, "May I help you?"

"Yes," one of the commander's replied. "We are looking for a man named Elisha."

"I'm afraid you must have taken the wrong road," Elisha said. "But if you follow me, I'll be glad to show you where he is." Then he led them right into Samaria.

The Syrians thought they were entering Dothan. Once the whole army had entered Samaria, the royal city of Israel, Elisha prayed, "Lord, open their eyes so that they may see where they really are." Then the Lord allowed the Syrians to see that they were in Samaria.

When King Joram saw the Syrian army standing meekly before him, he was shocked. Joram turned to Elisha and said, "Shall I kill them, my father?" Like many in Israel, the king addressed the old prophet with respect, calling him "father."

"Do not kill them," Elisha said. "Would you kill captives who surrendered to you? They are defenseless here in our midst.

"No," continued Elisha, "give them food and water. Let them eat and drink. After they have refreshed themselves, send them back to their master in Syria."

So King Joram ordered his servants to prepare a great feast for them. After they finished eating and drinking, he sent them away in peace and they returned home.

Elisha had given the king wise counsel, and Joram had done well to heed it. From that time on, Syria stopped raiding the land of Israel.

TBC 114

'He Drives Like Jehu'

TBC Book One, Chapter 115
2 Kings 9:1-37

Now was the time: Elisha called for a young man in the school of prophets. "I have a mission for you. Take this flask of oil and travel quickly to Ramoth Gilead. Find Jehu, the commander, and speak to him privately. Anoint him king over Israel. Then run away quickly!"

When the young prophet arrived at Ramoth Gilead, he found the commanding officers sitting together at a table. "I have a private message for you, commander," he said.

"For which one of us?" Jehu asked.

"For you, commander." So Jehu went inside the house and the young man followed.

Once Jehu was seated, the prophet poured oil on his head and said, "The Lord says, 'I anoint you king over God's people, Israel, for you are to destroy Ahab's entire household to pay for the lives of my prophets, who were killed by Jezebel. As for her, dogs will eat her dead body.' "

Then the young man fled out of the house, racing past the officers.

"Is everything all right?" they asked Jehu. "What did that madman want?"

Everything had happened so quickly. Jehu was still puzzling over what the young man had done and the words that he spoke. When the officers persisted in asking why the young man had come, Jehu finally spoke up: "He said, 'The Lord says, "I anoint you as king over Israel." ' "

Jehu had not taken the prophet's words seriously—until he saw the commanders' response. They all took off their cloaks and spread them at his feet as one would do for a king. Then one of them blew a trumpet and shouted, "Jehu is king!"

When Jehu realized they were serious, he called the commanders together and began to make plans. They would begin by leading their army to Jezreel. If the prophet's words really were from God, then they must deal with Ahab's household.

Meanwhile, in Jezreel, Ahab's son, King Joram, was recuperating from a battle wound. While King Ahaziah of Judah was there visiting him, a report came from the watch tower: "I see troops approaching. They are moving rather quickly."

"Send a messenger," ordered the king. "Find out if they come peacefully."

When the messenger did not return, they sent out a second man on horseback.

The man at the lookout post said, "The second messenger isn't returning either. I can't see who is in the lead chariot, but he drives like Jehu."

""Hitch up my chariot," the king commanded his servants. "I will see for myself."

King Ahaziah followed Joram in his own chariot. They met Jehu at the plot of ground that had belonged to Naboth. Joram called out, "Have you come in peace, Jehu?"

Jehu shouted his reply for all to hear: "How can there be peace when your mother's witchcraft and idolatry are rampant?"

Immediately, Joram wheeled around and shouted out a warning, "Treachery, Ahaziah!"

Joram raced away, but Jehu drew his bow and shot him between the shoulders, piercing his heart. Ahab had shed innocent blood to take that field; now his son Joram would die there.

When Ahaziah saw what happened to Joram, he fled in his chariot. But Jehu pursued him, shouting, "Kill him, too!" So Jehu's men shot arrows and managed to wound Ahaziah. He escaped to Megiddo, where he soon died. His servants took his body to Jerusalem for burial.

As Jehu advanced toward Jezreel, Jezebel began putting on her make-up and fixing her hair. When Jehu arrived, she called out from her window, "Have you come in peace?"

Jehu shouted, "Who is on my side? Who? Show it now by throwing her out the window!"

Palace officials did as Jehu commanded, and Jezebel now lay dead. Horses trampled her body and she received no burial, for dogs had eaten her flesh. The word of the Lord had come true.

TBC 115

Israel's Most Zealous King

TBC Book One, Chapter 116
2 Kings 10:1-36

All the Samaritan leaders had received the same heart-stopping message. Jehu knew that 70 princes were scattered throughout Samaria, Ahab's grandsons and potential heirs to the throne. Samaria's leading officials were raising the boys to prepare them as leaders. So Jehu sent a letter telling them to fight for the throne if they wanted one of those princes to become king.

The men were terrified when they read his letter. "If Jehu defeated two kings," they said, "how can we possibly resist him?"

"We can't," said another. "I say we support him. What choice do we have?"

So they all agreed to send back this message: "We do not wish to appoint any of the princes as king. We will do whatever you wish."

Then Jehu sent another letter: "If you really are on my side and will obey me, prove it: Kill all the sons of Ahab's household and bring me their heads by tomorrow."

The officials agreed to his terms. Though none of them realized it, God was using Jehu to bring judgment on Ahab. The men killed all the princes of Israel. In those days, conquerors would sometimes show their power by displaying the heads of the kings they defeated. So the officials placed the heads in a basket and delivered them to Jehu as he had ordered.

When the basket arrived, the people of Jezreel stared in horror. Jehu told the people he had killed the king because the Lord God had ordered him to do so. But he pretended to have nothing to do with the other deaths. He told them God had decreed that Ahab would have no survivors. This persuaded the people to support him.

Then Jehu ordered that all of Ahab's household who remained in Jezreel be killed—his friends, his servants, and even his chief officials. He used the deaths of the princes as his excuse for killing the officials, and in this too, the people supported him.

As Jehu traveled toward Samaria, he met some relatives of King Ahaziah. They were traveling to Jezreel to see Joram. They had no idea that Jehu had killed Joram and wounded their own king. When Jehu learned they were related to Ahaziah, he killed them, too.

Jehu continued his mission, to destroy Ahab's entire household. In the distance, he saw Jehonadab, a man who feared the Lord and raised godly children; all the people respected him. Jehu reached down and helped Jehonadab into his chariot. "Come with me," he said, "and see my zeal for the Lord." When they reached Samaria, Jehu killed the rest of Ahab's family.

Only one more task remained. From the palace in Samaria, Jehu assembled all the people. He announced a worship ceremony for Baal and required all of Baal's prophets to attend. "Ahab served Baal a little," he said, "but I will serve Baal much."

At Jehu's command, they prepared for the special assembly. All the ministers of Baal crowded into Baal's temple, filling it completely. Then Jehu pretended to honor Baal's prophets by giving them robes. This would clearly identify which men were the prophets of Baal.

As Jehu and Jehonadab entered the temple, Jehu told the prophets, "Make sure no servants of the Lord are in here—only ministers of Baal." They had no idea he had posted soldiers outside the temple. Then Jehu sacrificed burnt offerings, pretending to worship Baal.

After sacrificing the burnt offerings, Jehu left the temple and spoke to the guards and officers: "Go in and kill all of them. Let no one escape, or you will pay for it with your own life." So they killed Baal's prophets, burned their sacred stone, and destroyed Baal's temple.

Because Jehu obeyed the Lord, he ruled Israel for 28 years, and God promised that his family would reign for four generations. But Jehu did not follow God with his whole heart, for he had allowed his people to worship the golden calves. So from that time on, God began to reduce Israel's territory.

TBC 116

The Youngest King of All

TBC Book One, Chapter 117
2 Kings 11:1-12:21;
2 Chronicles 22:10-12; 23; 24

While Jehu gained a firm grip on ruling Israel, terrible things happened in Jerusalem, beginning with the burial of Judah's King Ahaziah. His mother ordered that all of Judah's princes be killed, even her own grandchildren. She would rule Judah, killing anyone who threatened her reign.

All of the young princes were placed together in one room. Ahaziah's half-sister, Jehosheba, realized what this meant. Somehow she had to rescue her young nephew, one-year-old Joash. Quickly she slipped into the room and motioned to the woman who nursed Joash.

"Follow me," she whispered. Jehosheba led them to a small bedroom and hid them there while the queen carried out her wicked plans. Some time later, when no one could see them, she brought them to the temple and kept them hidden there.

Jehosheba's husband, Jehoiada, served as a priest in the Lord's temple. For six years they cared for Joash while Athaliah ruled as queen. She had no idea the prince remained alive.

When young Joash was seven, Jehoiada decided it was time to call for Judah's commanders. After making them take an oath to obey the Lord, he showed them Joash.

Other than the child's aunt, they were the only ones who knew a prince was still alive. So they formed a plan to make Joash king. On the Sabbath, when people came to worship, Jehoiada would then give the commanders the shields and spears kept in the temple.

With a crowd of people inside the temple and guards stationed throughout, Jehoiada brought out the king's son. Then he anointed him and crowned him king of Judah.

Athaliah heard a ruckus outside her window. A great many people were shouting, "Long live the king!" When she looked out her window, she tore her robes and cried out, "Treason!"

Jehoiada ordered the commanders to capture Athaliah and anyone who followed her. They caught her near the horse gate of the palace grounds and put her to death. Then they destroyed the temple of Baal. Like her father, Ahab, she had worshiped the idols of Baal.

After presenting the young king with a copy of the book of God's Law, Jehoiada led the people in affirming their covenant to serve the Lord. They also vowed to serve the king. The people rejoiced as Joash took his place on the palace throne, and Jerusalem enjoyed peace.

Now Joash was only seven when he became king, but his uncle, Jehoiada the priest, guided him until he was old enough to make his own decisions. One of the first decisions he made on his own was to order the priests to collect money to repair God's temple.

But the priests ignored his orders. Years went by until finally Joash summoned them and rebuked them. Then he ordered that a chest be set at the temple so people could donate money and know it would be used to repair the temple. The people gave gladly and workers were hired.

God blessed Jehoiada the priest with long life. When he died at age 130, the people buried him with the kings because of the good he had done in guiding Joash and protecting him.

After Jehoida died, however, Judah's officials persuaded Joash to turn away from God and worship idols. The people then began to set up Asherah poles and idols. The Lord sent prophets to warn them, but they would not listen. Finally, the Lord spoke through Zechariah, Jehoiada's son, "Because you have turned away from the Lord, he will turn away from you."

But instead of listening, Joash's advisors plotted how to kill the prophet. King Joash gave orders to stone Zechariah, even though his father had saved Joash's life. As the prophet lay dying, he turned to his cousin Joash and said, "May the Lord see this and hold you accountable."

Less than a year later, the Syrians (Arameans) plundered Judah and Jerusalem with only a small army. Before they withdrew, they wounded Joash. As he lay in bed, his own officials killed him for having murdered Zechariah. God's judgment on King Joash was now fulfilled.

TBC 117

As the Future Unfolds

TBC Book One, Chapter 118
Joel

While Joash reigned over Judah, and Jehu's family ruled Israel, the Lord revealed himself to a prophet named Joel, showing him the future of both nations. Now, thousands of years later, some of those things have already happened; some have yet to take place.

Joel predicted that terrible times lay ahead for Israel and Judah. He compared it to a plague of locusts, insects that look like grasshoppers. When they multiply quickly, hundreds of thousands being born, they fly in groups so large that they block out sunlight, as if it is night.

Few creatures are as destructive as locusts. They keep in formation like a well-trained army. They eat everything that is green, stripping crops, shrubs, and trees. They even eat the bark, often causing trees to fall by the weight of so many at once.

God revealed to Joel that, in the same way, an army of people would sweep through Israel and Judah, too many to count and terribly destructive. Joel said this would happen in four stages. Perhaps this refers to the four great empires that eventually conquered much of the world.

But still another invading army is yet to come. Joel calls that time "the day of the Lord." This refers to a time yet to come. As an act of judgment, the Lord will permit a military campaign unlike any the world has ever seen.

Joel recorded his prophecies to answer one key question: What can Israel do?

The prophet answers by quoting the Lord: "Even now," says the Lord, "turn back to me with your whole heart, with fasting, weeping, and sorrow."

Joel urges the people: "Let each person cry out to God, 'Spare your people, O Lord. Do not let the nations say, "Where is their God?" ' "

The prophet predicts that the Lord will then hear their cry and have compassion for his people. His anger will turn toward the army from the north that threatens to invade Israel. After dealing with that army, the

Lord will bless his land and restore what was destroyed. God's people will praise him for what he has done, and Israel will know that the Lord is their God.

Joel also predicted a time when the Lord would pour out his prophetic spirit on men and women of all ages. This would precede another unusual event, when strange things will begin to happen in nature and in the sky.

These unusual happenings will signal a time of judgment yet to come for all people. The nations of the world will one day join forces to attack Israel, not knowing that God has permitted this for a reason—to judge all nations for how they have dealt with Israel. Israel's Valley of Jehoshaphat will become God's valley of judgment.

Armies from many nations will join in a worldwide alliance, thinking they can conquer Israel. They will not realize they are challenging God himself, for the people of Israel belong to the Lord. As those military forces advance toward Jerusalem, God will shock the whole world.

The Lord Himself will come as a judge, and the world will be terrified. There will be terrible times in those last days, and many will die. But of those who survive, God will choose to save some of them, and everyone who calls on the name of the Lord will be saved.

All nations of people will become so wicked that God will decide, "That's enough—no more." The Lord compares it to a harvest of grapes that are ripe, ready to be picked, ready to be crushed. God's winepress must crush mankind's wicked rebellion against the Lord.

At the most terrifying moment of God's judgment, he will provide a refuge for his people. The Lord will destroy those who have violently attacked Israel. Never again will nations invade Jerusalem. Only then will everyone throughout the entire world know that Jerusalem is indeed the holy dwelling place of God Almighty.

TBC 118

The Rise and Fall of Amaziah

TBC Book One, Chapter 119
2 Chronicles 25:1-28

The king's officials watched with pleasure as Amaziah, son of Joash, took his father's place on the throne. They assumed young Amaziah would bear no hard feelings for the death of his father. After all, it was they who crowned Amaziah. The young man seemed to welcome their counsel, and everyone was eager to see how Judah would be governed under King Amaziah.

He began his reign at age 25. In those early years he did what was right in God's eyes, just as his father had done at the beginning of his reign. So the Lord blessed King Amaziah and gave him success—until he turned away from the Lord.

Early in his reign, after he firmly established himself as king, Amaziah ordered the deaths of the officials who had murdered his father. But he did not take revenge by killing their sons; he obeyed God's Law, which said children could not be put to death for their father's sins.

Amaziah gathered the men of Judah and divided them into military groups, according to their families. Then he assigned commanders over each group. After learning that Judah had only 300,000 men who could serve in their military, he hired another 100,000 from Israel.

Amaziah made plans to attack the Edomites, but before he marched out with his army, a prophet appeared to him with a warning: "These troops from Israel must not march with you, for the Lord is no longer with Israel. Even if you fight valiantly, God will cause your enemies to win because Israel's men are among you."

"But what about the payment I made? I gave their king almost four tons of silver!"

The man of God replied, "The Lord can give you much more than that."

So Amaziah dismissed the men from Israel and sent them home.

When the Israelite soldiers realized they would be sent home, they were furious. The silver that was paid went to their king, not to them. They were to gain their wages by taking plunder from the battle, valuables that belonged to their enemies. So on their way back to Israel, they raided the towns in Judah, killing 3,000 people and taking their wealth as plunder. The people in those towns were left defenseless because all their fighting men were with Amaziah.

Meanwhile, King Amaziah led his army toward Seir. At the Valley of Salt, they attacked the Edomites and killed 10,000. Then they captured another 10,000 and led them to their deaths.

After defeating the Edomites, Amaziah brought back their gods to Judah. He bowed to them and offered sacrifices. This kindled the Lord's anger. So he sent a prophet with a message: "Why do you worship a god that could not even save its own people from your army?"

The king interrupted the prophet. "Who made you an advisor to the king?" he shouted. "Stop speaking, or you will lose your life!"

So the prophet stopped. Then, as he was leaving, he turned around and said, "God has decided to destroy you because you have done this and have not listened to my counsel."

Amaziah ignored the warning. He was thinking about the towns the Israelites had raided. After consulting his advisors, he sent a challenge to King Jehoash, the grandson of Jehu.

Jehoash replied, "You defeated Edom and now you have become arrogant and proud. Stay in Judah. Why bring your own downfall?"

But Amaziah refused to listen. So Israel struck first, attacking Judah and capturing its king. Judah's soldiers fled as the Israelites brought Amaziah back to Jerusalem and broke down the city wall. They took many valuables, as well as some hostages. Then they returned home to Samaria.

Though God had turned his back on Israel, he let them defeat Judah to bring punishment on Amaziah. From the time Amaziah first turned away from the Lord, people in his kingdom began plotting against him. He tried to flee, but they caught him, and he died at their hands.

TBC 119

Running Away from God

TBC Book One, Chapter 120
Jonah 1:1-17; 2:1-10

The prophet Jonah could not believe what God was telling him to do: "Go to the great city of Nineveh and preach against it. Its wickedness has reached the point I must judge it."

Jonah thought, *When has a prophet of God ever gone to a Gentile nation to warn it?* Nineveh was a huge city in Assyria, and the Assyrians were long-time enemies of Israel.

After the Lord spoke to Jonah, the prophet boarded a ship and headed for Tarshish. But Tarshish was in the opposite direction of Nineveh. In the past, Jonah had always delivered the messages God had given him. This time he was afraid, not of the Ninevites, but of what might happen if they heard God's warning. . . . There was only one thing to do. He would run away.

But no matter where Jonah would have traveled, he could not have escaped the Lord's presence. A violent wind seemed to follow him after he boarded the ship. It stirred up such great waves that even the sailors grew terrified. They had never seen anything like this. Soon they began to throw cargo overboard to lighten the ship. Nothing seemed to help. The sailors grew so desperate that they all began to call on their gods to save them, but still the storm raged.

Finally, the captain of the ship went below deck and found Jonah sleeping. "How can you sleep through this?" he shouted. "Get up and call on your god! Maybe he will help us."

The violent storm had come so suddenly that the sailors had only one explanation for it: Someone on board must have done something terrible to anger the god who had raised this fierce storm. So they drew lots to find out who was the guilty person. The lot pointed to Jonah.

"Who are you?" one of them asked. "Where do you come from?"

Another cried out, "I want to know what god is causing this!"

"I am a Hebrew," replied Jonah, "and I worship the Lord. He is the God of heaven, who made both the sea and the land. He has sent this storm because I was running away from him."

At this the men were terrified. One of them shouted, "How could you do this to us?"

All the while they were talking, the sea became even rougher. The captain turned to Jonah once again. "How can we appease your God so he will make the sea calm down for us?"

"Throw me into the sea," Jonah replied, "and it will calm down. I know it is my fault that you are facing this storm. So now do what you have to do."

But the captain and his men refused to throw him overboard. In a storm like this, they knew he would surely drown. So they tried to row back to land, but the sea grew even wilder.

Finally, the men looked at one another helplessly. They knew what they must do. As they grabbed hold of Jonah, one of them cried out, "O Lord, please do not kill us for taking this man's life. Do not hold us accountable for this."

Then they picked up Jonah and threw him overboard. Immediately the storm died down and the sea grew calm. When the men saw this, they realized that Jonah's God was indeed the Lord, and they feared him greatly. So they offered a sacrifice and made vows to him.

The sailors assumed that Jonah must have drowned. They had no idea that God had sent a huge sea creature, one large enough to swallow a man. It swallowed him whole. For three days and nights, Jonah remained inside its belly. And from there he prayed and made his own vows.

On the third day, the Lord caused the creature to vomit Jonah onto dry ground. Some time later, Jonah looked back on those three days and wrote: "In my distress I called out to you, and you heard me. It seemed like I was in the depths of hell, but you answered my cry.

"Water surrounded me and seaweeds wrapped around my head. I was fainting away. But you brought my life up out of that pit, O Lord my God. So now I will sacrifice to you with a voice of thanksgiving. And I will keep the vow that I have made."

TBC 120

The Pouting Prophet

TBC Book One, Chapter 121
Jonah 3:1-4:11

Seldom does a disobedient servant get a second chance. The vow Jonah promised to keep may well have been an agreement to speak God's words to anyone, anywhere. Once again the Lord told Jonah: "Go now to the great city of Nineveh and say what I tell you."

So this time, Jonah did as the Lord commanded and traveled to Nineveh. It was indeed a great city, situated on the Tigris River, in the region of the world now known as Iraq. It may have taken the prophet days just to walk through it from one end to the other. As he walked, Jonah loudly proclaimed the message God gave him: "In 40 days, Nineveh will be overthrown!"

The people of Nineveh took his words to heart. They decided there was only one way to avert God's judgment—humble themselves before God. First they proclaimed a fast and put on ragged old clothes: They were mourning for their sins. Everyone participated, from the wealthy and powerful to the poorest. When news of this reached the king, he too humbled himself. The king took off his royal robe, put on ragged clothes, and sat down in the dust.

Then the king issued a decree: "Let no person or animal taste anything. No one is to eat or drink, not even water. Let each person turn from his wickedness and violence and call on God. Perhaps God may change his mind and turn away his anger so we won't perish."

The Lord did indeed see that the people of Nineveh were turning away from their wicked ways and calling out to him. Just as they had hoped and prayed for, God held back from punishing Nineveh. But he sent no message to tell them of his decision.

When Jonah began to sense God might not send the destruction, he became very angry.

"I knew it!" Jonah said out loud. He spoke as if the Lord were right beside him, listening to him. "I was afraid this would happen. That's why I fled to Tarshish. For I know that you are a gracious, compassionate God, slow to anger and full of lovingkindness."

Jonah did not mind telling the Ninevites God was about to destroy them. But he did mind that they could repent and find God's mercy. The Assyrians had always been enemies of Israel and were growing ever more powerful. Nineveh was their capital, and Jonah wanted it destroyed. The prophet was so upset by the Lord's decision that he asked God to let him die.

"Do you have any right to be angry?" the Lord replied.

Jonah did not want to hear that. Still pouting, he walked just east of Nineveh, made a shelter, and sat down. The 40 days were not over yet. So he watched to see what would happen. If the Ninevites turned back to their old ways, surely God would bring judgment. Meanwhile, the Lord caused a vine to grow there, and Jonah was quite pleased to have its shade.

But at dawn the next day, the Lord caused a worm to chew the vine and cause it to wither. When the sun rose, God caused a scorching east wind to rise up. The sun blazed on Jonah's head, and he grew faint. Without shade from the vine, Jonah felt hot and miserable.

Once again he said, "It would be better for me to die than to live."

Then God said to him, "Do you have a right to be angry about the vine?"

"I do," Jonah said. "I am angry enough to die."

The Lord replied, "You speak about this vine as though it were yours. You cared about what happened to it. But you never planted it, you never tended it, you never caused it to grow. The plant sprang up overnight and it died the next night.

"Should I not have compassion on that great city? Nineveh has more than 120,000 little ones, children who are not yet old enough to know their right hand from their left. Nineveh also has many animals. Should I not be concerned about that great city?"

Jonah had overlooked an important truth: God's mercy extends to all.

TBC 121

Powerful—and Proud of It

TBC Book One, Chapter 122
2 Chronicles 26:1-22; 27:1-9;
2 Kings 14:21, 22; 15:1-3, 5-7

A great celebration took place in Jerusalem, and the people shouted for joy. Everyone rejoiced to watch 16-year-old Azariah take the place of his father, Amaziah, as the new king of Judah. Since a teenage boy could not rule the kingdom by himself, he would rely on the guidance of a wise counselor named Zechariah.

Zechariah taught young Azariah (later known as "King Uzziah") what it meant to fear the Lord, to show his respect for God by obeying him in all things. For many years, Uzziah did just that. He turned to God for guidance and did what pleased the Lord. During those years, God blessed him and made him a successful king.

The Lord granted Uzziah victory as he waged war against the Philistines and neighboring Arab tribes. Then he built up those towns and claimed them for Judah. The Ammonites also paid tribute to Uzziah. He had become so powerful that his fame spread to Egypt.

Uzziah had lookout towers built in Jerusalem. He also built towers in some of the towns in the desert so he could be warned of invading armies. He even had wells dug for his livestock. Many people worked in his fields and vineyards, for he loved growing crops.

King Uzziah developed a well-trained army, a powerful force of 307,500 men. They were always battle ready and worked together well, thanks to Uzziah's organizational skills. He followed his father's example, grouping the men by families, with family leaders in command.

More than any king before him, Uzziah focused on developing weapons to give his army a decisive advantage. He made sure his entire army was equipped with shields, spears, helmets, armor, bows, and slings. Perhaps his greatest achievement was his decision to command skilled men to devise other weapons—machines that could be used on Jerusalem's towers to shoot arrows and hurl large stones. So the king grew even more famous.

But after Uzziah became powerful and well-known, he also grew proud. One day he went into the temple to burn incense, something only a priest could do. Azariah the high priest, with 80 other brave priests, followed him inside and tried to stop the king before he sinned.

"Uzziah," he said, "you know it is not right for you to burn incense here. The Lord commanded that only the priests, Aaron's descendants, are to do that. You must leave at once, for you have been unfaithful. God will no longer honor you."

As Uzziah stood holding the lit censer, he yelled at the priests in rage. "How dare you order the king of Judah! You are the ones who will leave this temple!"

While Uzziah continued to shout, leprosy broke out on his forehead. The priests saw it first and gasped in amazement. Then they ran outside, fearful that it would spread to them.

Suddenly Uzziah stopped shouting. He looked down at his arms and saw what the priests were pointing at. So that was why they all ran out—the Lord had inflicted him with leprosy.

From that day on, King Uzziah had to live in a separate house, away from his family, for leprosy was contagious. Like anyone with a skin disease, he could never again enter the temple.

Uzziah lived with leprosy until the day he died. During those years, his son Jotham took charge of the palace. Uzziah's reign lasted 52 years, longer than any other king of Judah. But it was Jotham who ruled Judah during Uzziah's last years. Crowned at age 25, Jotham did what was right in God's eyes. But he did not remove the high places, altars that were frequently used to sacrifice offerings to other gods.

The Ammonites tested young King Jotham by refusing to pay tribute. So Jotham waged war against them and defeated them. The Ammonites then paid him a yearly tribute of silver, wheat, and barley. And Jotham continued to grow powerful, because he chose to obey the Lord.

TBC 122

Visions of the Future

TBC Book One, Chapter 123
Amos

David was not the only shepherd boy chosen to do great things for God. While King Uzziah reigned in Jerusalem, God chose a shepherd from Judah, a man named Amos, to go to Israel with an important message.

Jeroboam II reigned as king over Israel and his people enjoyed peace. They also grew wealthy. But how they gained their wealth displeased the Lord.

God revealed to Amos what was about to happen, not only to Israel, but also to the other nations surrounding them. Some would sell God's people as slaves. Some were so violent that one day they would kill the babies inside Israel's pregnant women. None of these things had happened yet. But when they did, God would judge those nations by destroying them.

God would judge Judah, too, for the people had rejected the Lord's commands and turned to false gods. First, however, he would judge their sister nation in the north, Israel.

Israel's own judges were taking bribes from those who were rich. They gave judgments that favored rich people and ruled against those who were poor.

Of all the families on earth, God had chosen Israel as his people and made his descendants into a nation. But the Israelites disobeyed him by worshiping golden calves. And instead of loving God, they loved riches. Since God punishes the ungodly, surely he would also punish those who knew they were doing wrong.

Israel's leaders lived a life of luxury and ease. The people gave offerings and tithes, thinking this would satisfy God. But God knew they did not love him. Over the years he brought famines, plagues, and drought to turn them back to him. But they refused.

So God decided that judgment must come. They would be taken captive by foreigners, like fish caught on hooks. They had only one way to escape. . . .

"Stop seeking evil," the Lord warned. "Seek me. You oppress honest people and take advantage of the poor. Turn back to what is just and right."

The Israelites had heard prophecies about "the day of the Lord." They looked forward to that time, for they thought, *God will punish our enemies. Then we will be vindicated.*

But Amos said, "You are wrong. It will be a terrible time for the whole world—including you."

The leaders of Judah and Israel knew the prophets predicted judgment on them. Both nations enjoyed so much prosperity that they did not worry about the future. The people thought, *Surely God's judgment won't happen in our lifetime.* So they continued to live for pleasure.

One day the Lord showed Amos a vision of locusts destroying Israel. Amos pleaded for Israel, and God relented. Then the Lord showed him destruction by fire. Again Amos begged for mercy, and God listened to him. Finally, the Lord showed him a plumb line, used to measure walls.

Amos realized that God has a measurement of what is right and true, and Israel was far from God's standard. The Lord then showed him a basket of ripe fruit.

"The time is ripe," the Lord said. "No longer will I spare them."

It was too late to pray for mercy.

The people of Israel loved their wealth and prosperity. They were eager for each Sabbath to end so they could open up their shops and earn money. Then they would cheat their customers and take advantage of the poor, forcing them work as their slaves just to survive.

One of the last visions Amos saw was the Lord standing by an altar, a vision that may relate to the end times. In that vision Amos heard the Lord speaking to him.

"My eyes are on this sinful kingdom," he said, "and I will destroy it—but not completely. In the end, I will save a small remnant, not only from Israel, but from those who bear my Name among all nations."

TBC 123

Where Is the Love?

TBC Book One, Chapter 124
Hosea

Sometimes God would command a prophet to do strange things to get the people's attention. Shortly after Amos prophesied to Israel, the Lord chose yet another man to deliver God's word to his people. He used the personal life of Hosea as an illustration to show the Israelites what they were doing and why it was wrong.

The Israelites had done a lot of things that were sinful in God's eyes. But there was really just one issue at the heart of all their sin—they had stopped loving God.

They were just like a married person who breaks wedding vows and chases after someone else. So the Lord told Hosea to marry an unfaithful woman named Gomer. Why would he want his prophet to do that? Because she behaved just like the Israelites did toward God.

Even though Gomer was an unfaithful woman, Hosea loved her. In fact, he loved Gomer the same way that God loved Israel.

In time she became pregnant and gave birth to a son. The Lord said to Hosea, "Name him Jezreel, because I'm about to punish Jehu's family for the people Jehu murdered at Jezreel." So the child's name became a symbol, revealing what God was about to do.

Though Gomer was married and the mother of Hosea's child, she pursued other men. In time she became pregnant again and gave birth to a daughter. Hosea did not even know whether the child was his. But he kept Gomer as his wife. In obedience to the Lord he named the child "Lo-Ruhamah," which means "not loved."

"This is to show that I will no longer love Israel," said the Lord, "but I will love Judah."

After Gomer had weaned Lo-Ruhamah, she got pregnant again and gave birth to another son. Hosea knew that this child was not his, and the name God selected for him was fitting.

"Call him Lo-Ammi," the Lord said. (The name meant "not my people.") "For you, O Israel, are no longer my people, and I am not your God."

Meanwhile, just as Israel had turned away from God, so also was Gomer becoming more unfaithful to Hosea. She lived with other men, loving them instead of loving Hosea. In spite of this, the Lord told Hosea, "Take Gomer back as your wife and love her."

Hosea paid her to return to him, just as other men had paid her to come away. "You must live with me now," he said. This too symbolized the people of Israel. In time they would have no king, no sacrifices, no gods, and no guidance. But in the end, they would seek the Lord.

Hosea told the Israelites: "When you finally do seek the Lord, you will not find him. You broke your covenant with him by worshiping idols. So your sacrifices will do no good. God says to you, 'I desire mercy, not sacrifice. To make me God of your lives is what matters.' "

Then Hosea prophesied about Israel's future: "Because you have been unfaithful to God, who loved you, you will not remain in this land. Punishment is coming. You will eat forbidden food in Assyria. You disobeyed God; now you will be wanderers among the nations."

Hosea compared Israel to hard, dry ground, land that is no good for growing seeds. "Plow up your hardened ground," he said, "so you can sow the seeds of righteousness and reap the fruit of God's love. Seek the Lord. Keep seeking him until he comes to you."

But the people of Israel trusted the strength of their army, instead of the Lord. Israel was like God's child. But as the child grew, it refused to come into his arms and ran the other way.

"Return to the Lord your God," pleads Hosea. "Maintain love and justice. Ask God to forgive you." This message holds true for Israel even today.

One day Israel will say to God, "you are my husband." And God will respond. He will make a covenant with all creation, and he will say to Israel, "You are my people forever."

TBC 124

A Divine Appointment

TBC Book One, Chapter 125
Isaiah 6:1-13; 1:11-2:22; 3:13-15; 5:1-22

At the end of Uzziah's reign, a prophet named Isaiah saw a startling vision. Standing in front of the temple, he saw the Lord seated on a throne. Winged angels (seraphs) cried out, "Holy, holy, holy is the Lord Almighty! The whole earth is full of his glory!"

At the sound of their voices, the thresholds shook and the temple filled with smoke.

"Oh no!" Isaiah cried. "I'm doomed to die. I am just a person with unclean lips, and I have seen the Lord Almighty!"

What he meant was that he knew he was not worthy to speak even praises to God. So one of the angels flew to Isaiah and put a hot coal to his lips.

"There," he said. "Your guilt is taken away and your sin is now paid for."

Then Isaiah heard the Lord say, "Whom shall I send? Who will go for us?"

"Here am I," Isaiah answered. "Send me!"

So the Lord said, "Go to these people and say, 'May you always hear but never understand, always see but never take it to heart.' "

Isaiah asked, "For how long will this happen?"

God answered, "Until the cities and land lie in ruins. But my holy seed will remain."

So Isaiah accepted God's invitation. He would deliver his words and write them down for future generations, like ours today. For at least 47 years, perhaps as many as 60, Isaiah prophesied to the southern kingdom, Judah, warning God's people of what would happen.

Like the Israelites, the behavior of those living in Judah had grown disgusting. They, too, thought their sacrifices and prayers would please God.

But God saw what they were doing. Leaders ruled favoring the rich people who bribed them, while the poor suffered with no one to plead their case.

The people acted religious, but they refused to do the things that really please God. They did not watch out for orphans and widows, the people in their society who needed help.

For this reason, the Lord said, "As gold is placed in fire to remove impurities, so also must my people suffer judgment to be purified."

Then the Lord showed Isaiah what would happen to God's people in the distant future. Some of these things are still yet to happen. In the last days, for example, all nations will honor the Lord in Jerusalem. Weapons used for war will one day be turned into tools that help people.

But before that day when the Lord is exalted, mankind must first be humbled. Isaiah said that the people loved possessions rather than God. What was true in Isaiah's time is also true today.

The prophet spoke of "the day of the Lord," a time that is yet to come. In that day, God will shake the earth so violently that people will hide in caves, fearing the end of the world.

Isaiah describes how the Lord will take his place as Judge against the elders and leaders of his own people: "You have ruined my vineyard," says the Lord, "and you have become wealthy by plundering those who are poor. How dare you crush my people and grind down the poor!"

Israel and Judah were like a vineyard that produced only bad grapes. God saw no justice among his people, only bloodshed and distress. People held parties to get drunk. They loved their music but ignored the God of creation. So God would send them into exile.

Those who did not ignore God were guilty of their own arrogance and pride. This would lead to their downfall. They were eager to see God's judgment because they thought they were safe. *Judgment will happen to others,* they thought, *not to us.* But they were wrong. . . .

TBC 125

Judah's Fateful Treaty

TBC Book One, Chapter 126
2 Kings 16:1-20; 2 Chronicles 28; Isaiah 7:1-25

Dark days loomed for Judah when 20-year-old Ahaz ascended to the throne as Judah's new king. Unlike his father, Jotham, or his grandfather, Uzziah, Ahaz chose to imitate the kings of Israel. He burned incense at the high places and even sacrificed his own sons in the fire.

But terror gripped the young king when he heard news from the north. Rezin, the king of Aram (also known as Syria), had joined forces with Israel's King Pekah, leading their armies to invade Judah. Already Aram had conquered Elath, and the Edomites moved into that territory.

The people trembled with fear as the armies now advanced against Jerusalem. Judah suffered heavy losses and thousands of women and children were also captured. But when the prophet Oded warned Israel this would bring God's judgment, the Israelites finally let them go.

The Lord then sent Isaiah to King Ahaz. The prophet's son accompanied him. His name, Shear-Jashub, hinted at the future of God's people. It meant "a remnant will return."

"Tell Ahaz not to fear," said the Lord. "Tell him, 'The head of Aram is only Rezin. The head of Israel is only Remaliah's son. Within 65 years, Israel will be shattered.' "

So Isaiah delivered the message to Ahaz. At God's prompting, he added, "Ask the Lord for a sign to prove that my words are true."

Although the Lord offered the sign, Ahaz refused, saying, "I will not test the Lord."

Isaiah sighed in exasperation. "Must you try God's patience?" he said. "All right—if you will not ask for a sign, the Lord himself will give you one.

"Here is the sign: A virgin will give birth to a son and name him Immanuel. He will eat curds and honey until he is old enough to know right from wrong. But before he reaches that age, the land of these two kings will be conquered.

"The Lord will then bring you and your people a time unlike any since Israel broke away from Judah. The armies of Egypt and Assyria will swarm over this land. The Lord will send the King of Assyria, and he will destroy your kingdom the way a razor strips off hair.

"This land, now rich in crops and vineyards, will become a desolate wasteland, covered by briers and thorns. Cattle and sheep will graze here, and people will live off curds and honey. Wild animals will multiply and hunters will come with bow and arrow."

Despite Isaiah's words, Ahaz turned to Assyria instead of turning to God. He sent the temple's silver and gold to King Tiglath-Pileser with this message: "Let's make a treaty. I am now your servant and my kingdom is your vassal. Come rescue us from Aram and Israel."

The king of Assyria came, just as Ahaz requested, and conquered Damascus. He captured their people and killed King Rezin. Judah had escaped their grip. But now Judah, too, would be subject to Assyria. So Ahaz met Tiglath-Pileser in Damascus.

While Ahaz was in Damascus, he saw an altar used for pagan worship, and that gave him an idea. *Surely the gods of Damascus had enabled Aram to win battles,* thought Ahaz. *Perhaps they also helped Tiglath-Pileser gain his victory.*

So King Ahaz sent instructions to Uriah the priest and ordered him to build a similar altar in Jerusalem. Ahaz hoped the pagan gods would help him, too.

Upon returning to Jerusalem, Ahaz sacrificed to the pagan gods he had recently learned about. The king then led Judah to follow his example. He even shut the doors of the temple, preventing his people from worshiping there. Then he set up pagan altars throughout Judah.

After reigning for 16 years, Ahaz died. His body was laid to rest in Jerusalem, but it was not placed in the tombs of the kings. His son, Hezekiah, was crowned as the new king of Judah. People wondered, *Will he be like his father?* They did not have to wait long to find out. . . .

TBC 126

If They Only Knew . . .

TBC Book One, Chapter 127
Micah

What kind of a person does God choose as a prophet? He chooses all kinds, with various temperaments and abilities, but he also uses that person's background and personality to shape his message. While God chose Isaiah to deliver his messages to kings, he chose Micah to address God's concerns for those in small towns and villages, like the one where Micah grew up.

Micah predicted the downfall of both Samaria and Judah. What he saw grieved him, and it angered God.

Greedy landowners had forced poor people to give up their property. Even other prophets were guilty of greed. Some of them gave prophetic predictions just to make money. And the leaders who governed them were just as guilty. Instead of ruling justly, they made decisions that favored those who bribed them.

Despite all their wicked behavior, the people thought God was on their side because of the covenant he made with their forefathers. They were certain that no disaster would befall them.

But Micah told them the truth—Jerusalem would be destroyed. Yet he also revealed to them the big picture. In the end, God would raise up the city that bears his Name, and he would bring back his people. And one day, in the distant future, all nations would worship the Lord.

In the near future, however, Jerusalem would be surrounded and cut off. For quite some time following that event, it would seem to them as though God were abandoning Israel. But one day a new king would be born in Bethlehem, from Judah's smallest clan. Micah said that this Shepherd-King would be like no other, that he would bring peace to the whole world.

Looking at the distant future, Micah saw an enemy invade Israel's borders. By then, God's remnant of chosen people would be in nations all over the world. At that time, God will destroy everything that mankind has trusted in—weapons, wealth, and worshiping other gods.

Micah pictured the Lord as a judge, and he delivered God's words as they were spoken to him: "My people," says the Lord, "what excuse do you have? I rescued you from Egypt's slavery. I sent you leaders like Moses, Aaron, and Miriam. You deserved to be destroyed back in Gilgal. Yet I blessed you and brought you into the land."

Then Micah himself urged the people, saying, "How should you respond to God? Would he be pleased with thousands of burnt offerings? Would it help if you offered up your own child?

"You may ask, 'Then what does God want from us?' Just this—to do what is right, to love mercy, and to walk humbly with God."

Already it was too late—the time had come for discipline. They had used violence and deceit to gain wealth. So God would destroy everything they had gained. They followed the example of wicked kings by worshiping idols. So God would give them over to their enemies.

Micah speaks poetically, as if he were the voice of all Israel: "What shall I do? Everything I enjoyed is gone. The godly have been swept away. Violence is everywhere, and leaders conspire with rich people. I can't trust anyone. So I will turn to God."

Then Micah speaks as the voice of God's people in the end times: "Do not gloat, my enemy! I have fallen, but I will rise again. When you mockingly say, 'Where is your God now?' I will watch your downfall. The whole earth will become desolate as a result of people's deeds."

The prophet pictures the Lord as a shepherd tenderly using his staff to guide and feed his sheep. Just as God performed miracles to deliver his people from Egypt, so also will he deliver "the remnant of his inheritance." Only then will the nations learn to fear God.

Micah concludes with praise: "Who can compare to you, O Lord? You have chosen to pardon your remnant people. You do not stay angry forever. You delight to show us your mercy. You will again have compassion and keep the promise you made to our fathers, Jacob and Abraham."

TBC 127

Israel's Last Kings

TBC Book One, Chapter 128
2 Kings 10:32, 33; 14:23-27; 15:8-30; 17:1-33

Deceit and treachery marked the last years that kings reigned in Israel. Over the years since Jehu's reign, Israel's kings had worshiped the golden calves at Bethel and Dan, and they led their people to do the same. So God allowed surrounding nations to capture land from Israel. All the Israelites suffered badly. Finally, God showed mercy and Israel regained power.

Under King Jeroboam II, the Israelites won battles for their land and managed to prosper once more. But just as the prophets warned, Israel's love of wealth choked out their love for God and his people. After Jeroboam's reign, one king after another was murdered.

The prophecies about Jehu's family were soon fulfilled. Jeroboam's son, Zechariah, ruled for only six months when a man named Shallum killed him and made himself king. Zechariah was the last of Jehu's family to rule as king. Just as the Lord predicted, Jehu's dynasty would end in its fourth generation.

The final kings who rose to power in Israel were treacherous. Shallum reigned only a month before he too was murdered. A violent man named Menahem had conquered territory in Israel, sparing no one—not even babies. In Samaria, he attacked and killed King Shallum.

Menahem ruled Israel for 10 years, and the wealth gained under Jeroboam soon vanished. Tiglath-Pileser of Assyria invaded Israel, and Menahem offered him 37 tons of silver so he could remain Israel's king. So Israel became Assyria's vassal kingdom, just as Judah had done. Making a yearly tribute payment was like buying peace from a powerful nation. It would stop Assyria from overrunning them and would ensure that Assyria rescue them when others threatened to attack.

When Menahem died, his son Pekahiah became king of Israel, but he reigned for only two years. One of his chief officers, Pekah, led a group of soldiers in conspiring against the king. They killed him in Samaria's royal palace, and Pekah took over the throne.

Pekah reigned for 20 years. During that time he joined forces with Aram (Syria) to challenge Judah in battle. But he lost much territory to

King Tiglath-Pileser, when Judah turned to Assyria for help. Finally, a man named Hoshea conspired against Pekah and succeeded in killing him.

Under Hoshea's reign, Israel continued to pay tribute to Tiglath-Pileser, then to Shalmaneser, who became Assyria's next king. Unlike Israel's previous kings, Hoshea did not worship idols of Baal or bow to the golden calves. Yet he, too, was evil.

Although King Hoshea had agreed that Israel would serve Shalmaneser as a vassal kingdom, he secretly sent messengers to Egypt. Once he thought he was assured of Egypt's alliance, he stopped paying tribute to Assyria. King Hoshea knew that Shalmaneser would be angry. Assuming that would lead to a battle, he believed Egypt would then help defend Israel.

When Shalmaneser discovered that Hoshea was joining forces with Egypt, his army quickly invaded Israel. But Israel's capital city, Samaria, was well-fortified. For three years the Assyrian army kept it under siege. Finally the Assyrians broke through, and when they did, they captured Hoshea and deported the Israelites to Assyria.

Israel had ignored the warnings of the prophets and became just as wicked as the nations that God had driven from the land. That's why the Lord allowed Assyria to take them away.

The Assyrians made a practice of deporting people far from their native land. Then they would repopulate that region by sending in foreigners that they had conquered.

But when the Assyrian king sent foreigners to replace the Israelites in Samaria, strange things happened. Because they did not worship the Lord, God sent lions to attack them. Knowing that Israel's God must have caused this, the king sent an Israelite priest to teach the people how to worship God. So the foreigners worshiped the Lord as well as their own pagan gods.

TBC 128

A Man After David's Own Heart

TBC Book One, Chapter 129
2 Kings 18:1-8; 2 Chronicles 29-31

Six years before Assyria carried off the Israelites and planted other people in Israel, a new king came to power in Israel's sister kingdom to the south, Judah. At age 25, young King Hezekiah took his place on the throne, and he was nothing like his father, Ahaz.

Hezekiah loved the Lord. So God blessed him and caused him to succeed.

On his first day as king, Hezekiah opened the doors to the temple, which had been shut by his father. Then he summoned all the priests and Levites for a special meeting.

"Our fathers have sinned," said King Hezekiah. "That's why many have died in battle. Let us now consecrate ourselves and this temple."

Sixteen days later, the priests and Levites finished preparing the temple for worship. The next morning, Hezekiah gathered all the city officials. While sacrifices were made, the Levites played instruments and sang praises, and everyone bowed in worship.

After making sacrifices, the whole assembly knelt down and dedicated themselves to God. Then the Levites praised the Lord with psalms that had been written by David and Asaph the prophet. Everyone sang praises joyfully and bowed their heads in worship.

Now that the temple was open for service and enough priests had been consecrated, Hezekiah invited all the Israelites to celebrate the Passover in Jerusalem. He sent messages not only to his own people in Judah, but also to the tribes in Israel, urging all of them to return to the Lord.

Many people, however, made fun of Hezekiah's messengers. But some of the people from Asher, Ephraim, Manasseh, and Zebulun humbled themselves and came to Jerusalem.

Meanwhile, the people in Judah united to obey the king and follow God. So a large assembly came to celebrate the Passover.

It had been so long since anyone had celebrated the Passover that many of those who came had not prepared themselves according to God's requirements. So Hezekiah prayed that the Lord would look beyond that and pardon each one who had set his heart on seeking God. The Lord heard him and honored that prayer.

The people celebrated the Passover (called "Feast of Unleavened Bread") for seven days. King Hezekiah provided 1,000 bulls and 7,000 sheep and goats for the entire assembly. The officials also showed generosity in providing 1,000 bulls and 10,000 sheep and goats.

Not since Solomon's reign was there a celebration like this. Everyone was full of joy, even the foreigners among them who were not Jewish. For God had made a provision for Gentiles, too; those who had shown their faith by being circumcised could join in the celebration.

Because the people worshiped God wholeheartedly, this naturally led into serving him. When the celebration ended, the service to God began: Israelites traveled all over Judah and portions of Israel, destroying the high places and pulling down altars.

For King Hezekiah and the priests and Levites, service also meant organizing the temple. They instructed the people on the need to tithe, to give a portion of all they owned to the Lord. Then they encouraged the people to provide still other offerings beyond the required ones. This would allow priests and Levites to devote themselves fully to carrying out their duties.

The people responded by tithing a portion of all their crops, firstfruits, flocks, and herds, as well as other valuables. They were so generous that special storerooms now needed to be built. So Hezekiah and his officials praised God and blessed all His people.

TBC 129

When Death Comes Knocking

TBC Book One, Chapter 130
Isaiah 38:1-8; 2 Chronicles 32:1-5;
2 Kings 18:1-8; 20:1-11

The young new king of Judah began to flex his muscles as the ruler of a small but thriving nation. Before becoming king, Hezekiah had probably ruled jointly with his father, when Shalmaneser, king of Assyria, conquered Samaria. Shalmaneser died soon, and his brother Sargon became king of Assyria. Sargon, who deported the Israelites, ruled forcefully.

Eighteen years later, Sargon died in battle, fighting a rebellious vassal kingdom. This gave hope to other vassal kingdoms: perhaps now they could rebel and refuse to pay tribute. In the midst of this turmoil, a man named Sennacherib succeeded his father as king of Assyria.

Hezekiah knew that Assyria was weakened by the death of Sargon. It would take time for Assyria's new king to gain full control against so many rebelling nations. For some time Hezekiah had wanted to rebel against Assyria. He reasoned that now was the time to break away from Assyria and stop paying tribute.

Hezekiah knew that he must strengthen Judah if his people were to stand up to the forces of Assyria. So weapons were made, Jerusalem's walls were repaired, and watchtowers were built.

Hezekiah then organized his army. They began to exercise their military strength and gain more power as they waged war on old enemies. Hezekiah defeated the Philistines who had seized land from Judah during his father's reign.

After regaining their territory from the Philistines, King Hezekiah put pressure on nearby nations in Phoenicia and Palestine. He believed their only hope against a powerful force like Assyria was to create a united front with other nations that wanted to break free from their role as vassal kingdoms. So while Babylon stirred up rebellion in the north, Judah led its own revolt in the south, persuading the nearby countries to rebel against Assyria.

Hezekiah knew Sennacherib would eventually attack Jerusalem. So he and his officials devised a plan: They would block off the Gihon Spring so the Assyrians would have no water. Then they would channel the stream through tunnels leading into Jerusalem.

During this time, King Hezekiah became ill and was concerned about a boil that had developed. Wanting a word from the Lord about his sickness, he sent for the prophet Isaiah.

Isaiah came to him and said, "The Lord says, 'You will not recover. You will die. So put your house in order.' " That meant he was to prepare his family and his kingdom for his death.

Hezekiah could hardly believe the prophet's message. He was not ready for this. Turning his face to the wall, he prayed: "Remember, O Lord, how I have walked before you faithfully and with wholehearted devotion, how I did what was right in your eyes." Then he wept bitterly.

Meanwhile Isaiah reached the middle court of the palace grounds when the Lord said, "Go back to Hezekiah. Tell him I have heard his prayer and seen his tears. I will add 15 years to his life. I will also rescue Jerusalem from Assyria for my name's sake and for David's sake."

Isaiah returned and delivered the Lord's message. Then he took some figs, wrapped them in a warm, wet cloth to create a poultice, laid it on the boil, and waited. When he finally spoke again, he said, "In three days you will be well and able to go to the temple."

Hezekiah asked, "What sign can you give that I will indeed be healed in three days?" He did not want to make the same mistake as his father. He knew he could ask God for a sign.

Isaiah replied, "Shall the Lord cause the sundial to go forward ten steps or backward ten steps?" Apparently, Hezekiah measured time by watching the shadows on a certain set of steps.

"It would be simple to make the shadow appear to go forward. So have it go backward." Isaiah prayed and Hezekiah watched as the shadow went back up ten steps. This was a miracle! The king recovered, and three days later, he went to the temple and worshiped the Lord.

TBC 130

Testing a King's Heart

TBC Book One, Chapter 131
Isaiah 39:1-8; 36; 37; 2 Chron. 32:6-8;
2 Kings 18:13-16; 19:35-37

If only King Hezekiah had known the temptations that he would face in those God-given 15 years. Word spread that the king had recovered from his deadly illness, and the people of Judah were not the only ones who knew about the sundial miracle. Babylon's king then sent messengers to congratulate King Hezekiah on his recovery and to inquire about the miracle.

The envoys also brought news from their king, Merodach-Baladan: Babylon could use a strong ally against Assyria. And Hezekiah was eager to impress them. He did not know that the Lord had left him to test him, to reveal what was in Hezekiah's heart.

Hezekiah showed the envoys all the wealth he had acquired, storehouses full of silver, gold, spices, and oils. He showed them the armory of weapons he had built up. But instead of giving glory to God for his recovery and his wealth, his heart had become carried away by pride.

After the envoys left the palace, Isaiah went to Hezekiah. "Who were those men?" he asked. "What did they want?"

"They came from a distant land," said Hezekiah, "from Babylon."

"What did you show them?"

"Everything," Hezekiah said, "all my treasures."

Then Isaiah said, "The time will come when all the wealth in your palace will be carried off to Babylon. And some of your descendants will be taken away to serve Babylon's king."

King Hezekiah consoled himself by thinking, *At least this won't happen in my lifetime.*

But Hezekiah's hopes of peace were dashed when Assyria invaded Judah. Sennacherib had defeated Babylon. Now he laid siege to Judah's fortified cities. Jerusalem would be next.

Hezekiah summoned his people and tried to encourage them to take heart. "Do not be afraid," he said. "We have the Lord to fight for us."

While Sennacherib fought the strong city of Lachish, his field commander challenged Jerusalem. Hezekiah sent officials to negotiate a peace treaty. Using gold stripped from the temple and the palace treasures, he sent out his tribute—11 tons of silver and one ton of gold.

But Sennacherib wanted more than their wealth. He wanted them to surrender so he could deport them. And the man he sent to conquer them was skilled at demoralizing his enemies.

Shouting loudly in Hebrew, so people could hear, the commander called out: "Don't listen to Hezekiah! The Lord will not deliver you! When has any god ever stopped Assyria?"

But the whole time he spoke, the people kept silent. They knew what he was trying to do.

Hezekiah and his officials tore their clothes in grief. Then they contacted Isaiah.

The prophet replied: "Do not be afraid. The Lord will put a spirit in King Sennacherib that prompts him to return to Assyria after hearing a report. There he will be killed with a sword."

Meanwhile, the commander withdrew his forces so he could help Sennacherib attack Libnah. But by then, Egypt's army was on its way. Judah would have an ally.

So Sennacherib sent Hezekiah another message, hoping to force a surrender: "Do not let your god deceive you. Did any gods deliver all the nations my forefathers destroyed?"

Hezekiah spread out Sennacherib's letter and prayed. "O Lord, Almighty, listen to how he has insulted the living God. Assyria has destroyed many nations. Now deliver us so that all kingdoms may know that you alone are God."

The Lord listened to his prayer and sent Isaiah to him. "The Lord says, 'Because you have prayed, I will save this city for my name's sake and for David's sake.' "

The angel of the Lord killed 185,000 Assyrian soldiers by a plague. So Sennacherib returned to Nineveh. Years later, two of his own sons killed him in a temple.

TBC 131

The Turning Point

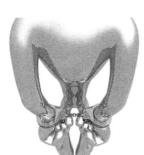

TBC Book One, Chapter 132
2 Kings 21:1-26; 2 Chronicles 33:1-25

In the 15 years added to Hezekiah's life, he fathered a son who would change Judah's destiny. No king of Judah reigned longer or did more evil than Hezekiah's son Manasseh. At age 12 he began ruling in partnership with his father. But after Hezekiah died, Manasseh killed many innocent people. Then he showed loyalty to Assyria by worshiping its pagan gods.

Manasseh followed the evil practices of the nations that God had driven out of the land. He rebuilt the high places his father had destroyed. He built altars to Baal and Asherah poles. He even placed pagan altars in the temple, the sacred place that bears God's name.

Perhaps imitating the Babylonians and Assyrians who practiced astrology, Manasseh also put altars in the temple courts to worship the stars. He practiced witchcraft and divination, consulting mediums and spiritists. He even sacrificed his own sons in the fire as offerings.

God had promised never again to make his people leave the land he gave them—if they obeyed God's Law. Manasseh, however, led them away from the Lord and refused to listen to the prophets' warnings. Some think he had the prophet Isaiah sawed in two.

Manasseh had done more evil than the wicked Amorites. Because of him, Judah had returned to idolatry. And because of him, it was time for God's judgment.

The Lord said, "I am going to bring great disaster on Judah and Jerusalem. When people hear what I am going to do, it will make their ears tingle."

From the day they left Egypt, hundreds of years earlier, the sins of God's people had been mounting. So God would use the same standard against Judah that he used against Israel: "I will wipe out Jerusalem. I will forsake my remnant and hand them over to their enemies."

Despite this message, Manasseh and his people still refused to heed God's warnings. So the Lord stirred up the army commanders from the king of Assyria. They returned to Judah and invaded the land. Assyria's forces conquered Judah and captured King Manasseh. They put a hook in his nose, bound his feet in shackles, and then took him away to Babylon. There the Assyrian commanders would crack down on all the vassal kings suspected of rebellion. If Manasseh planned to sever their ties, the Assyrians would cure him of such notions.

Never had Manasseh faced such a terrible ordeal. But he knew why all this was happening. In his greatest moment of need, Manasseh humbled himself and turned to the Lord. He prayed that God would permit him to return to Jerusalem. The Lord was so moved by his sincere, humble prayer that he granted his request.

When Manasseh realized that his captors had decided to let him return to Judah, he knew that the Spirit of the Lord had prompted his captors to make that decision. Now Manasseh knew for certain that the Lord was God.

As soon as he returned to Jerusalem, Manasseh got rid of the foreign gods and removed the altars from the temple. He gratefully sacrificed peace offerings and thanksgiving offerings.

Manasseh then commanded his people to worship the Lord God. But the nation's many years of idolatry were hard to erase. The people now sacrificed to the Lord, but they did it at the same high places that were used for pagan worship.

After reigning for 55 years, Manasseh died and was buried in the palace garden. His 22-year-old son, Amon, succeeded him as king. But Amon did not walk with the Lord. He worshiped idols and did much evil, just as his father had done most of his life.

Two years after he was crowned, some of Amon's own officials conspired against him and killed him. The people of Judah knew this was wrong, so they found the men who did it and put them to death. But now who would take Amon's place as king? His eight-year-old son.

TBC 132

The Boy on the Throne

TBC Book One, Chapter 133
2 Kings 22:1-23:30;
2 Chronicles 34; 35

At the age of eight, young Josiah became king of Judah. He was born to Amon when his grandfather, Manasseh, turned to the Lord. The young king had advisors to help him, and when he was 16, he made one of the most important decisions of his life—he began to seek the Lord.

Throughout his life, in fact, Josiah made decisions that pleased God. When he was 20, he traveled throughout Judah and began to destroy places of pagan worship. He must have regained much of Israel's territory, for he destroyed many idols throughout Israel, too.

By the time he was 26, King Josiah turned his attention to repairing the temple. During his reign, money had been collected at the temple door. Josiah ordered that the money be used to cover the cost of repairing the temple and paying the workers.

While gathering the money, Hilkiah the high priest found the Book of the Law in the temple. He brought it to Shaphan, the king's secretary, and Shaphan read it to Josiah. When King Josiah realized the many ways Judah had disobeyed God, he tore his clothes in grief.

Josiah sent his officials to find a prophet. So they went to Huldah, a prophetess, and she sent this word from the Lord: "The Lord says, 'I will bring disaster on this place, but not in your time, Josiah, because you humbled yourself and wept when you heard my words.' "

The king knew he must turn his people back to the Lord. So he summoned all the people to the temple. Standing before them, he read aloud what the book said about God's covenant. Then he led the people to pledge that they would keep that covenant and obey the Lord.

Josiah ordered the people to destroy all their objects of idolatry—altars, shrines, Asherah poles, household gods, and all the high places, as well as the idolatrous priests. At Bethel he fulfilled a previous prophecy by digging up bones and burning them on the altar to desecrate it.

On the fourteenth day of the first month that year, King Josiah led all the people in celebrating the Passover in Jerusalem. He appointed priests to specific duties. Then he instructed the Levites on the right way to carry the holy ark of the covenant.

Josiah commanded the people to form groups according to their tribe and family. The Levites would then spread out among them and slaughter the Passover lambs. The king and his officials generously provided thousands of sheep and goats for the people's offerings.

The priests sprinkled the blood over the altar while other Levites skinned the animals. Burnt sacrifices were offered for each family. Then the meat was roasted and served. Meanwhile, the musicians played. Not since Samuel had the people celebrated like this.

Josiah ruled for another 18 years. The Assyrians began to weaken, so Babylon and the Medes joined forces to conquer Nineveh, Assyria's capital. Many years had passed since Jonah preached to the Ninevites. They had returned to their wicked ways, and judgment was coming.

When the Babylonian army advanced toward Haran, Egypt sent an army to help Assyria. But Josiah's army blocked them. Josiah was acting as an ally to Babylon, in hopes of breaking Assyria's stronghold. Yet the Lord had not called him to take that stand.

Egypt's King Neco sent a message to Josiah, urging him to turn back: "Listen, King of Judah, what quarrel do I have with you? It is not you or your people that I am attacking. It is the Lord himself who has told me to do this. So stop opposing God's will, or he will destroy you."

But Josiah was determined to defeat Assyria. He wondered if Neco's words were true. Would God punish him for engaging in this battle?

So Josiah disguised himself and returned to the battle. He led soldiers to cut off Neco's army from helping Assyria. On the plains of Megiddo, archers shot Josiah. He died soon after in Jerusalem. With great mourning, Josiah was buried with honor in the tombs of his fathers.

TBC 133

Peeking into the Future

TBC Book One, Chapter 134
Zephaniah

Young Josiah had reigned for at least 10 years when the prophet Zephaniah foretold of God's coming judgment. He began prophesying years before Josiah died, while the young king was still reigning. In fact, his words may have influenced Josiah a great deal. Zephaniah warned that God would destroy Judah's idols and those who worshiped them. He also warned of a future day of judgment that would come upon the whole world.

Referring to that judgment yet to come, God spoke through Zephaniah: "I will sweep away everything from the face of the earth, both men and animals, birds and fish. Only rubble will be left to the wicked when I cut off mankind from the face of the earth."

Referring to Judah, the Lord said, "I will cut off every remnant of Baal, every pagan priest, those who worship the stars and bow down to Molech, those who turn from the Lord and refuse to seek him." And that indeed happened during Josiah's reign.

Then the prophet foretold what he saw in the distant future, the final judgment of God upon all mankind. The Lord says he will pour out his wrath on the world because of man's sins. What God does at that time will terrify everyone. Things that people rely on, like wealth, will not help them at all.

After describing how awful that day will be, the prophet urges the people of his nation, saying, "Gather together before God's judgment comes and seek the Lord. You who do obey the Lord, humble yourselves before him. Perhaps the Lord will shelter you on that day."

The prophet also predicts the judgment soon to come upon Judah's neighbors. The Philistine cities of Gaza and Ashkelon would come to ruins. Judgment would fall on Ashdod and Ekron when they least expect it, and Judah's shepherds would gain their coastland.

The Moabites and Ammonites, descendants of Lot, were Israel's ongoing enemies. They had constantly mocked God's people and tried to conquer them. Because of their pride, God would destroy them like Sodom and Gomorrah. And he would give their land to his people.

Nineveh had become the capital city of mighty Assyria. The people who lived there felt secure. They thought no other city in the world was as great as theirs; surely no harm would come to them. But they were wrong. God would destroy both Nineveh and Assyria. In fact, not long after Zephaniah prophesied this, Nineveh was conquered by Babylon.

Sometimes a prophet speaks of a group of people as if he is describing a person. That is, the prophet personifies an entire group. Zephaniah says Jerusalem "obeys no one. She refuses to accept correction. She does not trust in the Lord nor turn to him. Her leaders oppress people and violate God's Laws."

Still speaking through Zephaniah, the Lord says: "I have destroyed cities and cut off nations. I thought surely then you would fear me and accept my correction. But still you acted corruptly. Now you must wait for the day that I pour out my wrath on all the nations."

After God brings judgment on all the nations, his people will finally turn back to him and serve him, from all parts of the earth. Among those living in Jerusalem, God will have destroyed those who are haughty and proud. Only the meek and humble who have trusted the Lord will remain to worship him.

Jerusalem stands as a special place, the city where God has chosen to reveal himself to the whole earth. Though his people are destined to face terror, in the end, God will deal with their enemies. Then the Lord himself will give his people a special place of honor, among all peoples of the earth.

TBC 134

How the Mighty Have Fallen

The discipline on God's people was about to end.

TBC Book One, Chapter 135
Nahum

The time for judgment had finally come. For hundreds of years, the cruel, powerful nation of Assyria had oppressed Israel and Judah. God had allowed this to happen to bring judgment on his people. But now the time had come for judgment on Assyria. Like Zephaniah, the prophet Nahum lived during Josiah's lifetime. He revealed to God's people what the Lord was about to do to Assyria.

Nineveh had become Assyria's capital. God had once spared the city from judgment because the Ninevites repented. But now they had again become proud, arrogant, and as cruel as ever. Their wicked actions made them enemies of God. He would soon punish them.

Yet the Lord himself is good. He protects those who trust in him and cares for them in times of trouble. But those who rise up against the Lord do not stand a chance. Sennacherib had plotted evil against God's people, and now God's judgment would come.

The Assyrians had conquered other peoples and forced them to help fight Assyria's battles. God had allowed Assyria to gain power for his own purposes. But now God would break Assyria's stronghold. He would destroy the Ninevites as well as their gods.

The Assyrians' King Sennacherib had once surrounded all of Jerusalem with his army. Recalling that time, Nahum predicted a day when God's people would face a similar threat. In that distant day in the future, however, they will look to the mountains and see a messenger of peace. Then they will celebrate and worship the Lord, for their enemies will be destroyed.

But in regard to the near future, the prophet addresses the Assyrians in a mocking tone: "You are about to be attacked, Nineveh. Guard your city and brace yourselves!"

The discipline on God's people was about to end. God would restore their splendor and send warriors on chariots to punish Nineveh.

The Tigris River was on the west side of the city, and a moat surrounded the other three sides. Nineveh's soldiers would open the flood gates to drive away their enemies. But instead, the walls would collapse, for God had decreed that Nineveh would be destroyed. Assyria's enemies would take all the gold, silver, and treasures that they had stripped from other nations.

"I am against you," the Lord declares. "I will burn up your chariots. Like a lion you conquered your enemies. Now the sword will devour your young."

No other nation had dealt so cruelly with its enemies as the Assyrians. But now all the evil they had done would come back upon themselves. God would destroy Nineveh and bring Assyria to ruins. Then all the nations would see what happens to a kingdom that opposes God.

As if speaking to the city of Nineveh, Nahum says, "Do you think you are any better than Thebes?" It was a great city in Egypt, protected from attack by the Nile River. But just as Assyria had devastated Thebes, so also would a conqueror destroy Nineveh.

"Draw water to prepare for a siege," Nahum says. "Stoke up the fire for building bricks to repair your walls."

But water and fire are also symbols of judgment. Nahum says that Assyria's merchants, like locusts, have multiplied and devoured everything in sight.

Assyria's guards and officials are also compared to a swarm of locusts, unable to fly in cold weather. But just as locusts fly away when the sun appears, so also will Nineveh's leaders vanish. And all who hear about Nineveh's downfall will clap their hands in joy.

TBC 135

The Weeping Prophet

TBC Book One, Chapter 136
Jeremiah 1:1 - 6:30

While Josiah was still reigning over Judah, God raised up a young man who became known as "the weeping prophet." Jeremiah, the son of a priest named Hilkiah, grew up in the land of Benjamin. During Josiah's thirteenth year as king, the Lord began to speak to Jeremiah.

"Before I formed you in the womb," said the Lord, "I knew you, and I appointed you as a prophet to the nations."

"Ah, Sovereign Lord," Jeremiah said, "I wouldn't know what to say; I am so young."

"Do not say that," the Lord replied. "Go where I send you and say what I tell you. Do not be afraid of those I will send you to, for I will be with you, and I will rescue you."

Then the Lord touched his mouth and said, "I am putting my words in your mouth. Today I appoint you over kingdoms and nations, to tear down and to build up."

The Lord then gave Jeremiah a vision.

"What do you see, Jeremiah?" the Lord asked.

"I see the branch of an almond tree," he replied. It was also called the "wakeful tree."

"You have seen correctly," the Lord said. "It means I am watching to fulfill my word."

God gave Jeremiah another vision and said, "Now what do you see?"

"I see a boiling pot tilting away from the north."

The Lord explained: "I will use the kingdoms of the north to pour out disaster against Judah. For my people have forsaken me and worshiped other gods.

"You must stand up to these people and say whatever I tell you. Do not be terrified by them or I myself will terrify you. I am making you an iron pillar, a bronze wall to stand against the people of Judah. They will fight against you, but I will rescue you.

"Speak to the people in Jerusalem and say, 'When I led you in the wilderness, you were devoted to me. But since then you have defiled my land. You exchanged my Glory for worthless idols. You have forsaken me, the living water, for cisterns that cannot even hold water.' "

In spite of King Josiah's efforts, Judah remained guilty: "I sent Israel away from this land because of her idolatry," the Lord said. "But Judah learned nothing from watching that. So now I find that rebellious Israel is more righteous than Judah who pretends to worship me."

Through Jeremiah, the Lord urged his exiled people to repent: "Confess your guilt and return to me, faithless Israel. One day I will give you shepherds after my own heart and bring you back to Zion. In the end, Judah will join Israel and come from a northern land to this land. Then all nations will worship at my throne in Jerusalem."

Jeremiah used symbolic images to speak to the people of Judah and Jerusalem: "Break up your unplowed ground; do not sow among thorns. Circumcise your hearts. An army from a distant land will surround Judah because she has rebelled against the Lord."

The Lord said, "Jeremiah, if you can find even one honest person in Jerusalem who seeks the truth, I will forgive this city." But there was no one.

So the Lord told Jeremiah, "Just as my people have forsaken me and served foreign gods, now they will serve foreigners in another land.

"Everyone is greedy for wealth," said the Lord. "Even the prophets and priests are deceitful. They have falsely reassured my people, comforting them with predictions of peace. But I see an army coming, and it will purify my people the way fire purges metal."

The Lord had given Jeremiah strong messages to deliver. But that was only the beginning of what lay ahead for this young prophet. . . .

TBC 136

Jeremiah's Mission

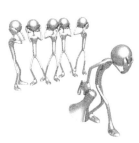

TBC Book One, Chapter 137
2 Kings 23:31-37;
Jeremiah 7:1-15; 26:1-24; 11:1-23

All of Judah felt a deep sense of loss. Their gallant king, Josiah, had died after challenging Egypt in battle. Jeremiah honored him by composing songs that lamented his death. Josiah's 23-year-old son, Jehoahaz, then ascended to the throne, but only for three months.

Judah was now forced to pay tribute to Egypt. The pharaoh removed Jehoahaz from the throne, for he was a wicked king. He replaced him with another son of Josiah, Eliakim, and changed his name to Jehoiakim. The 25-year-old king taxed the people to pay Pharaoh.

Jeremiah stood at the temple gate and said, "You think you are safe because God's temple is here. But the truth is you must change your ways. Stop oppressing foreigners and widows and orphans. Stop shedding innocent blood and worshiping other gods.

"The Lord says, 'Do you think you can steal and murder, commit adultery and lie in court, then stand before me? This house bears my Name, and I am watching. I first made a dwelling for my Name in Shiloh, and look what I did to it because of Israel's wickedness!' "

No sooner had Jeremiah finished speaking, when the priests, prophets, and others suddenly grabbed him. "You must die!" one of them shouted. "How dare you prophesy in the Lord's name that this temple will be like Shiloh and this city deserted!"

They took Jeremiah and tried him before city officials, demanding he be sentenced to death. Jeremiah replied, "What I spoke were God's words. You must change your ways. Do to me whatever you want. But if you kill me, God will judge you for shedding innocent blood."

The officials said, "This man should not be killed! He has spoken in the name of the Lord."

Then an elder spoke persuasively, "The prophet Micah predicted that Jerusalem would become a heap of rubble. Did King Hezekiah have him killed? No, the people repented, so then God relented from judging them."

Before Jeremiah spoke these words, another prophet of the Lord had once delivered the same message. At that time, King Jehoiakim and his officials sentenced the man to death. He escaped to Egypt but was caught there, brought back, and put to death.

But the Lord protected Jeremiah, for his mission was far from over. He went to each of the gates of Jerusalem and gave yet another message. He said, "The Lord says, 'Keep my Sabbath day holy; do not bring loads of merchandise through these gates on the Sabbath. If you disobey, my fire will consume Jerusalem.'"

The Lord sent Jeremiah throughout Judah to remind the people of the terms of his covenant. "God told our forefathers, 'Obey me, and you will be my people, and I will be your God. I will give you this land.' But they disobeyed him and brought down God's curses."

Then the Lord told Jeremiah, "Both Israel and Judah have sinned and broken our covenant, just as their forefathers did. So I have decreed disaster for them. Judah has as many gods as it does towns. Do not pray for them any longer, for I will not listen to their pleas."

Meanwhile, in Jeremiah's hometown of Anathoth, the men were plotting to kill him. By killing him now, he would have no descendants to carry on his name. In their thinking, that would be the ultimate punishment. But the Lord had other intentions, and he revealed their wicked plans to Jeremiah.

"I will punish them," the Lord told Jeremiah. "It is they who will die with no descendants."

TBC 137

'Why Do the Wicked Prosper?'

TBC Book One, Chapter 138
Jeremiah 12:1-17; 16:1-17:18; 7:16-10:25

Jeremiah knew God so intimately that he could talk to him about anything. So one day he opened up about something that troubled him deeply. "Why do wicked people prosper?" he asked. "They say prayers, but they don't love you. They don't even know you. Why don't you judge them?"

God knew that Jeremiah felt betrayed, especially since even his own friends from childhood had plotted to kill him.

"Do not let these things cause you to stumble," the Lord said. "I must warn you, it is going to get worse. Right now even your own family is speaking out against you."

The Lord continued: "Judgment is coming, Jeremiah. My household, too, has turned against me. So I will forsake them. Those who shepherd my people will ruin my vineyard. Because of them, this land will become desolate. An army of destroyers will be my sword.

"The surrounding nations will think this is their chance to seize this land. So I will uproot them too. But I will also have compassion. One day I will bring these nations back to their own land. And if they worship me as Lord, I will plant them among my people.

"Because of the disaster that is coming, Jeremiah, you must not marry and have children while living in this land. The people here will die of deadly diseases, of sword and of famine. Do not show sympathy for those families, for I have withdrawn my love.

"When the people ask why I have decreed disaster, say, 'Because your fathers turned away from the Lord to worship other gods. And you have behaved even more wickedly than they did. So you will be thrown into another land where you will serve other gods.'

"A time is coming, though, when I will draw all of my people out of the countries where I have banished them. I will send many fishermen to catch them. Then I will send many hunters because of their sin. In the end, all the nations will know my power and might.

"Cursed is any person who puts his trust in man's power, anyone who has turned away from the Lord. But blessed is the one who trusts the Lord. Like a tree by a stream, he always bears fruit. The Lord searches minds and hearts; he rewards each one as he deserves.

"Jeremiah, do not pray for these people. Do you know what they are doing even now? They are making offerings to a god they call Queen of Heaven.' All their sacrifices to me are worthless, for they refuse to obey me. But when you tell them that, they will not listen.

"They have set up idols in the house that bears my Name. They have sacrificed their sons and daughters. So I will now let them be slaughtered, with their bones exposed to the very sun, moon, and stars that they worshiped. And those who are captured will wish that they had died.

"Say to these people, 'No one repents of his wickedness. Even birds obey their appointed time to migrate, but my people do not heed my requirements. Do not boast about your wisdom, your strength, your riches. Only one thing is worth boasting about—boast that you know me.' "

Jeremiah prays, "O Lord, there is no one is like you. Man's idols are a fraud; they have no life. They will perish. You alone are Maker of all things."

Then Jeremiah returned to the people and shouted, "Gather your belongings! Prepare to leave. For the Lord will hurl you out as captives."

TBC 138

Like Clay in the Potter's Hands

TBC Book One, Chapter 139
Jeremiah 18:1 - 20:18

God speaks to his people in many ways, and almost anything can serve as a symbol of his plans. One day the Lord sent Jeremiah to a potter's house. When he arrived, he saw the potter working at his wheel. The clay pot he held was marred, so he threw it back on the wheel to shape it again. While Jeremiah watched, the Lord spoke to him.

"Jeremiah, you must say, 'O House of Israel, like clay in the potter's hand, so are you in my hands. If I plan to tear down a nation and it repents, then I will have mercy. But if I plan to build up a nation and it does evil, then I will change my plans.' Say to the people of Judah, 'The Lord says, "I am preparing disaster for you. So turn from your evil ways, each one of you, and change your behavior."'

"But I know they will not listen," said the Lord. "Like wind I will scatter them. I will turn my back on the day of their disaster."

So Jeremiah told the people all that the Lord had commanded him to say. But instead of taking his words to heart, they plotted against him and dug a pit for him.

"Lord," Jeremiah prayed, "hear what they are saying! You know how I had prayed on their behalf. Lord, judge them as you planned."

Some time later, Jeremiah took a clay jar and stood at the Potsherd Gate.

"You have made this a place of foreign gods," he said. "You have also shed innocent blood by sacrificing your children. So the days are coming when this will become the Valley of Slaughter.

"The Lord says, 'I will make Judah and Jerusalem fall by the sword. Their enemies will lay siege to Jerusalem. The siege will be so terrible that people will eat the flesh of their own sons and daughters. Finally, they will even eat the flesh of one another.'"

Then Jeremiah threw the jar to the ground and smashed it to pieces.

"The Lord Almighty says, 'I will smash this nation and the city of Jerusalem, just as this jar is smashed beyond repair. For all these houses where you worshiped the starry hosts and other gods are defiled.'"

Jeremiah completed his mission to prophesy in Topheth then returned to Jerusalem, where he stood in the court of the temple. Again he spoke out about the disaster the Lord would bring upon Jerusalem and Judah. When the priest Pashhur heard what he was saying, he was furious. He ordered that Jeremiah be beaten and put in stocks.

It seemed to Jeremiah that every time he obeyed the Lord and spoke his words, it only brought him grief. "O Lord," he cried, "everyone is against me. All day long people mock me. Even my friends plot against me. I wish I had never been born!

"Sometimes I think, 'That's it. I'm not going to mention anything about the Lord. I won't speak his words anymore.' But then I can't live with myself. His word is in my heart. It's like fire in my bones. I can't hold it in. I have to speak his words.

"But I know, O Lord, that you are with me like a mighty warrior. You will cause my enemies to stumble. O Lord Almighty, you who examine the righteous and search a person's mind and heart, let me see your vengeance on them, for I have committed myself to you."

The next day, Pashhur released Jeremiah from the stocks. Then Jeremiah faced him and said, "You will see your friends killed by sword. Judah and all its wealth will be handed over to Babylon. There you will die, you and all those to whom you have prophesied lies."

TBC 139

The Cup of God's Wrath

TBC Book One, Chapter 140
Jeremiah 25:1-38; 46-51

Time was running out for Judah. The word of the Lord came to Jeremiah during Jehoiakim's fourth year as king, the year Nebuchadnezzar became king of Babylon. Standing before the people, Jeremiah said, "For 23 years now I have spoken to you again and again, but you have not listened.

"Again and again the Lord has sent his prophets to you with his words, 'Turn from your evil ways so you can stay forever in the land I gave you. Do not provoke me to anger by worshiping what your hands have made. You are only bringing harm to yourselves.' "But you did not listen. Therefore, the Lord Almighty says, 'I will send my servant Nebuchadnezzar, king of Babylon, against this land and the surrounding nations. It will become a desolate wasteland, and you will serve the king of Babylon 70 years.

" 'After those 70 years are fulfilled, I will punish Babylon and its king for their guilt. I will make it desolate and do to it all I have done to these nations. Then Babylon will be enslaved by many nations; I will punish its people according to their actions.' "

God often spoke symbolically to his prophets, as if to paint a picture in words. In a vision to Jeremiah one day, he said, "Take this cup from me. It is filled with my wrath. Make Jerusalem, Judah, and all its neighbors drink from it. All nations on earth will drink from this cup."

Jeremiah prophesied what would happen to Egypt: "The Lord says, 'I am about to bring my punishment on Pharaoh, on Egypt, and on her gods. I will also punish those who have relied on Egypt for protection. They will be handed over to Nebuchadnezzar and taken in exile.' "

Before Egypt fell to Babylon, Jeremiah predicted that Pharaoh would attack the Philistines in Gaza. But this was just a shadow of greater judgment yet to come. Babylon would invade like a flood. Overcome by terror, the Philistines would abandon their own children.

The Moabites, descendants of Lot, were proud of their warriors. Over the years Moabite marauders invaded Judah, and they gained much wealth.

Jeremiah prophesied that God would use Babylon to destroy Moab. The Moabites, too, would be taken into exile.

Jeremiah also predicted the destruction of Ammon and Edom, as well as Damascus, Kedar, Hazor, and Elam. The Ammonites, also descendants of Lot, had trusted in their great wealth. And the Edomites were fierce. But nothing could stave off God's judgment.

Although the Lord would permit the Babylonians to destroy the temple and to slaughter many people, they would still be held accountable. Babylon, too, would suffer God's punishment. Jeremiah predicted a day when God would raise up the Medes to conquer Babylon.

These were not the only nations that would drink from God's cup of wrath. The prophecy given to Jeremiah also speaks of the distant future, a time yet to come. In that day, the Lord will bring judgment against all mankind, against every nation on earth.

Just as the shepherds over God's people had failed them, so also in the end times will spiritual leaders see that they have failed. Like fine pottery that falls to the ground, they will be shattered. In that day, there will be no place to escape from God's judgment.

TBC 140

A Shocking Revelation

TBC Book One, Chapter 141
Habakkuk

Great changes were about to take place for the entire nation of Judah, and even the prophets were surprised by what God had planned. The Lord sent his people yet another prophet, Habakkuk, who lived during the time of Jeremiah. While Jeremiah spoke of things soon to happen to Judah, Habakkuk spoke of distant things yet to come upon the whole world. Through Habakkuk, God's people overhear a conversation between God and the prophet, one that God wants us to hear.

Like Jeremiah, Habakkuk knows the Lord intimately, and he is not afraid to be honest with God. "O Lord," he says, "I keep calling out to you, and it's as though you do not listen. I see violence everywhere. Justice is never served. The wicked overrule the righteous."

The Lord replied, "I will deal with the wicked, and you will be amazed at how I will do this. In your lifetime, I will raise up the Babylonians, those ruthless people, and they will sweep across the nations. They will advance like a vulture swooping to devour."

Habakkuk is shocked. "O Lord, my Holy One, I know you have appointed them to execute your judgment. I know you cannot tolerate wrongdoing, for you are pure. Why, then, do you choose such a wicked people to swallow up those more righteous than they are?"

Instead of answering him, the Lord said, "Write down what I am telling you and preserve it. I am revealing to you what will happen in the distant future, in the end times. I speak of one who is arrogant and greedy. He will take captive all nations.

"His victims will say, 'Woe to him who has become wealthy by conquering other nations and robbing them of what they possess.' You have made yourself powerful by crushing other peoples and shedding much blood. Those who are left will make you their victim.

"The Lord is sovereign over all creation. Though mankind struggles to achieve great things apart from God, their labors are in vain. In the end, it will just bring more judgment upon them. The destruction of lands, cities, and people will bring God's wrath.

"Of what value is an idol, since it is made by man? Woe to the person who thinks an idol will come to life. It is covered with silver and gold; no breath of life is in it. But the living God reigns in his holy temple; let all the earth bow to him."

Habakkuk then records his prayer, a song of praise so God's people will lift their hearts to the Lord, no matter what hardships they face: "O Lord, I stand in awe of you. Your actions among your people are famous. When you revealed yourself, the mountains shook."

Habakkuk uses poetic phrases to paint pictures. "Were you angry with the waters when you rode your horses and your chariots?" God had delivered his people from Egypt by parting the Red Sea. But Egypt's chariots and horses were swallowed by the waters.

The prophet alludes to the past and hints at the future as though both have already happened. "Sun and moon stood still at the glint of your arrows (perhaps a reminder of Joshua's famous battle). Then he says, "You threshed the nations to save your people."

Habakkuk confesses, "I tremble at your coming judgment. Yet I will wait patiently for you to deal with our enemies. Though the land becomes barren and our livelihood fails, I will rejoice in the Lord. For you will one day set my feet on higher ground."

TBC 141

One Last Chance

TBC Book One, Chapter 142
Jeremiah 36:1-32; 2 Kings 24:1-20;
Jeremiah 45:1-5; 35:1-19

God decided to give his people one more chance. In the fourth year of King Jehoiakim's reign, he commanded the prophet Jeremiah to write down the words of the Lord. "Write down everything I have told you" said the Lord. "When the people of Judah hear of these coming disasters, perhaps they will turn away from their wickedness."

At this time, the Assyrian Empire was crumbling, and Egypt feared the rise of Babylon. So Pharaoh Neco sent his army to help the Assyrians defend the city of Carchemish. But Prince Nebuchadnezzar defeated them, and Egypt lost its control over Judah.

Egypt's defeat marked a turning point. Babylon was quickly rising in power. Perhaps now God's people would listen. Jeremiah dictated his prophecies to an assistant, a scribe named Baruch. He would send the scribe to the temple to read the scrolls aloud, for Jeremiah was not free to leave.

After Baruch had written down all of Jeremiah's prophecies, Jeremiah said to him, "The Lord has also given me a message for you, Baruch. For he has heard you complaining about your situation. He has heard you say to yourself, 'The Lord has added sorrow to my pain.'

"The Lord says to you: 'I am about to uproot what I have planted. You are disappointed because you had hoped for great things for yourself in this life. Let go of those ambitions. For I will bring disaster on all these people, but I will allow you to escape with your life.' "

After hearing the Lord's word to him, Baruch took the scroll and went to the temple. It was now the ninth month of Jehoiakim's fifth year, and the king had proclaimed a fast for those in Jerusalem. Standing in an upper courtyard, Baruch read to the people from the scroll.

One of the those listening to Baruch was Micaiah, the grandson of Shaphan, who was one of the king's officials. Micaiah told his father and the other officials what Baruch had said. Immediately, they summoned Baruch.

When Baruch arrived, one of the officials motioned him to a chair. "Please, sit down," he said, "and read to us what you just read to the people."

So Baruch read to them. When he finished, they looked at one another in fear.

"We must tell these words to the king," said one of the men. "Did Jeremiah dictate all this?"

"Yes," Baruch replied.

The man looked at Baruch with concern. "Then both you and Jeremiah must go and hide while we read this to the king."

The men urged King Jehoiakim and his other officials to hear Jeremiah's words. The king agreed. But what he did then made them even more afraid of what the Lord might do. After every three or four columns that were read, the king cut off each portion and threw it into the fireplace.

Then the king ordered Jeremiah and Baruch be arrested. But the Lord had hidden them. While they were in hiding, they learned what the king had done. At God's command, they rewrote all of Jeremiah's words, and the Lord gave them even more words of prophecy.

Some time later, the Lord sent Jeremiah to the Recabite tribe to offer them some wine. But the Recabites replied, "Our forefather Jonadab, son of Recab, said we must never drink wine nor settle down with houses. We must always live in tents as nomads."

The Lord wanted Judah to learn a lesson from them: "In every generation this family obeyed its forefather. But my people have not obeyed me or listened to my prophets. So I will judge them. But I will bless Jonadab; he will always have a relative to serve me."

TBC 142

Turning a Deaf Ear

TBC Book One, Chapter 143
2 Kings 24:1-9; 2 Chronicles 36:6,7;
Jeremiah 13:1-14:6; 15:1-4; 22; 23

Judah's worst nightmare was now coming true. Not long after Nebuchadnezzar defeated Egypt's army, Babylonian forces invaded Judah and forced King Jehoiakim to pay tribute as a vassal. After three years, the king rebelled against Babylon and broke his agreement. So the Lord allowed raiding parties from Babylon and other nations to destroy Judah.

Nebuchadnezzar's army attacked Jerusalem, pillaged the temple, and captured King Jehoiakim. They bound in him bronze shackles, intending to take him to Babylon, but apparently, he died in Jerusalem. His 18-year-old son, Jehoiachin became the new king. But like his father, he too was wicked. He ruled for only three months.

Meanwhile, the Lord continued to speak to Jeremiah. He commanded him to buy a linen belt and wear it, without letting it touch water. Then God told him to hide the belt in a crevice. Many days later God commanded him to dig up the belt, but by then it was ruined. The Lord was using this as an illustration.

He said to Jeremiah, "The people of Judah and Jerusalem have stubbornly turned to other gods. So I will ruin them just like this belt. As a belt is bound to a man's waist, so have I bound Israel and Judah to me, but they have not listened."

The time was coming when the Lord would make them helpless, as if they were in a drunken stupor. He rebuked both Jehoiachin and his mother, the queen, warning them that all Judah would go into exile. The allies they trusted in would become their captors.

During this time, the Lord sent a drought. No rain meant no crops, and food was getting scarce.

The famine was so bad that Jeremiah prayed, "O Lord, we have sinned. But do not forsake us. Help us, for we bear your name."

The Lord replied, "These people are being punished for their sins."

Then the Lord told Jeremiah, "Do not pray any longer for the well-being of these people. Although they fast and make offerings, I will not listen to them. I will destroy them by death, famine, and plague. Those who are predicting peace are false prophets.

"Even if Moses and Samuel were to stand before me and pray, my heart would not go out to these people. Send them away from my presence. Some are destined to die by plague, some by sword. Some will starve to death, and some will be taken captive."

Judah's kings also faced judgment. Jehoahaz died in captivity because he treated his people like slaves to build a bigger palace for himself. Arrogant Jehoiakim also died in captivity. Wicked Jehoiachin and his queen mother would also both be exiled to Babylon.

God held the leaders responsible. The Lord said, "You have caused my flock to be scattered and driven away. But one day I will give them other shepherds. I will raise up a son of David as King. Then I will gather the remnant of my people from all nations."

Judah's spiritual leaders were also guilty. The Lord said, "The prophets speak visions from their own minds, proclaiming peace. But who among them has ever stood in my council? For if they had, they would have turned my people from their evil ways."

The Lord said, "I am against those prophets who speak lies in my name. They speak their own words as if it is the word of the Lord. But my word is like fire and like a hammer that breaks a rock in pieces."

Then he added to Jeremiah, "Let the one who really has my word speak it faithfully."

TBC 143

Nebuchadnezzar's Nightmare

TBC Book One, Chapter 144
Daniel 1:1-21; 2:1-49

Of all the possessions Nebuchadnezzar had plundered, the most valuable had nothing to do with gold or silver. When Nebuchadnezzar's army invaded Judah and raided the temple, they also captured some young men from the royal family. All were handsome and intelligent, and all would be trained to serve Nebuchadnezzar. Among these young men were four particularly outstanding individuals, Daniel, Hananiah, Mishael, and Azariah.

In Babylon they were given choice foods from the king's table. But eating it would cause them to break God's Laws. So Daniel requested they eat only vegetables and drink only water.

"You will grow weak," their guardian replied.

But Daniel convinced him to let them try it for ten days.

At the end of those days, Daniel and his friends looked healthier than those who ate the king's food. So they continued with their own meals, and God blessed them with tremendous knowledge and wisdom. In fact, they surpassed all the other young men who served the king.

Early in his reign, King Nebuchadnezzar had a troubling dream. He summoned his wise men and demanded they tell him what he had dreamed and what it meant. He knew that if he had asked only what the dream meant, they might lie rather than admit they did not know.

Finally, one of the astrologers spoke up: "There isn't a man on earth who can do that! What the king is asking is too difficult."

His answer made the king furious. He ordered all the wise men killed—including Daniel and his friends. Arioch, the commander of the guard, came to take them to their fateful judgment.

Sensing that their lives were in danger, Daniel spoke to the guard tactfully and learned what had happened. When he realized that one man's reply now meant the death of them all, he asked if he might have time to try to answer the king's question. The commander delivered Daniel's plea, and the king granted his request.

All night long, Daniel and his friends prayed earnestly for God to reveal the answer. The next day, Daniel appeared before the king.

"Can you tell me my dream and interpret it?" the king asked.

Daniel replied, "No person can do that, O King. But there is a God in heaven who does reveal mysteries, and he is the one who has revealed it to me.

"You saw a large statue, its head made of gold, its chest and arms silver, its belly and thighs bronze, its legs iron, and its feet partly iron, partly clay. Then a rock, not cut by man, smashed the statue's feet and became a mountain. It filled the whole earth.

"Here is the interpretation: You, O King, are the king of kings. The God of heaven has given you dominion, might, and glory. He has placed in your hands mankind and the beasts of the field and birds of the air. As ruler over them, you are that head of gold.

"The silver is a lesser kingdom to rise up after yours. The bronze is a third world kingdom. The iron is a fourth kingdom that will break all others. The feet show it will be partly strong, partly brittle. Its people are a mixture and will not remain united.

"But the God of heaven will set up a kingdom that will never be destroyed. It will crush all those kingdoms and bring them to an end. That is the meaning of the rock not carved out by human hands. God has shown you what will happen in the future, O King."

Immediately King Nebuchadnezzar fell prostrate before Daniel. "Surely your God is the God of gods, the Lord of kings, and the revealer of mysteries," he said.

Thanks to Daniel, all the wise men were saved. Then the king appointed Daniel as a ruler over Babylon. And right away, Daniel knew where he could find three faithful assistants. . . .

TBC 144

'We Will Never Bow'

TBC Book One, Chapter 145
Daniel 3:1-30

On the plains of Dura in Babylon, all of King Nebuchadnezzar's officials gathered for a special occasion. The king had ordered that a statue be built, nine feet high, nine feet wide, and plated with gold. It was now time to dedicate the statue, and according to the king's edict, everyone must participate.

A herald called out, "This is what the king commands, O peoples, nations, and men of every language. When you hear the music play, fall down and worship the image of gold. Anyone who does not do this will be thrown into a blazing furnace."

As soon as the people heard the sound of the music, they all fell down and worshiped the image. Many nations were represented, for the Babylonians had conquered many. But of all the people they had conquered, only the Jews refused to appear and bow down.

One of the king's astrologers realized that some individuals were missing. He approached Nebuchadnezzar and said, "O King, live forever! Did you notice those three Jews you appointed over Babylon have ignored your decree? They refuse to worship your image."

Nebuchadnezzar was enraged that anyone would dare to defy him. So he summoned Daniel's friends, whose Babylonian names were Shadrach, Meshach, and Abednego.

When they appeared, the king remembered these were the same men appointed by Daniel. With his voice now calm, he said to them, "I will give you another chance to bow to the image. If you refuse, you will be thrown into a blazing furnace. Then what god can save you?"

The three men looked at one another. Then one of them spoke up to render their reply.

"O King Nebuchadnezzar," he said, "we do not need to defend ourselves in this matter. Our God is able to save us from the furnace—and from you. But even if he chooses not to, we want you to know that we will not worship your gods or this image."

Their reply made the king furious, and his attitude toward them suddenly changed. He ordered that the furnace be made seven times hotter than it was. Then he commanded some of his strongest soldiers to tie up the three men and throw them into the furnace.

The three men were fully robed as the soldiers tied them up. The soldiers moved quickly to appease the king. But the fire was so hot that the soldiers themselves were set aflame while they shoved Shadrach, Meshach, and Abednego into the blazing furnace.

The king was seated a short distance away, and he didn't bat an eye when his men were burned to death. He continued to stare intently. Then all of a sudden, he leaped up and shouted, "Were there not three men that that we tied up and threw into the fire?"

"Yes, there were," replied one of his advisors.

"Look!" the king exclaimed. "There is someone else in there! Who is the fourth man? He is not tied or harmed! Why, he looks like a son of the gods!"

The king drew closer to the furnace and shouted, "Shadrach, Meshach, and Abednego, servants of the Most High God, come out!" At his command, they stepped out. The officials crowded around them in disbelief. They were unharmed! Their clothes were not even scorched.

Nebuchadnezzar raised his hands in amazement and said, "Praise to the God of Shadrach, Meshach, and Abednego! He has sent his angel to rescue his servants, for they trusted him. They were willing to give up their lives rather than serve any other god.

"I hereby issue a new decree," the king announced. "From this time forward, any people from any nation who say anything against their God will be cut into pieces and their houses will be turned into rubble. For no other god can save as he does."

Then Nebuchadnezzar turned to the three and announced that they would be promoted.

TBC 145

Bad Figs in Jerusalem

TBC Book One, Chapter 146
2 Kings 24:15-25:3; 2 Chronicles 36:12;
Jeremiah 24; 27-29; 34; 30; 31

Daniel and his friends were not the only Jews deported. King Jehoiachin and his mother, as well as Judah's army, its craftsmen, and its leaders were also taken. Then Nebuchadnezzar appointed Jehoiachin's uncle, Mattaniah, as Judah's new king, and he renamed him Zedekiah.

At this time, the Lord gave Jeremiah a vision of two baskets near the temple. One held good figs, the other bad.

"I will watch over the exiles for their good and bring them back," he said. "But like bad figs, Zedekiah and those in Jerusalem will be destroyed."

Early in Zedekiah's reign, the Lord commanded Jeremiah to wear a yoke around his neck as he sent this message to the kings in the surrounding nations: "I will hand over your country to Nebuchadnezzar. If you do not submit to his yoke, your people will perish."

Jeremiah also spoke to King Zedekiah, then to the priests and all the people: "Serve the king of Babylon and you will live. If you resist, this city will be ruined.

"There are some who claim to be prophets, and they are telling you that peace will come to Jerusalem. They also say that the things which were seized from the temple will soon be returned to their rightful place. I tell you, don't listen to what those prophets are saying. Believe me, even what is left in the temple will be taken to Babylon, and they will not be returned until the Lord restores them."

Not long after that, a prophet named Hananiah met face-to-face with Jeremiah. Boldly, Hananiah turned to him and said, "The Lord says, "I will break Babylon's yoke. Within two years, Jehoiachin and the things taken from the temple will be returned."

Jeremiah calmly replied, "A prophet is from God only if his predictions come true."

Hananiah grabbed Jeremiah's yoke, yanking it off his neck. Then he broke it and said, "So also will God break Nebuchadnezzar's yoke."

Jeremiah later returned to him with a message from the Lord: "Because you have preached rebellion against the Lord, you will die this year." Two months later, Hananiah died.

Jeremiah then sent a letter to the Jews who were exiled in Babylon with Jehoiachin: "The Lord says, 'Settle in Babylon. Marry and raise families. Pray for peace and prosperity. In 70 years I will bring you back. When you seek me with all your heart, then you will find me.' "

In spite of the Lord's warnings, Zedekiah rebelled against the king of Babylon. In the ninth year of Zedekiah's reign, Nebuchadnezzar marched his army to Jerusalem and surrounded it. For the next two years, Jerusalem would be cut off from the outside world by Nebuchadnezzar's army.

In all his years as king, Zedekiah had done evil before the Lord. When Jeremiah had delivered God's word, he had refused to humble himself. And after taking an oath in the Lord's name, pledging loyalty to Nebuchadnezzar, he had broken his agreement.

While Nebuchadnezzar's army battled Judah's last two fortified cities and the city of Jerusalem, the Lord again sent Jeremiah to King Zedekiah with a message: "The Lord says, 'I will hand this city over to the king of Babylon. Then you will be captured and taken away.' "

As to the future, the Lord told Jeremiah to write in a book: "A time of great trouble is coming for my people Israel and Judah, like the pain of labor before a child is delivered. But I will restore my people to this land, and I will raise up a King from David.

"Finally, in that day, I will be their God, and they will be my people. I will bring them from the land of the north and gather them from the ends of the earth. I will plant the house of Israel and Judah with the offspring of men and of animals. In that day, they will all know me."

TBC 146

Visions of Glory

TBC Book One, Chapter 147
Ezekiel 1-7

From the thousands captured by Nebuchadnezzar stood a young man by the Kebar River, a man who saw visions. It was as though heaven were opened to him. The young man, Ezekiel, was from the priestly tribe of Levi, and God's hand was upon him. Ezekiel was called to prophesy.

Ezekiel saw what looked like a windstorm, with lightning bolts, surrounded by brilliant light. The fiery center looked like glowing metal, and four creatures were in it, each one with four wings and four faces—that of a man, a lion, an ox, and an eagle.

Above the creatures he saw a throne that looked like sapphire. There, on the throne, sat one who looked like a man, but he was so radiant that he glowed. Brilliant light surrounded him, like a rainbow—like the glory of the Lord. And the moment he spoke, Ezekiel fell facedown.

"Son of man," the figure said, "stand up."

Then God's Spirit raised him to his feet.

"I am sending you to the Israelites," he said, "to a rebellious nation. They may not listen, for they are stubborn. But they will know a prophet is among them. Do not be afraid to speak."

The Lord handed him a scroll. It contained words of sorrow and trouble on both sides, for God's message was to fill Ezekiel's mind.

"Now go to your people in exile," he said. "But I know they won't listen." Then it seemed that the Spirit had carried him to the exiles near the Kebar River.

After seven days, the Lord said, "Son of man, I have made you a watchman. If a righteous man becomes evil and you do not warn him, he will die, and I will hold you accountable. But if you warn him and he listens, he will live and you will have saved yourself.

"Now go to the plains," he said. There Ezekiel again saw God's glory, and he fell facedown. The Spirit entered him and raised him to his feet.

"Go in your house," the Lord said to him, "and stay there as if you are unable to go out." What Ezekiel was doing symbolized what would happen to Jerusalem.

Ezekiel was then told to say nothing while he drew a picture of Jerusalem on a clay tablet. He was to make it appear surrounded by enemies. Then the prophet lay down and put an iron pan between himself and the city. This, too, symbolized what would happen—the siege would be strong and Jerusalem would be separated from God.

For 390 years the nation of Israel had sinned by worshiping idols and forgetting what pleases God. So God let them be exiled by the Assyrians. Judah later committed the same sins and did it for 40 years. Now God was judging Judah and its chief city, Jerusalem.

Ezekiel now shaved his head and his beard. He used the hairs to show what would happen to the people in Jerusalem. One third he burned, revealing what would happen inside the city. One third he struck with a sword, to show what would happen outside of it. And one third he scattered in the wind. Only a few strands did he save.

The Lord said to Ezekiel, "I will cut off Jerusalem's supply of food and water. It will be so bad that people will eat the flesh of their own family members."

Then Ezekiel faced the mountains, and God's Spirit moved him to prophesy: "The Lord says, 'I will destroy all your high places.' "

The exiles may have envied their kinsmen who lived in Jerusalem and Judah. But Ezekiel told them that they were much more fortunate than those living in Judah.

"Those outside Jerusalem will die by the sword," he said. "Those inside the city will die by plague and famine. And those who survive will flee to the mountains. Finally they will realize that their wealth cannot save them."

TBC 147

The Fate of Jerusalem

TBC Book One, Chapter 148
Ezekiel 8-13

The exiled Jews knew there was something special about Ezekiel. One day, as the elders sat before him, the Spirit of God overcame him. Suddenly he saw Jerusalem and the glory of God. At the north gate he saw the altar that had angered God's jealous Spirit.

"Son of man," said the Lord, "see what they are doing—detestable things that will drive me far from my sanctuary."

Through a hole in the wall, he saw 70 elders secretly worshiping idols. In the courtyard he saw women mourning for the god Tammuz and 25 men worshiping the sun god.

Then the Lord called six angels who guarded Jerusalem. With them was a man in linen who held something with which to write.

"Go throughout the city," the Lord told the man, "and put a mark on the forehead of those who grieve over these detestable things. Then kill the rest. Begin at my sanctuary."

Still seeing a vision, Ezekiel watched as those without a mark were being killed.

"Defile the temple with their bodies," the Lord commanded.

Ezekiel fell facedown and pleaded. "O Lord," he said, "have mercy on them."

"They are guilty of bloodshed and injustice," the Lord replied.

Then Ezekiel saw the throne and the creatures he had seen by the Kebar River. He realized now that they were cherubim.

Once again the Lord spoke to the man in linen. "Take fiery coals from the cherubim and spread them over Jerusalem." As soon as he said this, God's glory left the temple's threshold.

The Spirit then showed Ezekiel the east gate of the temple, where 25 leaders were mocking what Jeremiah had said. And they were all thinking the same thing: *We are more righteous than those who were exiled. We are safe here.*

The Lord then told Ezekiel to prophesy against them. But Ezekiel fell facedown, crying out, "Will you completely destroy your remnant?"

The Lord replied, "I will gather those scattered among the nations. They will return and obey me wholeheartedly."

When the vision no longer appeared, Ezekiel told the exiles everything.

Some time later, the Lord said to Ezekiel, "Pack your belongings so the people can watch you. At dusk, dig a hole in your wall and crawl out. Put your pack on your shoulders and cover your face so you cannot see the land. The people will wonder what this means."

So Ezekiel did just that. The next day he explained: "The prince in Jerusalem will try to escape with his belongings. The Lord will then scatter his troops. He will be caught and taken to Babylon but will never see it. Those spared from sword, famine, and plague will be exiled."

Then the Lord told Ezekiel to eat and drink in front of the people and to tremble while doing it, as if fearful. Ezekiel did just as the Lord had commanded him.

The prophet then gave them time to ponder his actions. They even discussed among themselves what this could mean. Finally, Ezekiel explained the meaning: "The people in Jerusalem and Judah will eat and drink in fear and anxiety, for their land will be stripped bare."

For years God's people had ignored his prophets. They had grown cynical. "The days go by," they said, "and every vision comes to nothing." Even those who did believe the visions were deceiving themselves. They consoled themselves by thinking, *This disaster won't happen in my lifetime.* Yet the Lord had said those visions would soon be fulfilled.

Meanwhile, other prophets predicted peace for Jerusalem. They were simply saying what people wanted to hear. Soon the Lord would put an end to the false prophets and their visions.

TBC 148

'Do Not Mourn, Do Not Gloat'

TBC Book One, Chapter 149
Ezekiel 14; 17; 18; 20-22; 24-26; 28

The news about Jerusalem jarred the exiles. If there were any way to spare their countrymen of this terrible ordeal, surely Ezekiel would know. So the elders came to him, hoping that God's judgment on their homeland could somehow be averted.

But as they appeared, God whispered to Ezekiel, "Should I even let them appeal to me? These men have set up idols in their hearts. They love things that separate them from me."

Ezekiel told them, "You need to turn away from all your wrongdoing. God will set himself against anyone who wants a word from a prophet but refuses to repent. As for Jerusalem, even if men like Noah and Job prayed, they could save only themselves."

Some time later, Ezekiel revealed more about Jerusalem: "The prince took an oath in God's name, promising to submit to Nebuchadnezzar. But he will break his word, and this will bring down God's punishment. When he tries to escape, he will be caught."

Meanwhile, in Babylon, the exiles resented the discipline of being captured and deported. They said that God was punishing them for their fathers' sins.

But Ezekiel shook his head, saying, "No, God disciplines each one for his own sin. If a wicked person repents, God will forgive all his sins. But if a person turns away from God, his sins will be held against him."

On another occasion, the elders again came to Ezekiel to inquire of the Lord.

Ezekiel said, "The Lord says, 'You may not inquire of me. You are just like your forefathers who left Egypt. They wanted to be like the other nations. So they worshiped idols.' "

Soon after this, the prophet learned from God that Nebuchadnezzar would seek an omen to decide which nation he should attack, the Ammonites or the Israelites. The lot would point to Israel.

The Lord told Ezekiel, "Judah's prince will soon remove his crown, and no one will reign until I crown my Chosen One."

Meanwhile, the people in Jerusalem grieved God's heart. Orphans, widows, foreigners, and the poor were all treated badly. Others were being killed when they had done no wrong. The leaders gave no justice. And instead of seeking God, people turned to idols.

During this time, back in Babylon, Ezekiel's wife suddenly died. But God forbade him to mourn for her death. Ezekiel knew that the Lord had his reasons.

The prophet said, "Just as the one I loved has died, so also will the temple and our relatives in Jerusalem be destroyed. The Lord says, when this happens, you must not mourn."

Soon after Ezekiel gave this prophetic word, Nebuchadnezzar's army surrounded Jerusalem. Yet the house of Israel was not the only nation about to be judged by God.

Ezekiel prophesied, "The Lord says, 'You Ammonites and Moabites rejoiced over Israel's downfall. So I will destroy you also. Then you will know that I am Lord.' "

Ezekiel also predicted that God would punish Edom for being so hostile to the Israelites. One day the Israelites would return to this land, and they would destroy the Edomites as a nation. God would also destroy the hostile Philistines who were living on the coast.

The people of nearby Tyre were pleased when they learned that Jerusalem seemed helpless against Babylon. With Jerusalem in ruins, they could prosper from the trade that would now go to them. For this attitude, God would allow Babylon to lay siege to Tyre as well.

Tyre's king was proud of his wealth and his accomplishments. The people looked back on a time when Tyre had overcome a siege by the Assyrians. Behind their pride and arrogance was a spirit of rebellion, the same spirit that worked in the garden of Eden, when God's anointed cherub rebelled and led mankind to do the same. And that attitude would bring their downfall.

TBC 149

Jeremiah's Plight

TBC Book One, Chapter 150
Jeremiah 34:8-22; 37; 38; 39:15-18; 21

Jeremiah had no inkling that his life would soon be in danger. While Zedekiah reigned, Jeremiah was free to come and go as he pleased. Zedekiah, his officials, and the people paid no attention to him—until Babylonians surrounded Jerusalem. Then Zedekiah begged Jeremiah to pray for them.

During the siege, King Zedekiah made a covenant on behalf of all the people in Jerusalem. Everyone would set free any slaves they had who were Jewish. For God had commanded that every seven years, the Hebrew slaves among them should be freed, but the people had not obeyed.

After freeing the slaves, Zedekiah and his people learned that Egypt had sent an army to help fight Babylon. The Babylonians withdrew their troops to attack Pharaoh's army. Thinking they were now safe, the people changed their minds and took back their slaves.

Jeremiah rebuked them and warned that the Babylonians would return. Then he started to leave for Benjamin to claim his share of some property. But at the Benjamin Gate, the captain of the guard, Hananiah's grandson, accused him of deserting to the Babylonians.

The officials agreed and had Jeremiah beaten and imprisoned in a dungeon cell and left him there. Some time later, Zedekiah sent for him secretly to get a word from the Lord.

"You will be handed over to the king of Babylon," Jeremiah said.

The prophet then begged not to be sent back to the dungeon. So from that time on, Jeremiah was guarded in the courtyard and given bread daily.

As Jeremiah predicted, the Babylonians returned. Zedekiah sent a message to Jeremiah. But the Lord gave him a message that the king would not want to hear.

"I myself will fight against you," said the Lord. "I will hand over to Nebuchadnezzar both you and all those in this city who survive. The king of Babylon will show no mercy."

Then Jeremiah stood before all the people and said, "Whoever stays in this city will die. But whoever surrenders now will escape with his life."

When the king's officials heard Jeremiah's words, they raced to tell Zedekiah.

"This man should be put to death!" they urged. "He is going to discourage the soldiers as well as all the people. His words will only bring harm."

Zedekiah replied, "Do with him whatever you wish."

Immediately, the men went to Jeremiah, tied him in ropes, and lowered him into a well in the courtyard. No water was in the well, and Jeremiah sank helplessly in the mud.

When one of the royal officials, a Cushite named Ebed-Melech, heard what happened, the wickedness of the people galled him. He refused to let Jeremiah die in that muddy pit.

Ebed-Melech went directly to the king. "My lord," he pleaded, "do you realize these men acted wickedly with Jeremiah the prophet? They threw him in a well. He will starve to death!"

The king replied, "Take 30 men with you and lift him out before he dies."

So Ebed-Melech called for 30 men. Together they found rags and worn-out clothes in a room under the treasury. They tied the rags to the ropes so Jeremiah could put padding under his arms. Then they lifted him out. From that time on, he remained in the courtyard.

Some time after this incident, the Lord told Jeremiah to deliver a message to Ebed-Melech, the man who had rescued him. The prophet gladly relayed God's words.

Jeremiah went to him and said, "I have a word for you. The Lord Almighty says, 'I am about to fulfill my words to bring disaster against this city. But I will rescue you. You will escape with your life because you trust me.' "

TBC 150

Zedekiah's Moment of Decision

TBC Book One, Chapter 151
Jeremiah 32; 33:14-26; 38:14-28; 39; 52;
2 Kings 25; 2 Chronicles 36

Things looked grim for the people of Judah. In the tenth year of Zedekiah's reign, Babylonia's army had held Jerusalem under siege for a year. Because of his prophecies, Jeremiah remained a prisoner in the palace courtyard. But the Lord continued to speak to him.

The Lord said, "Your cousin Hanamel is going to come to you and offer you his field at Anathoth, for you are his closest relative, and you have the right and duty to buy it."

When the Lord's prediction came true, Jeremiah remembered his words. He knew God was prompting him to buy the property. So he weighed out 17 shekels of silver and signed the deed. Still a prisoner, he had Baruch put his documents in a clay jar to protect them.

After finishing the transaction, Jeremiah praised the Lord for the miracles he performed in Egypt and for bringing his people to this land. Then he praised God for his promise: Although Jerusalem would be conquered, his people would one day return to this land.

The Lord responded, saying, "Is anything too hard for me? I am about to hand this city over to the Babylonians, who will set it on fire. Both Israel and Judah have turned their backs to me. I taught them again and again, but they would not listen or respond to my discipline.

"And yet, just as I brought calamity, I will one day bring prosperity and gather them back to this land. Then they will never turn away, and I will make an everlasting covenant with them."

Meanwhile, the siege continued, and King Zedekiah grew more desperate. He was beside himself wondering what he should do. So he sent for Jeremiah and met with him privately.

"I have a question for you," the king said, "and you must hide nothing from me."

Before the king could pose his question, Jeremiah said, "Why should I say anything? If I answer, you will have me killed, won't you? And if I gave you counsel, you would not listen."

So the king swore an oath to Jeremiah, promising not to harm him.

Then Jeremiah said to him, "If you surrender, your life will be spared and this city will not be burned down. You and your family will live. But if you refuse, you will not escape."

Zedekiah replied, "If I surrender, then the Babylonians might hand me over to the captive Jews who already surrendered to Babylon. They would surely mistreat me."

"No, Nebuchadnezzar's men won't hand you over to them," Jeremiah said. "But if you refuse to surrender, you will be humiliated and mocked by the women from your own palace."

As Jeremiah left the king's presence, Zedekiah pondered his words. But the longer he thought about surrendering, the more fearful he became. Surely there must be some way he could slip out of the city and escape before it fell! Zedekiah knew he didn't have much time. In spite of Jerusalem's high walls and strategic location, the Babylonians were preparing to attack.

For years the people had scorned God's messengers and despised his words. The only remedy now was God's wrath. After a two-year siege, the Babylonians broke down the city's wall. Pouring into Jerusalem, their officials now took seats of authority as Judah's rulers.

When Zedekiah and his soldiers saw what happened, they fled, using the garden pathway. But they were captured near Jericho. The king was then forced to watch the Babylonians kill his own sons. Then they put out his eyes, bound him in shackles, and took him to Babylon.

Nebuzaradan, the commander, seized everything of value. Then he set fire to the temple, the palace, the houses—every place where people had sacrificed to false gods. He left only some poor people who owned nothing. To them he gave fields and vineyards to tend for the king.

Nebuchadnezzar appointed Gedaliah, the grandson of Shaphan, as governor over those left in Judah. The soldiers who had fled came out of their hiding to meet with him at Mizpah. Gedaliah promised them: "If you submit to Babylon, all will go well with you."

TBC 151

Defiant to the End

TBC Book One, Chapter 152
Jeremiah 40 - 44

The king of Babylon ordered his chief commander, Nebuzaradan, to find Jeremiah, for the prophet had urged the people to surrender. Days later he found the prophet bound in chains among the captives of Jerusalem.

"The Lord has decreed disaster for this place," Nebuzaradan told Jeremiah, "but you are free to go. Come with me to Babylon if you wish, and I will make sure you are cared for."

Jeremiah hesitated, then he turned to leave. The commander called out, "Jeremiah! You may return to Judah if you wish and live with Gedaliah, the grandson of Shaphan. He has recently been appointed as governor over Judah. But you do whatever you want."

During their time of war, many Jews had been scattered throughout Moab, Ammon, Edom, and the surrounding areas. When they heard that Gedaliah was appointed governor, they returned to Judah. Gedaliah encouraged them to settle in the land and serve Babylon.

The people obeyed Gedaliah, and they harvested an abundance of wine and summer fruit. Then one day, an officer named Johanan came to Gedaliah with a serious concern.

"I have just learned that Ishmael is planning to murder you. Shall I secretly kill him?"

"No, don't do such a thing!" Gedaliah said. "Surely this is not true."

But Ishmael was of royal blood, a descendant of David, and he was indeed planning a coup. When Ishmael and ten of his men were eating a meal with Gedaliah, they pulled out their swords and killed him. Then they turned against the Jews loyal to Gedaliah and killed them, too. They also killed the Babylonian soldiers stationed nearby.

The next day Ishmael saw 80 men approaching Mizpah, mourning the destruction of the temple. They knew nothing about Gedaliah's death. Ishmael met them, weeping as he came. He was pretending that he, too, was grieved. Then he led them into the city, and his men killed them.

Ten of them, however, saved their lives by offering the grains, oil, and honey they had hidden away. Taking them and the rest of the people as his captives, Ishmael set out for Ammon. But Johanan and his soldiers caught up with them, and Ishmael fled to the Ammonites.

After rescuing the people, Johanan led them away from Mizpah. The officers were afraid of the Babylonians because Gedaliah had been murdered. So they went to Jeremiah, whom they had also rescued. "Ask the Lord what we should do," they said, "and we will do it."

Ten days later, the Lord gave Jeremiah his response. Jeremiah called the people and said, "The Lord says, 'If you stay in this land, I will have compassion on you. You need not fear the king of Babylon. But if you leave and go to Egypt, you will all die by sword, famine, or plague.' "

When Jeremiah finished giving the Lord's words, Johanan and all the arrogant men said, "You are lying, Jeremiah! The Lord did not really say that. Surely Baruch is behind this. You are probably going to hand us over to the Babylonians." So they decided to leave and go to Egypt.

Jeremiah and Baruch were forced to go with them. As they approached Tahpanhes, the Lord told Jeremiah, "Take some large stones and bury them at the entrance of Pharaoh's palace. Then say, 'Nebuchadnezzar will attack Egypt and set his throne over these stones.' "

The remnant of Jews settled throughout Egypt, and they insisted on worshiping other gods. So the Lord spoke through Jeremiah, saying, "Have you forgotten why I destroyed Judah and Jerusalem? Now you will perish in Egypt. You will die by sword, famine, and plague."

The people defied him, saying "We will keep doing this."

Jeremiah replied, "Then go ahead. But you will all perish, and here is God's sign: He will hand over Pharaoh Hophra to his enemies."

Just as Jeremiah had predicted, a rebel force did indeed overcome Pharaoh. Soon after that, Nebuchadnezzar invaded Egypt.

TBC 152

'Your Time Will Come . . .'

TBC Book One, Chapter 153
Obadiah

How you will be ransacked! Your wealth will be pillaged.

On the lofty mountain crags south of the Dead Sea lived a proud nation of people who had somehow managed to survive the invasion of Babylon. They were not deported as the Jews and other nations were. So they thought they were secure. But they were wrong.

This nation of people, the Edomites, were descendants of Esau, Jacob's twin brother. For many generations, Esau's descendants held a grudge against Jacob's descendants. The Edomites refused to cooperate in ways that would have helped the Israelites.

Now that the Jews were deported to Babylon, only a small number were left to care for the fields and vineyards in Judah. So the Lord sent them a prophet named Obadiah, who gave to them a word of encouragement. But what served as an encouragement to them was first of all a message of warning to their neighbors, the Edomites.

Speaking through Obadiah, the Lord said, "You descendants of Esau have made your home on the heights of the mountains. You have thought, 'No one can attack us here.' You take great pride in knowing you have not been conquered. But I will cut you down to size, and you will fall."

The Edomites had used their rocky clefts like vaults to hide their wealth. With that in mind, the Lord said, "If thieves were to take you off guard, would they leave behind anything of value? How you will be ransacked! Your wealth will be pillaged.

"Your own allies will force you down from the mountains and drive you to the border. The nations you have trusted as your friends, those with whom you have traded, will now set a trap for you. They will deceive you and overpower you, and you will have no hint of it."

The Edomites had acquired a great deal of knowledge from their contacts with both Egypt and Babylon. But even the wisest of their people would not detect the disaster about to come upon them. For this reason, the prophet added, "Even your warriors will be terrified in that day."

Although their founding fathers were brothers, the Edomites were pleased over the downfall of Judah. Obadiah likened Judah's invaders to

"foreigners who were casting lots for Jerusalem." The Edomites' attitude made them just as guilty as Judah's invaders.

"You should not look down on your brother in the day of his troubles," the Lord warned. "You should not rejoice at Judah's downfall, nor should you use that as a reason to boast. You should not plunder them, nor should you capture those who are fleeing.

"The day of the Lord's judgment is drawing near for all nations. As each nation has done, so will it be done to them. Just as my people drank from the cup of my wrath, so will all nations drink from that cup, and they will be totally destroyed.

"But on Mount Zion there will be deliverance—it will be holy. The house of Jacob will possess its inheritance. The house of Israel and Judah will be like a flame that sets on fire the house of Esau and consumes it. Edom will not survive as a nation."

The nation of Edom may well symbolize all those who oppose the Lord, just as the Edomites opposed Israel. God will thwart those opposed to him and give their land to others.

"Mount Zion will rule over the mountains of Esau," predicted the prophet, "and the kingdom will be governed by the Lord."

TBC 153

Ezekiel the Watchman

TBC Book One, Chapter 154
Ezekiel 29; 33-35

No one should have been surprised. Before Jerusalem fell to the Babylonians, Ezekiel had prophesied against Egypt. When Babylon first threatened to attack, the Israelites had turned to Egypt instead of the Lord. Egypt's pharaoh was proud of his power. So God would use Nebuchadnezzar to humble him as well as his people.

Seventeen years after Ezekiel prophesied against Egypt, his predictions came true. Although the Pharaoh had won back territory lost in the battle of Carchemish, he now faced a humiliating defeat. Egypt became as weak as the other nations that were conquered by Babylon.

But that's getting ahead of the story. . . .

After two years of being under siege, the city of Jerusalem was conquered and much of it destroyed. For 12 years now Ezekiel had been in Babylon, where God had made him a watchman. And as such, he warned his people to turn away from their sin.

The exiles were still saying that God was not fair. Ezekiel continued to tell them: "If a righteous person turns away from God and starts doing wicked things, God will not remember the good things he used to do. Likewise, if a wicked person repents and turns to God, God will not remember his sin."

After the exiles learned of Jerusalem's fall, the Lord told Ezekiel: "Son of man, hear what your countrymen are saying: 'Come quickly! Ezekiel has a word from the Lord!'

"To them, you are just an eloquent speaker," said the Lord. "They love to hear to you speak, but they don't do what you tell them."

Back in Jerusalem too, the few who were left did not obey the Lord. As for them, the Lord revealed that they would soon be overcome by wild animals and plagues.

Ezekiel cried out, "Woe to you leaders! You did not shepherd the people. The weak and sick were left helpless. You ruled them harshly."

God likens his people to a flock of sheep whom he entrusts to the "shepherds" or leaders. And the Lord is grieved by what he sees: "You shepherds have plundered the sheep, and I'm holding you accountable. I will remove you shepherds and rescue my flock from you."

Just as God's chosen people were scattered during their exile, so also will a scattering take place in the last days. Then the Lord himself will come and gather his people from all nations. He will shepherd them with compassion and destroy those who oppressed them.

The Lord will gather all his "sheep," for he has created all people. But not all people honor him as their chief shepherd. For he says, "Some of you have taken advantage of others and turned them away from my flock. I will judge you, and I will rescue my sheep.

"I will place over my sheep one shepherd, a descendant of my servant David. Then I will make a covenant of peace with my people and the land in which they live. At that time I will send them showers of blessing to make their land fruitful. They will feel secure and at peace.

"No longer will my people be terrorized by other nations. No longer will they fear wild animals seeking to devour them. No longer will they be victims of famine. For you, O house of Israel, are my people, the sheep of my pasture, and I am your God."

Ezekiel spoke these words of comfort to encourage God's people both then and now. But to those like the Edomites, who wished harm on God's people, the Lord said, "When you spoke against them, you spoke against me. The destruction you wished upon them will come upon you."

TBC 154

Valley of Dry Bones

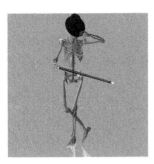

TBC Book One, Chapter 155
Ezekiel 36-43; 47; 48:5

When God spoke to the prophets of long ago, he gave messages not only for the people living back then, but also for us today. Some of the most exciting messages (and also the most puzzling) are those revealed to Ezekiel. In his final words, he speaks of a period yet to come, perhaps even in our lifetime.

Ezekiel predicts a time when the nations of the world will turn against Israel. But the Lord has chosen Israel for a special purpose—to show the world that he is real, he is holy, and he is active in our lives. For this reason, God promises to put his Spirit in his people.

Ezekiel says the Lord will then gather his people from all nations and return them to the land of their forefathers. Though people will have made it a barren place, God will make it fruitful, like the Garden of Eden. Everyone will know this is the work of the Lord.

One day the Lord gave Ezekiel a peculiar vision. He saw a valley full of dry bones. The Lord asked, "Son of man, can these bones live?"

Ezekiel replied, "O Sovereign Lord, you alone know."

"Prophesy to these bones," the Lord said. "Tell them, 'Hear the word of the Lord!' "

As Ezekiel spoke, he heard a rattling sound. The bones began to rise and join together. Then the Lord clothed them with flesh and tendons. The Lord said, "I will put breath in you, and you will come to life. Then you will know that I am the Lord.

"Son of man, prophesy these words: 'Come from the four winds, O breath. Breathe into these who were slain, that they may now live.' "

Then they came to life and stood up, a massive group of people.

"This is the whole house of Israel," the Lord said.

"They thought their hope was gone. Now I want you to tell them: 'This is what the Sovereign Lord says, "I will open your graves, my people, and bring you back to Israel. Then you will know I am the Lord. I will put my Spirit in you and settle you in the land." ' "

The Lord told Ezekiel, "Take a stick and write on it: 'The Israelites who belonged to Judah.' Then take another stick and write: 'The Israelites who belonged to Joseph.' Now join them together, for I will make my people one nation with one shepherd."

The Lord revealed that a nation from the north would lead many others against Israel: "They will arouse my anger. So I will cause an earthquake in Israel and send torrents of rain, hail, and burning sulfur on them. The whole earth will tremble at my presence."

The nations who join forces against Israel will suffer a horrible defeat. Even those on the coastlands who think they are safe will suffer from God's wrath. It will take months just to bury the dead. Then Israel will gather their weapons and use them for fuel.

Finally, the Lord allowed Ezekiel to look beyond God's judgment, to a time when he would build a new temple. He saw the glory of the Lord enter through the east gate.

"Son of man," the Lord said, "this is the place of my throne. This is where I will live, among the Israelites forever.

"A river will flow from the temple, with many trees on both sides. Every month they will bear fruit that people can eat. The trees that draw water from my temple will have leaves that bring healing. From then on, this city where they lie will be known as: 'The Lord Is There.' "

TBC 155

A Dream Come True

TBC Book One, Chapter 156
Daniel 4:1-37

One day King Nebuchadnezzar decided that he wanted to tell his people a story, a true story about himself and the Lord. In fact, he decided that the whole world should hear this story. So he called his scribe to write down the words, and this is what he said. . . .

I was at home in my palace, content and prosperous, until one night. I had a nightmare that frightened me. The images and visions I saw were so terrible that I called for all my wise men. I told them my dream, but none of them could interpret what it meant.

Finally, Daniel came, and I knew he could interpret the dream. So I told him what I saw, an enormous tree in the middle of the land. Its top reached the sky, and the whole world could see it. Its beautiful leaves provided shelter; its fruit fed every creature.

Then I saw an angel. He called out, "Cut down the tree. Trim its branches, strip off its leaves, and scatter its fruit. Let the animals and birds flee. But let the stump and roots, bound with iron and bronze, remain in the ground, under the grassy field."

The angel continued: "Let him be drenched with heaven's dew and live with the animals and plants. Let him have the mind of an animal for seven years. The Most High is sovereign. He gives kingdoms to whomever he wishes and sets over them the lowliest of men."

As I turned toward Daniel, he looked very troubled.

"Don't be afraid to tell me what it means," I said.

Daniel replied, "Oh, my lord, if only the dream applied to your enemies! You are that tree, great and strong, but what will happen to you is not good.

"The Most High has decreed that you will be driven away from people and will live with wild animals, eating grass like cattle. This will continue for seven years, until you acknowledge that the Most High is sovereign and gives kingdoms to whomever he wishes. The stump and roots were left to show that your kingdom would be restored when you admit that Heaven rules.

"O King, I suggest you turn away from your sins by doing what is right and being kind to those who are oppressed. Perhaps God will then change his mind."

But I soon forgot Daniel's advice.

A year later, as I was admiring my kingdom, I said to myself, "See what I have accomplished! Is this not the great Babylon that I have built as my royal residence, that I gained by my mighty power for the glory of my majesty?"

No sooner had I said that, when a voice spoke from heaven: "This is what is decreed for you, King Nebuchadnezzar. Your royal authority has been taken away. You will live like an animal for seven years, until you acknowledge that the Most High is sovereign."

Immediately, what was said to me came true. God had given me the mind of an animal, and I was driven away. I ate grass like cattle. My body became drenched with heaven's dew. My hair and nails grew long. After seven long years, I looked up toward heaven for mercy.

At that moment, the Most High restored my sanity. Then I praised and honored the Eternal One. He does as he pleases; no one can hold him back. He restored my kingdom and blessed it even more. All his ways are just. And those who are proud, he is able to humble.

TBC 156

Fate of the World

TBC Book One, Chapter 157
Daniel 7:1-28

Of all the prophets God had raised up, no one saw the world's destiny more clearly than the prophet Daniel. Many years after Nebuchadnezzar reigned, his grandson sat on his throne as king, and now Daniel him was the one who began to have strange dreams.

In one of his dreams, he saw four beasts rising from the sea. One looked like a lion with wings. Suddenly its wings were torn off and it stood on two feet like a man.

The second beast looked like a bear, and it held three ribs between its teeth. It was told to eat all the flesh it wanted.

Then Daniel saw the third beast. That one looked like a leopard, but it had four wings and four heads. It was given power to rule.

When Daniel saw the fourth beast, he was terrified. This powerful beast had large iron teeth. It crushed its victims and devoured them. Then it trampled everyone else. But when he looked more closely, he noticed something different about this beast—it had ten horns.

Daniel stared at the ten horns, wondering what they stood for. Then suddenly, another horn appeared, a small one. As it rose up, three of the first horns were uprooted. The little horn had eyes like a man, and it spoke in a boastful way.

Meanwhile, Daniel saw heavenly thrones being set in place. The Holy One appeared, "the Ancient of Days," and he sat down like a judge in court. Special books were opened. The beast was judged: He was destroyed and thrown into a blazing fire.

Then Daniel looked up again and saw someone like a Son of Man coming in the clouds. As the figure drew closer, he was led to the Ancient of Days. Then the Ancient One gave him authority, majesty, and power. People from every nation bowed down to worship him.

But Daniel could not forget what he saw initially, the portion of the dream that portrayed the beasts. He was still very troubled by those images. So in his vision, he approached someone standing nearby and asked what they meant.

He was told, "The four beasts stand for four great kingdoms that will come to power. But in the end, God's people will rule."

Daniel wanted to know more about the fourth beast. He watched the beast again, this time as it was making war against the saints—God's people. It was so powerful that it defeated them—until the Ancient of Days came in judgment. Then the Ancient One took the kingdom from the beast and rewarded it to the saints.

Daniel was told, "The fourth beast stands for the last great kingdom on earth. It will be more powerful than the others before it. It will conquer the whole world. The ten horns you see stand for ten rulers who will come from this kingdom.

"The small horn that you saw stands for another leader who will rise up later. This one will be different from the ones before him, and he will overpower some of the nations. He will speak against the Most High and will oppose God's saints for three-and-a-half years.

"But the court of heaven will meet, and the ruler's power will be taken away. Then power to rule over all the kingdoms under heaven will be given to the saints, the people of God Most High. His kingdom will never end, and all rulers will worship him."

Daniel wrote down a description of all that he saw, but he never discussed it with anyone. All the things Daniel saw were symbols, to show what would happen in the future. Some of those things have already happened. Some have yet to be fulfilled. . . .

TBC 157

Those Who Would Rule the World

TBC Book One, Chapter 158
Daniel 8:1-27

Two years after Daniel's strange and perplexing dream, God gave him another startling vision. He saw himself standing beside the Ulai Canal in the fortress of Susa, a prominent city in Persia (now called Iran). Daniel began to see things as if he were really there.

He looked up and saw a ram with two long horns standing near the canal. One of the horns later grew longer than the other. The ram charged toward the west, then toward the north, and finally toward the south. No animal could stop him, for he was powerful.

While Daniel tried to understand what this might mean, a goat suddenly came from the west, crossing the whole earth without touching the ground. This goat had a large horn between his eyes, and he charged the ram so hard it shattered its two horns.

The ram had taken such a fierce beating that it could not even stand. The goat trampled on the ram, and no one could stop it. The goat then became very great and powerful, until his horn broke off. Four other horns grew up in its place. Daniel understood that the horns symbolized ruling power. In fact, all of these details were symbols, and if you understood the symbols accurately, they revealed a great deal about what was destined to happen.

From those four horns came another. It started small but grew to the south and to the east, toward the Holy Land. It grew until it reached the heavens, and when it did, it threw down some of the starry host.

This horn symbolized a ruler who would set himself up as if he were God. He would refuse to let people sacrifice to God, and he would ruin their place of worship. Because of rebellion, the saints would be powerless against him. The ruler would succeed in everything he did.

Daniel was told that "truth would be thrown to the ground." Then he heard two holy beings speaking to each other, purposely talking loudly enough for Daniel to hear.

The first one said, "Once these things start happening, how long will it take for this vision to be fulfilled?"

The other one replied, "It will take 2,300 days; then the temple will be purified."

While Daniel wondered what this meant, he saw an angelic being that looked like a man. A voice from the canal shouted to the figure: "Gabriel, tell this man what the vision means."

As Gabriel walked closer, Daniel fell to the ground. Then Gabriel raised him to his feet.

"Son of man," he said, "this is what will happen in the end. The two-horned ram stands for the kings of Media and Persia. The shaggy goat stands for Greece; the horn is its first king. The four horns replacing it are kingdoms that will rise from it.

"These four kingdoms will reign until another ruler comes to power, a stern-faced man who is clever and deceitful. He will become strong and cause great devastation. This ruler will succeed at everything, destroying those who are mighty, even the holy people.

"He will consider himself the greatest man on earth. When other nations think they are secure, he will take them by surprise and destroy them. He will even challenge the Prince of God. In the end, he will be destroyed, but not by man's power.

"The vision you have seen must be recorded and saved, for it has to do with the distant future."

When Daniel awoke, he lay exhausted and ill for several days. Some of the things Daniel saw have already happened. Some have yet to happen. . . .

TBC 158

Good News for the Captives

TBC Book One, Chapter 159
Isaiah 40; 44:24-45:13; 47:1-52:12

Finally—a message from God that brought good news. The Lord promised his people that their exile to Babylon would not last forever. After a number of years, he commanded his prophets to speak words of encouragement. His people's time of discipline was coming to an end, and they had much to look forward to.

"Comfort my people," says your God. "Speak tenderly to Jerusalem, for her sins have been paid for. Hear the voice of one calling, 'Make way for the Lord! Every valley shall be raised up and every mountain made low. Everyone will see the glory of the Lord.' "

The Lord commanded his messengers to speak good news to his people, to reveal their future and the end times: "See, the Sovereign Lord is coming with power. He will tend his flock like a shepherd. He will gather his lambs in his arms, close to his heart."

God's people had grown discouraged. So his messengers said, "The Lord God, the Creator, understands everything. Those who trust in the Lord will be strengthened. They will soar like eagles. They will run and not get tired; they will walk and not grow faint."

Babylon's fall was drawing near. The Lord was revealing his plan many years before it would happen: "I summon you, Cyrus, as my anointed, even though you do not yet know me. I will enable you to conquer nations. You will rebuild my city and set the exiles free."

When God was angry with his people, he used Babylon as his tool of justice to punish them. But the rulers of Babylon were proud. Instead of turning to God, they relied on their magic spells. They studied the stars, thinking that would reveal their future. Now God's discipline on his people would end, and so would the kingdom of Babylon.

The Lord says he watches his chosen people and knows when they feel helpless. He says, "I will fight those who challenge you. All mankind will know that I am your Savior and Redeemer."

God's prophets pointed to a future Servant of God, who would say: "The Lord wakens me each morning and tells me what to say to those who are weary. Though I am mocked and beaten and my beard is plucked out, I will obey the Sovereign Lord who helps me."

Looking to a future time, when God's people will need encouragement, the Lord says, "Do not fear what mankind can do to you. Do not give in to feelings of terror when you see this great destruction. I am the Lord your Maker, and I have put my words in your mouth."

Just as Jerusalem saw great destruction during the time of Judah's exile, so also will it once again face a terrible time of ruin. God refers to this as "the cup of his wrath." But after that time, he will also make Jerusalem's enemies taste the same wrath of God.

In the end, the Lord will raise up Jerusalem as his holy city, and no one will be able to destroy it. For a time, God's chosen people will be conquered and mocked. But God's reputation is at stake. So he will rescue them, and they will know he is Lord.

When the Lord returns to Jerusalem, his people will see him coming, and they will shout for joy. Everyone on earth will see the Lord deliver his people. The Lord describes that time using imagery that would remind his people of another great time of deliverance, when they escaped their bondage in Egypt.

"The Lord will go before you," he says, "and the God of Israel will be your rear guard."

TBC 159

When the Messiah Comes

TBC Book One, Chapter 160
Isaiah 52:13-15; 53:1-12

The prophets spoke of someone special who would be sent by God to rescue his people—the Messiah. But they also said that this hero was destined to suffer greatly, that his body would become terribly disfigured. What will shock many, however—even world rulers—is what will happen in the very end.

The Holy Spirit led one prophet to describe the Messiah as if he had already lived: "He grew up like a tender shoot, a root out of dry ground. Nothing was special about his appearance." That is, he came from a humble family; he did not look like royalty.

Perhaps that is why God's people would not even recognize him. In fact, the prophet said, "He was despised and rejected, a man full of sorrow and familiar with people's suffering. Instead of honoring him, we looked the other way in disgust."

The prophet continues: "Surely this man came to take away our diseases. He took upon himself the burden of our sorrows. But when we saw him suffer, we thought God was judging him. We thought he was being punished for his sin, not ours. But the truth is, he was pierced for our wrongdoings: He was crushed by the weight of our sins."

Only a perfect sacrifice can bring peace with God. So the prophet goes on to say, "He took our punishment to give us that peace. Because of his wounds, we are forgiven.

"All of us are like sheep who have gone astray. We have wandered off in different directions, like sheep without a shepherd. But he is our shepherd, and he has sacrificed his life to save ours. For the Lord has laid upon him the sin of us all.

"He was treated terribly, and yet he said not a word to those who abused him and ridiculed him. Like a lamb who is being led to the slaughter, or a sheep who is about to be sheared, so also did he quietly accept what was being done to him.

"He was arrested and taken away to face judgment. He suffered the disgrace of dying without having any children, for he was sentenced to death.

"Yet who in his lifetime realized the reason why his life was cut short, that it was because of the sins of our people?

"He was sentenced to the death of a criminal and was assigned a grave with the wicked. He was with the rich in his death, given a proper burial. But in his life, he was treated just like the wicked, even though he had committed no violence. Nor was he guilty of deceit.

"Yet it was the Lord's will to crush him and cause him to suffer. Although the Lord made this man's life a guilt offering, he will have offspring, and his life will be continued. This is all part of God's will; the Lord's plans will prosper in his hands.

"After his soul has suffered, he will see the light of life. And he will be satisfied with what his suffering has accomplished. He will have made a way for many people to be made right with God. He has taken their sins upon himself and paid the price before God.

"So the Lord will honor him and divide the spoils of his victory, for he poured out himself to the point of death and let himself be treated like a law breaker. He took upon himself the sins of many and spoke up for those who had broken God's Law."

TBC 160

Listen Up!

TBC Book One, Chapter 161
Isaiah 55; 57 - 63; 65

Some of the most important things the Lord wants us to know are found in these writings of the prophets. One overriding message is: "Come to me, all of you who are wasting your efforts on things that cannot satisfy. Seek the Lord while he may be found. Call out to him while he is near."

Just as God sends rain and snow to nourish the earth, to water the crops before the moisture returns upward, so also is God's word. God's words go forth with a purpose. They accomplish what he desires. God's words always accomplish a purpose.

A time is coming when God's righteous people will perish. No one, however, will understand the reason why God is permitting this—to spare them from evil.

At that time, those who have a right relationship with God will enter into God's peace: They will find his peace through death.

The Lord says, "Though I live in a high and holy place, I also live with the person who is sorry for his sins. I will revive and comfort those who have humbled themselves before me. But those who do not will remain restless; they will never find peace."

God's people fasted, thinking God would then help them. But God knew they were hypocrites. They abused their workers and got into fights. So God said, "This is the fasting I desire—to stop oppressing people, to share your food with the hungry, to help the poor."

Sin separates people from God. When people do not practice justice, neither will they find it. More and more, people will turn away from truth and from justice. But in the end, the Lord will come, and he will bring justice, like brilliant light entering a dark place.

God's covenant people will think the Lord has forsaken them. But their time of sorrow will come to an end. Instead of being hated, they will become the pride of all nations. The Lord will allow them to possess the land forever, and God will be their light.

The prophet also reveals what the Messiah will say: "The Spirit of the Sovereign Lord is upon me. He has anointed me to preach good news to the poor, to comfort the brokenhearted, to set free the captives and those who are blinded by spiritual darkness.

"O Jerusalem, the nations will see your righteousness, and I will call you by a new name. In the meantime, those of you who call upon the Lord, do not stop praying for Jerusalem. Do not stop until I, the Lord, establish her and make her the praise of the whole earth."

When the Messiah comes, he will bring judgment against the nations of the earth. He says he will trample the nations in his wrath, the way grapes are crushed underfoot. And the blood of the nations will be poured upon the ground in judgment.

After God judges the nations, he will then create new heavens and a new earth. Nothing from the past creation will be remembered. At that time, people will live for hundreds of years. The wolf and the lamb will graze together. The lion will eat straw like the ox.

The Lord declares, "This is the person I hold in high regard—whoever is humble and broken in spirit, the person who takes my words to heart and trembles. But those who rebel will die and suffer eternal judgment."

In the end, all mankind will bow before the Lord.

TBC 161

The Writing on the Wall

TBC Book One, Chapter 162
Daniel 5:1-31

Unlike his forefather Nebuchadnezzar, King Belshazzar had never humbled himself before the Lord. In fact, he took the sacred goblets Nebuchadnezzar had taken from Jerusalem's temple and used them for a wild party. Everyone at this party got drunk, including the king.

The people at the party got so drunk that they began shouting praises to their gods of silver and gold. Suddenly, a large hand appeared in the room, and the fingers began to write on the wall. The king became so terrified that his legs shook and he fell down.

Then the hand disappeared and all that remained was some strange writing on the wall. The king called for his fortune tellers and wise men. He offered a reward to anyone who could read it. But no one could. So the king became even more terrified.

When the queen mother heard how alarmed he was, she entered the banquet hall and said, "O king, live forever! Do not worry! I know someone who can read this. He is a man with wisdom like that of the gods. He helped your grandfather. Call for the man named Daniel."

So Daniel was brought before the king.

The king looked down at Daniel and said, "I have heard the spirit of the gods is in you, that you have outstanding wisdom and insight.

"Some strange writing has appeared on my wall. None of my fortune tellers or wise men can decipher it and explain what it means. If you can read it and explain it, I will clothe you like royalty. I will give you a gold necklace and make you the third highest ruler in my kingdom."

Daniel replied, "You may keep your gifts and give your rewards to someone else. But yes, I can explain it.

"O King, the Most High God gave your forefather Nebuchadnezzar great power and glory. People from all nations feared him, for he had total control. But in time, he became arrogant and proud. So he was removed from his throne and stripped of his glory.

"He was driven away from people because God gave him the mind of an animal. He lived with the donkeys and ate grass like cattle. This continued for years, until he admitted that the Most High God is sovereign, and that God places over kingdoms anyone he wishes.

"But you, O Belshazzar, have not humbled yourself—even though you knew what happened to your forefather, Nebuchadnezzar. Instead, you have set yourself up against the Lord of heaven.

"You took the goblets from the Lord's holy temple and drank wine from them. Not only you, but also your nobles, your wives, and even your concubines drank wine from those goblets.

"Then you praised gods that are mere objects, unable to see or hear. But you did not honor the God who holds your life in his hands. For these reasons, the Lord God sent that hand.

"The writing says, 'Mene, mene, tekel, parsin.' It means God has numbered the days of your reign and brought it to an end. You have been judged and found guilty. Your kingdom is divided and given to the Medes and Persians."

Though Daniel wanted no rewards from King Belshazzar, the king commanded that he be clothed like royalty. Then he promoted him to the third highest ruler.

But that night, King Belshazzar lost his life. Just as Daniel had predicted, the Medes and Persians conquered Babylon, and a man named Darius was appointed by Cyrus to rule as king.

TBC 162

The Future, Decreed by God

TBC Book One, Chapter 163
Daniel 9:1-27

After Cyrus appointed Darius to rule Babylon, which would now become a part of Persia, the prophet Daniel made an important discovery. One day when he was reading the Scriptures, he carefully read the scrolls that were written by Jeremiah. There he learned that the destruction of Jerusalem would last for 70 years.

When Daniel discovered it had been God's will to let Jerusalem be destroyed, he realized that his people had rebelled against God. Right then and there, he dropped to his knees and prayed.

"O Lord God," Daniel cried out, "we have sinned! We have not listened to your servants, the prophets. We know you keep your covenant of love with those who love you and obey you. But we—all of us from Jerusalem, Judah, and Israel—are all covered with shame. O Lord, we also know you are merciful and forgiving, even though we have not obeyed."

It was Daniel's knowledge of God's love and mercy that gave him hope. This is what drove him to appeal to the Lord, to intercede on behalf of his people. He began by confessing their sins.

Daniel prayed, "The judgments written in the Law of Moses have been poured out on us because we sinned. You did what you said you would do by destroying Jerusalem. And after all this, we still have not turned from our sin. Nor have we turned to you.

"O Lord our God, you brought your people out of Egypt's bondage with your mighty power; the reputation you made for yourself is still known. We admit we have sinned—we have done wrong. We now ask you, righteous Lord, to turn away your anger from Jerusalem.

"O Lord, hear the prayers and requests of your servant. Look upon the destruction of Jerusalem, the city that bears your reputation. We ask not because we are righteous, but because we know you are merciful. Have mercy on that city and on the people that bear your Name."

While Daniel was still praying, one of God's holy messengers came to him in swift flight. It was the angel Gabriel, who had appeared to him before. Gabriel said, "As soon as you began to pray, Daniel, an answer was given, for God regards you highly."

The angel began to explain God's plan: "God has decreed a certain number of years before he will put an end to all sin and anoint the most holy one as ruler. It is 'seventy sevens.' Gabriel may have meant seventy seven-year periods, which is 490 years.

"An order will be given to rebuild Jerusalem. From that time until the time of the Anointed One there will be seven 'sevens' and sixty-two 'sevens.' The city will be rebuilt, despite troubled times. After sixty-two 'sevens,' the Anointed One will be cut off."

That leaves one group of time—the last 'seven.' Gabriel explained what will happen after the anointed one is cut off: "A ruler will rise up who will destroy both Jerusalem and the temple. Meanwhile, there will be wars, and God has decreed desolation.

"The leader who comes to power then will make a covenant with many for one 'seven.' In the middle of that time, he will put an end to sacrifices and offerings. He will set up something in the temple that is an abomination to God. So God has decreed desolation."

Today, 2,500 years later, some people believe that these events have already happened as predicted. Others think they have yet to happen. Perhaps both views are right. Some of these events may have already happened; perhaps they also picture what is yet to come. . . .

TBC 163

Daniel Breaks the Law

TBC Book One, Chapter 164
Daniel 6:1-28

One opportunity after another opened up for the Jewish man named Daniel. Soon after Cyrus conquered Babylon, he had appointed Darius the Mede as king. Then Darius set up 120 "satraps," leaders over certain regions. He then appointed three leaders over them, and one of them was Daniel. In fact, Daniel did so well that the king planned to promote him.

When the other chief leaders and satraps learned this, they were overcome with jealousy. So they met and discussed how they could get him in trouble with the king. But Daniel was so trustworthy and hardworking that there was only one way they could do it. . . .

They knew Daniel was devoted to God. Perhaps they could use his devotion as a threat to the king's authority. So they went to the king.

Their spokesman cried out, "King Darius, live forever! We have a plan that we would like you to consider. We all think you should issue this order: Let no one pray to anyone but you for the next 30 days. If anyone disobeys this order, that person should be thrown into the lions' den. We suggest you put this order in writing and seal it."

According to their laws, once the king issued a written decree, it could not be changed. Their idea appealed to the king. So he issued the statement and made it a law.

When Daniel heard about the new law, he went home, walked to his upstairs room, and did what he had always done. With the windows opened toward Jerusalem, he knelt and prayed to the Lord, giving thanks and asking for help. And he continued to pray three times a day.

When the other leaders saw Daniel praying, they went to the king and one of them said, "Did you not issue a decree that no one could pray to anyone but you? If anyone violates that law, shouldn't he be thrown into a den of lions?"

The king replied, "Yes, that is the law."

The spokesman continued: "Then we must inform you that Daniel, one of the exiles from Judah, is ignoring your law. He still prays to his God three times a day."

When the king heard that, he felt distressed, and all he could think about was how to save Daniel. But that was nearly impossible: He could not retract the law that he had just issued.

At sundown the leaders returned. "O King," they said, "remember that according to our laws, a decree issued by you cannot be changed."

The king knew he had no choice. "Yes," he said. "I know."

Reluctantly, he ordered his officials to seize Daniel and carry out the sentence for breaking this new law.

As Daniel was being thrown into the den, the king appeared. He called out to Daniel, "May your God rescue you!"

A stone was placed over the opening of the den. As the law required, the king and his nobles sealed it with their own signet rings. Then the king returned to his palace, but he refused to eat or be entertained. All night long, he tossed and turned, for he could not fall asleep.

At dawn the king got out of bed and hurried to the lions' den. He called out, "Daniel, servant of the living God, has your God been able to rescue you?"

"O King, live forever! My God has sent his angel to shut the lions' mouths."

The king was overjoyed. Immediately he ordered that Daniel be lifted out. He realized Daniel was unharmed because he had trusted in his God. He also realized who was really at fault. So he ordered that the very men who had accused Daniel now be placed in the lions' den.

King Darius then wrote a new decree: "I hereby order everyone in my kingdom to fear and respect the God of Daniel. He is the living God. His kingdom stands forever. He performs signs and wonders, and he has rescued Daniel from the power of the lions."

TBC 164

A Startling Vision

TBC Book One, Chapter 165
Daniel 10:1-11:12

Two years after Cyrus the Persian conquered Babylon, something remarkable happened to Daniel. After fasting from choice foods for 21 days, he saw a vision from heaven. As he stood there on the banks of the Tigris River, he saw an angelic being walk toward him.

Only Daniel saw the vision. But when the men who were with him saw his reaction, they were terrified. As they fled, Daniel was left alone, gazing at the vision. His body began to grow weak and his face turned pale. Dropping to the ground, he fell into a deep sleep.

A hand touched his shoulder, and Daniel raised himself on his hands and knees.

"Daniel," the angel said, "you are highly esteemed by God. Listen carefully to what I am about to tell you. Now stand up, for God has sent me to you."

So Daniel stood up, trembling the whole while.

"Do not be afraid, Daniel. Since the first day you decided to gain understanding from God and to humble yourself, your prayers were heard. For 21 days, the angelic prince of Persia prevented me from coming. Then Michael, the chief angelic prince, came to help me. I have come to explain what will happen to your people in the future."

As he spoke, Daniel bowed with his face to the ground, speechless. The angel touched Daniel's lips. But Daniel was so overwhelmed by the vision that he could hardly breathe.

Again the angel touched Daniel's lips, giving him strength. "Do not be afraid," he said to Daniel, "for you are highly esteemed by God. Peace! Be strong!"

As the angel spoke, Daniel began to regain his strength. "Speak, my lord," Daniel said, "since you have strengthened me."

The angel said, "I am about to return to fight against the angelic prince over Persia. When he is defeated, the prince of Greece will come to power. Michael, the prince of your people, supports me against both of them. But first I will reveal your people's future.

"Three more kings will rise to power in Persia. Then a fourth Persian will come to power by using his wealth, and he will try to invade Greece. But he will be defeated by a more powerful ruler. The new king's vast empire will be broken into four regions.

"The king of the south will grow strong. But one of his commanders will grow stronger and rule his own kingdom. In time, they will become allies. Then the daughter of the southern king will make an alliance with the northern kingdom, but both will lose their power.

"The princess will have a relative who takes her place. He will attack the king of the north and defeat him. This ruler will capture their gods and seize their valuables of silver and gold. He will take them back to his kingdom in the south, which is Egypt.

"Years later, the kingdom of the north will take revenge. He will invade the kingdom of Egypt but then retreat to his own country. His sons will prepare for a greater war. They will assemble a massive army and sweep their enemies like a flood.

"In spite of their large army, the kingdom of the north will be defeated. Egypt will capture its army and slaughter thousands. But the king of Egypt will be filled with pride. He will not remain victorious."

Daniel listened intently. When the angel paused, Daniel could not help but wonder, *What will happen then?*

TBC 165

The Future of His People

TBC Book One, Chapter 166
Daniel 11:13-35

It was almost 2,500 years ago, when an angel first appeared to Daniel in a vision and showed him what would happen to his people. He described a king of the south, which was then Egypt. The king of the north may have been Syria. Daniel listened as the angel continued to speak.

"The king of the north will raise a much larger army and advance toward the south. At that time, many others will also rise against the south. Violent men from among your own people will also rebel; their plans, however, will not succeed. But the king of the north will.

"After the northern king invades Egypt, no one will be able to defeat him. By invading Egypt, he will also have power over the land of Palestine" (the land once known as Israel and Judah). "He will make a treaty with Egypt's king by giving him his daughter in marriage.

"He will think his daughter's marriage will eventually allow him to rule Egypt. But his plans will fail. So he will turn toward the coast and conquer many islands. Another nation will then send its army to defeat him, for those island people are its allies.

"A new king will succeed the king of the north. He will appoint a person to collect tax money from the regions that he governs, including Palestine. But someone will secretly kill him. Then a vile, crude person will take the throne from the rightful heir.

"The people will not realize what the vile new king of the north is doing to win support. This king will also make a covenant with the prince of the south, but he will be lying to him. Meanwhile, he will conquer territories, using only small armies.

"The richest provinces governed by the southern king will start to feel secure and protected. Then the king of the north will take them off guard and invade their land. He will plunder them, then use that wealth to reward others so they will support him.

"The king of the north will then form a large army and attack the southern kingdom, which is Egypt. Egypt will also raise a large army, but it will be defeated.

"Then the king of Egypt will lose control, for those closest to him will plot against him.

"The king of the north and the king of Egypt will sit together, as if they are friends. But both will be lying. The northern king will then travel to the holy land. Driven by a great rage, he will attack its people then return to his homeland.

"Again the king of the north will invade Egypt. But another country will send ships from its western coastlands to stop him. Angry at being thwarted, he will again attack the holy land. He will reward those who turn against their own people to help him.

"The king will use his army to desecrate the temple and put an end to the daily sacrifices. He will then set up an altar to a pagan idol. Some of the people will actually support him and help him. But those who know their God will firmly resist.

"Those who are wise will continue to teach people the Law of God. For a time it will be very difficult: Some will die, some will be burned, some will be captured, some will be plundered. But even when it seems like they are failing, God has a purpose. . . ."

TBC 166

'Till the Power of the Holy People Is Broken'

TBC Book One, Chapter 167
Daniel 11:36-12:13

Daniel listened intently as the angel foretold what would happen to his people.
Today as we listen to his words, we look
back in history and see that those things
happened as he predicted. But the angel
had more to tell Daniel, some of which still has yet to happen.

"The king of the north will grow so powerful that he will do
whatever he wishes. He will set himself up above every god and speak
boastfully against the God of gods. He will be successful until God's wrath
has been fulfilled through him.

"He will show no regard for the worship others hold to. Instead, he
will use his wealth to make himself more powerful. It will seem like a foreign god is helping him as he attacks. He will honor those who honor
him, rewarding them with the land he conquers.

"As the time of God's wrath draws to an end, the king of the south
will challenge the king of the north. So the king of the north will raise up
a great army and a mighty fleet of ships. He will invade many countries,
sweeping over them like a flood.

"He will invade the holy land and conquer many other countries.
Edom, Moab, and the leaders of Ammon will avoid his control. But Egypt
will not escape; he will gain Egypt's wealth and its resources, as well as
that of the surrounding nations.

"Countries to the east and the north will plot against him. In rage,
he will react, destroying much and annihilating whole groups of people.
He will set himself up in Jerusalem. But he will meet his end, and when
he does, no one will help him.

The angel continued to speak to Daniel, describing what would
happen in the spiritual realm.

"In the end, Michael—the angelic prince who protects your
people—will rise up. There will be a terrible time of distress, like nothing
the world has ever seen.

"Your people—those whose names are written in the Book of Life—
will be delivered. Many who are dead will rise, some to eternal life, others

to everlasting shame. Those who are wise and lead many to God's right-eousness will shine with God's glory.

"Now, Daniel, close up and seal these words, for they speak of the distant future, the end times. At that time, people will frantically desire to know these things."

Suddenly, two other angels appeared. It was as though they were having a conversation that was meant for Daniel to overhear.

One of them called out, "How long will it be before these things are fulfilled?"

The other figure lifted his arms as if making a vow. "It will be for a time, times, and half a time. When the power of the holy people has finally been broken, then all these things will be fulfilled."

Daniel had questions. "My lord," he said, "what will happen then?"

"Go on your way, Daniel. These things are sealed up until the end times. Many will be purified by what happens then. The wicked will not understand, but those who are wise will."

The angel added, "From the time the sacrifices end until the idol is set up in the temple, there will be 1,290 days. Blessed is the one who will hold out to the end, 45 days later.

"Now, Daniel, you must go your way. Know that in the end, you will rise from the dead and receive your inheritance." And with that, the angel disappeared. But Daniel was left with the vivid memory of all that he had seen and heard.

He knew what he must do now—the very thing that the angel had instructed him to do.

So Daniel began to write down all he had seen and heard. He knew that someday, perhaps hundreds or thousands of years after he would die, those words would hold special meaning for God's holy people. Who knows? Perhaps they will be fulfilled in our lifetime. . . .

TBC 167

The Exiles Return!

TBC Book One, Chapter 168
Ezra 1:1-4:24

Two years before Daniel's final visions, the Lord moved the heart of Cyrus, king of Persia. This was during the first year after Cyrus conquered Babylon. To fulfill the prophecy that God had given Jeremiah, the Lord prompted Cyrus to make a decree.

"The Lord God of heaven has given me the kingdoms of the earth and appointed me to build his temple. Any of his people who wish may return to Jerusalem to rebuild the temple. Those who stay will help provide the materials and goods they will need."

Just as God had prompted Cyrus, so also did he inspire people to want to return to rebuild the Temple. Their friends and neighbors donated goods and valuables and livestock. Then Cyrus gave them the items that Nebuchadnezzar had taken from the temple.

So now, 70 years after being exiled in Babylon, the family heads of Judah and Benjamin led a group of 42,000 to return to Jerusalem. When they arrived, about four months later, they gave freewill offerings. Then each family returned to their home region throughout Judah.

Three months later they had all settled in their hometowns. Now they were ready to meet again in Jerusalem. They were wary of the other people living near them. But those fears did not stop them from their first task—to build the altar for burnt offerings.

Once they completed the altar, the people began making offerings to the Lord. They celebrated the Feast of Tabernacles with burnt offerings. Then they held other sacrifices and sacred feasts. But they had not yet laid the foundation for the temple.

The people decided to trade food, drinks, and oil for cedar logs from Sidon and Tyre. Once the logs began to arrive, they gave money to the masons and carpenters among them. In the second month of their second year back, they began to build the temple.

When the foundation was laid, the people were so happy that they held a celebration to praise the Lord. The priests dressed up in special robes. Some of the Levites played trumpets and cymbals. And the people shouted for joy.

But not all who were there felt happy. In fact, when the older people came and they saw the foundation, they were so disappointed they started to cry.

"Why this is so small!" they said. "Our temple was nothing like this!"

Only the older people had seen the original temple before it was destroyed.

Still the work on the temple continued, led by a man named Zerubbabel, one of their leaders. One day some of the neighboring people came and spoke to Zerubbabel: "Let us help you," said one of the men, "for we, too, seek your God. We have sacrificed to him ever since we were exiled here by the Assyrians."

But they were Gentiles, not Jews. Some of them, however, had married Jewish women who were left in the land. So Zerubbabel and the elders firmly told them, "No, you have no part in building this temple. We ourselves will continue to build it for the Lord, the God of Israel, just as King Cyrus has commanded."

Their reply made the neighboring people angry. From then on, the people in the region tried to stop the Jews from building the temple. They did things to make the Jews afraid. Then they wrote letters to officials, complaining about the Jews. Finally, their plan began to work. It wasn't long before the building stopped, and the Jews gave up working on the temple.

TBC 168

A Misplaced Mission

TBC Book One, Chapter 169
Ezra 5, 6; Haggai

Almost 20 years had now passed since all the exiles who were given their freedom returned to Judah, yet the temple was still not built. The Jews gave up the goal that brought them there. They now turned their attention to building themselves houses. So the Lord sent them the prophet Haggai.

"Have you ever wondered why your harvest is so small even though you planted much?" Haggai asked. "You have built up your own houses, while God's house remains a ruin. That is why God has sent this drought. The Lord says, 'Think about what you are doing.'"

Haggai's words did make them think. And when they realized that God had sent the drought, they feared the Lord.

"Now go and get timber," Haggai continued, "for the Lord says, 'I am with you.'"

With those words, the Lord inspired Zerubbabel, their governor, Joshua the high priest, and all the people. They decided they would return to what God had called them to do.

About a month later, the Lord gave another message through Haggai. "Who among you saw the former temple? How does this one compare to it? Does it seem like nothing to you? Do not despair. Be strong! I am with you, and that is my covenant. My Spirit is with you.

"A time is coming when I will again shake the heavens and the earth. I will shake all nations, and they will come to this house. The glory of this house will be far greater than the glory of the former one. In this place, I will grant my peace."

In time, the Lord sent yet another prophet to the remnant of his people, a man named Zechariah. He, too, urged the people to consider their ways and turn to God wholeheartedly.

"Remember what happened to your forefathers," said Zechariah. "Return to God and he will return to you."

One day Haggai asked the priests, "If a person carries consecrated meat in his garment, does the food that touches the garment become consecrated?"

"No," they said.

Then Haggai asked another question. "If the person became defiled by touching a dead body, would that defile the food?"

"Yes," they said in agreement.

Haggai continued, "So also it is with this nation. Whatever they offer there is defiled. Now think about this carefully. Before the foundation was laid, all their hard work was cursed by God; they barely survived. But from this day on, the Lord says, 'I will bless you.' "

That same day, the twenty-fourth day of the ninth month, the Lord sent Haggai to Zerubbabel with a message: "The Lord says, 'I will shake the heavens and earth and will overthrow the power of foreign nations. You are a symbol of what I promise to do on that day.' "

The news soon spread that the Jews had now returned to their work, building the temple. When the officials governing Palestine heard about it, they came to question them. But the Lord was watching over them. No one could stop them from their work without a legal document.

The governor then sent a letter to King Darius. (This King Darius lived and ruled sometime after Darius the Mede.) In that letter, the governor told Darius what the Jews were doing. He asked the king to check his records to see if their work was indeed ordered by King Cyrus.

Darius discovered that what the Jewish elders said was true. So he wrote back to the governor. King Darius not only told him to let the Jews continue, but he also ordered him to pay for their expenses. Once again, God had prospered his people, and the building of the temple continued.

TBC 169

The Four Horsemen of Heaven

TBC Book One, Chapter 170
Zechariah 1:7-6:8

Like Daniel, the prophet Zechariah received visions from the Lord. One night he saw a figure riding a red horse. Others appeared behind him on red, brown, and white horses. They reported to the angel of the Lord, "We have found the whole earth at peace and rest."

The angel of the Lord asked, "Lord Almighty, how long will you withhold your mercy from Jerusalem and Judah, whom you have been angry with for 70 years?"

The Lord answered by speaking words of comfort. Then he added, "But I am now angry with the nations that feel secure."

Zechariah then saw four horns. "What are these?" he asked.

"The ones who scattered the people of Jerusalem, Israel, and Judah."

Then four craftsmen appeared. The angel explained, "They have come to terrify those nations who scattered Judah's people."

Suddenly, Zechariah saw a man with a tape measure. "Where are you going?" he asked.

"To measure Jerusalem," the angel replied.

Then another angel added, "Tell him Jerusalem will be so large it will have no walls. The Lord himself will be a wall of fire around it."

The prophet's message conveyed a sense of urgency as well as reassurance: "Come and flee from the land of the north! declares the Lord. Escape to Zion, you who live in daughter Babylon! Concerning the nations that have plundered you, says the Lord of hosts: Whoever touches you touches the apple of my eye. I will plunder them just as they plundered you. . . . Sing and rejoice, O daughter Zion, says the Lord, for I am coming to dwell among you!"

The angel then showed Zechariah a vision of Joshua the high priest, standing before the Lord in dirty clothes. Satan stood nearby accusing him, but the Lord rebuked Satan. Then the angel commanded that Joshua be given new clothes, for his sin was taken away.

The angel said to Joshua, "The Lord Almighty says, 'If you obey me, you will govern my house. You and your associates symbolize things to come. I will bring my servant, the Branch. I will set a stone with seven eyes. And I will remove the sin of this land.' "

The angel aroused Zechariah, as if waking him. Then Zechariah saw a gold lamp stand with a bowl on top and seven candle lights. An olive tree stood on each side.

"Not by might, nor by power, but by God's spirit. Just as Zerubbabel laid the foundation, so also will he complete the task. Who despises the small temple? Someday people will rejoice.

"The seven eyes are the eyes of the Lord, watching throughout the earth. The olive branches are his anointed servants." Then Zechariah saw a scroll, 30 feet long and 15 feet wide.

The angel explained, "This stands for God's curse covering the land. One side declares every thief will be banished. The other banishes everyone who swears falsely in God's name."

Zechariah looked up again and saw a basket. The angel said it stood for the sin of the people. A woman appeared under the lid: she symbolized wickedness. Two women-like figures with wings carried it away the basket. It would be housed in Babylonia until the proper time.

Finally, Zechariah saw four chariots, coming out from between two mountains of bronze. The first chariot had red horses, the second had black horses, the third had white horses, and the fourth was pulled by dappled-colored horses. They were straining to go throughout the earth.

The angel said, "They are the four spirits of heaven, going out from the Lord's presence."

The black horses went north, the white ones raced west, and the dappled ones went south.

An angel called out to Zechariah, "Look—those heading northward have given rest to my Spirit in the land of the north." The prophet stared and wondered, *Now what could that mean?*

TBC 170

Too Marvelous to Imagine

TBC Book One, Chapter 171
Zechariah 6:9 - 8:23

While the people were rebuilding the temple, the Lord continued to speak to Zechariah. One day he instructed him to make a crown of silver and gold and place it on the high priest, Joshua. "Say, 'This man is named the Branch. He will branch out from this place and build the temple of the Lord.'"

Joshua symbolized a future leader who would rule as both king and priest. After crowning Joshua, Zechariah was to place the crown in the temple as a memorial.

The Lord added, "Someday, those who are far away will come and help build the temple of the Lord."

What the Lord said about the temple was puzzling. It sounded as though he were talking about the distant future. And yet, the temple would surely be finished within a few years. What did he mean when he said those who are "far away" will help build it? . . .

About a year later, in the fifth month, the people wondered if they should mourn and fast as they had each year at this time. The Lord answered through Zechariah: "When you fasted all those years, was it really for me? If so, then why didn't you obey me?"

The Lord spoke to them the same way he had spoken to their forefathers: "Practice justice. Show mercy and compassion. Do not oppress those who are disadvantaged—the widows and orphans, the aliens, the poor. Do not plot against each other."

Zechariah continued, "The prophets spoke these very same words to your forefathers, but they covered their ears and refused to listen. They were stubborn and hard-hearted. They turned away from the Lord's words and his Law. So the Lord Almighty became very angry with them.

"The Lord said, 'When I called, they did not listen to me. So when they called me, I would not listen to them either. Then I scattered them among all the nations and made them aliens. It is because of their actions that this pleasant land has become a desolate place.'"

Some time later, the word of the Lord again came to Zechariah, a word of encouragement for his people. "The Lord says, 'I will return to

Zion and live there. Jerusalem will be called the City of Truth, and my mountain will be called the Holy Mountain.

" 'In those days, men and women will live to a ripe old age. They will sit and watch the streets of Jerusalem, filled with boys and girls playing. Right now, this may seem too marvelous. But I will save my people and bring them back to Jerusalem.

" 'Listen, you who were there when the temple's foundation was laid. Be strong and finish building it. Remember when you let the temple lay in ruins? You had little money or food. Your enemies harassed you. But that time is over. Now I will bless you.

" 'Just as I made a decision to punish your forefathers when they angered me, so now have I decided to do good to Jerusalem and Judah. So do not be afraid. Be truthful with each other. Make just judgments in court. Love truth and peace just as I do.

" 'Someday, people from all over the world will say, "I am going to Jerusalem to see the Lord Almighty. Come with me!" People from powerful nations will come to seek out the Lord. And people will also seek counsel from the Jews, knowing that God is with them.' "

Four years after returning to the work, the people finished building the temple. They held a great celebration and dedicated it to the Lord. Hundreds of sacrifices were made as sin offerings. With great joy, all the people worshiped the Lord.

TBC 171

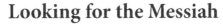

Looking for the Messiah

TBC Book One, Chapter 172
Zechariah 9 - 14

A burning question lingered among the Jews who had returned to Judea. Many years had now passed since the temple was rebuilt. The people wondered why their Messiah had not yet come to fill the temple with his glory. So the Lord described what must first take place. But he did it symbolically, with the Messiah speaking through Zechariah as a shepherd.

Zechariah says, The Lord my God said, "Pasture the flock marked for slaughter. Their own shepherds will sell them to make a profit. But I will not have pity nor rescue them." So I pastured the flock, especially those who were oppressed, and I removed three bad shepherds.

But the flock detested me, and I grew tired of shepherding them. I took my staff called Favor and broke it. It was my covenant protecting the flock from the nations. They paid me just 30 pieces of silver when I left. And the Lord told me, "Throw it to the potter."

Then I broke my second staff, called Union, ending the friendly bonds between Judah and Israel. The Lord said, "I will now raise a shepherd who will not care for the sheep. He will eat the meat of the choicest sheep. Woe to that worthless shepherd!"

Some time later, another prophetic word came, describing what would happen just before the Messiah reigns: "The nations of the earth will surround Judah and Jerusalem, but I will save them. My people will realize that I was the one they pierced, and they will mourn."

Zechariah says that after the Messiah comes and delivers his people from their enemies, he will put an end to idolatry. In that day, there will be no prophets, and if anyone claims to be a prophet from God, that person must die. His own friends and relatives will stop him.

But God decreed what would happen before then, revealing it through Zechariah: "Awake, O sword against the shepherd, though he is close to me. Strike him, and the sheep will scatter. Two-thirds will be struck down. One-third will be left to purify, like gold tested by fire."

The final event that will be fulfilled is called the "day of the Lord." The Lord describes that time, saying, "I will inspire all nations to gather together to fight against Jerusalem. The city will be captured, and half the people will be taken as exiles. But the rest will not be taken."

Though the Lord will incite the nations to gather for battle, in the end he will fight against them. The Messiah will stand on the Mount of Olives, near Jerusalem, and his presence will cause an earthquake. The valley it forms will provide an escape for his people.

The Messiah will then appear with all his holy ones. It will be an extraordinary day. Sunlight will disappear, yet there will be no cold or frost. Nor will there be dark of night. Living water will flow from Jerusalem to the sea. Finally, the Messiah will reign as King.

When the Messiah comes to his people's rescue, he will strike all the nations that fought against Jerusalem. Their flesh will rot, and their eyes will rot in their sockets. Others will be so terrified that they will fight one another. The wealth they leave behind will be gathered as plunder.

Some of the people, however, will survive. From then on they will travel to Jerusalem every year to worship the King of Kings. People from all nations will honor him. Only then will their land receive the rainfall it needs, for God will bless those who worship him.

TBC 172

A Royal Challenge

TBC Book One, Chapter 173
Esther 1:1-2:8

Just when it seemed they were safe and secure, a new threat loomed for Jews dispersed throughout Persia. More than thirty years after the temple was completed, the Persian king who supported that Jewish effort was succeeded by his son, Xerxes, grandson of Cyrus the Great. Though many Jews had returned to Jerusalem, most remained scattered throughout Persia. Some prospered and rose to prominence as public officials, like Mordecai, whose great grandfather was among the first exiles taken captive. From his strategic leadership position at the king's gate, Mordecai was one of the first to hear the news that came from the palace. . . .

For almost half a year, King Xerxes publicly displayed his great wealth and weapons of warfare. To show the world that the Greeks who dared to rival him were no match for his might and his majesty, he completed his grand display with a magnificent banquet at his winter palace in Susa. On the final day of the great feast, the king was drunk with revelry and decided to show off the beauty of his wife, Queen Vashti. So he sent his seven eunuchs to escort her.

Meanwhile, the queen hosted a banquet of her own for the women of nobility. When the king's attendants appeared, she beckoned one to approach. "Have you a message?" she asked.

"Yes, your majesty. The king has sent for you to appear before his honored guests."

A large circle of women surrounded the queen, and while the attendant stood waiting, a hushed silence fell upon the room. Vashti raised her eyes and looked out at the large crowd of women. Then she turned back toward the attendant. "You may leave now," she said.

"If it pleases your majesty—what message shall we take back to the king?"

A smile crossed her face as she glanced at the vast audience now standing before her. She turned once again toward the messenger. In a loud voice, she replied, "Tell him I am occupied."

When the attendant delivered the queen's message, King Xerxes was furious. How dare she challenge him, and in front of all his guests! *She will pay for this!* he thought. The king then summoned his wise men and told them what had happened.

"Now, according to our law," he said, "what shall I do? What punishment would befit such insubordination?"

The counselors requested a few moments to discuss the matter. This situation was more grave than the king realized. What would happen when news of this spread? Already hundreds of Mede and Persian women witnessed what the queen had done. If they followed her example, every man in the kingdom could face the same disrespect and misconduct.

"Your majesty," began the spokesman, "if it pleases the king, let him issue a royal decree. Since Queen Vashti refused to appear before you, henceforth may she never enter the king's presence. May her royal position be given to someone better. And may an edict be read in every province, in each person's language, that every man is ruler over his own household."

Both the king and his nobles were pleased with their counsel. But the task of finding a new queen would have to wait. King Xerxes found himself embroiled in one disastrous battle after another. Three years later he finally returned to Susa and remembered the royal edict.

Vashti was no longer queen. So one of the attendants proposed, "If it pleases the king, let a search be made for the most beautiful virgins from every province of your realm. Let them be placed under the care of the king's chief eunuch, Hegai. Let each one be given beauty treatments and placed in your harem. May the one who pleases the king most be crowned as Queen."

The king approved and the edict was issued. Girls from throughout the kingdom were selected for King Xerxes's harem. Among them was a beautiful young woman named Esther, the cousin of Mordecai. Her parents died when she was an infant, and Mordecai had raised her as his own daughter. Now, as she prepared to leave home, Mordecai whispered, "Promise me one thing. . . ."

TBC 173

Queen of Hearts

TBC Book One, Chapter 174
Esther 2:9 - 4:11

From the moment she entered the king's harem, Hegai knew there was something special about Esther. Yes, she was strikingly beautiful, but there was a quality that was also attractive. Was it her pleasant disposition? Or her soft-spoken nature? Or her responses? Often she would simply smile and say, "What do you think?"

Just as often, Hegai would smile to himself, musing the answer in his mind: *I think I have found a queen. . . .*

Hegai placed Esther in the best living quarters of King Xerxes's harem and provided her with choice delicacies. He assigned her seven maids from the king's palace, who helped with the year-long preparation of beauty treatments, six months of oils to soften her skin and six more months of perfumes and cosmetics. When that was completed, he would send her to the king.

Every day that year, Mordecai would walk near the harem courtyard to learn how Esther was faring. Each time she saw him, she recalled the vow she had made: No one must know that she is a Jew. Nor should she speak of her family background.

Finally, the day arrived for Esther to be presented to the king. She knew that once she entered the king's palace, she would never return to these quarters. She was destined for one of two fates: Either she would join the king's large harem of concubines, or she would be selected as the new queen of Persia. Hegai waved his arm as he gave the customary offer made to every maiden on this occasion: "Select whatever you wish to wear and whatever you wish to bring."

Only Esther would even consider such a winsome reply: "What would you suggest?"

Moments later, Hegai smiled with approval as he presented Esther to the king. He had done his part. Now it was up to her. Let her charm work its magic. . . .

The next morning, King Xerxes summoned his chief attendants and declared a royal holiday throughout his entire kingdom. He would host a magnificent celebration. Gifts would be presented to his nobles and chief officials for this grand event: Esther would be crowned queen.

As months turned into years, Esther enjoyed the favor of the king and of everyone who saw her. Her cousin, meanwhile, continued to serve as an official at the king's gate, the center for trade and legal matters. On this particular day, however, it also served as a meeting point for two disgruntled guards. While Mordecai appeared busy with his own matters, he overheard their every word—they were plotting to kill the king. Immediately, he sent word to Esther. She told the king, giving credit to Mordecai. The report proved true, and the men were hung.

Shortly after this, King Xerxes decided to reward a man named Haman by promoting him to chief official. The king commanded all his subjects to honor Haman by bowing down to him, and all the officials did so—except one. As a Jew, Mordecai refused to bow down to a mere man.

When the other officials told Haman that Mordecai refused to bow, Haman was furious. In his rage, he decided to do more than punish Mordecai—he would destroy all the Jews in Persia. Without naming their nationality, Haman simply told King Xerxes that he wished to deal with "a group of troublemakers" who refused to obey the king's laws. "If it pleases the king," he said, "let them all be killed on the thirteenth day of the twelfth month."

The edict was read throughout the kingdom, and in every province, Jews mourned in sackcloth and ashes. Outside the king's gate, Mordecai wailed loudly and bitterly. When servants told Esther, she was alarmed. So she sent for him, but he refused to change his clothes to enter the king's courtyard. Instead, he sent her a message, informing her of the king's edict: "I urge you, my child, go to the king. Plead for mercy on behalf of your people."

His message brought terror to her soul. King Xerxes had not sent for her for a whole month. And anyone who went to the king without being summoned could be put to death. . . .

TBC 174

For Such a Time as This

Mordecai's second message brought even more fear to Esther's heart. "Listen!" he said. "Do not think you will escape death because you are in the palace. Who knows—perhaps you were appointed queen was for such a time as this."

She knew he was right. Her only hope was that the king would hold out his golden scepter—permission to approach without forfeiting her life. She had her servant tell Mordecai: "Have all the Jews fast for three days. Then I will go to him. And if I perish, I perish."

After putting on her royal robes, Esther walked to the inner court and stood at the entrance. When the king looked up and saw her, he was pleased, and he held out his scepter.

Esther breathed a sigh of relief. As she entered, she touched the scepter and bowed.

"What is it, Queen Esther? Ask me for anything you wish, even up to half my kingdom."

"If it pleases my lord, the king, may he and the honorable Haman come to a banquet I am preparing."

King Xerxes smiled and accepted her invitation. Accompanied by Haman, the king attended her banquet that very day. As they sipped wine, the king again asked what she desired.

Esther replied, "May it please my lord, the king, and the honorable Haman to join me for yet another banquet tomorrow. Then I will answer your question."

When Haman went home that night, he boasted to friends and family about his exclusive invitation. His day was perfect except for one thing—that Jew still refused to bow. One man after another offered suggestions. Finally, one person said, "Why not build gallows to hang him?"

Haman stroked his chin, listening to the idea. He grew happy just thinking about it.

Meanwhile, King Xerxes lay awake in bed, wondering what Esther had in mind. To help him fall asleep, he ordered a scribe to read aloud the accounts of his reign. When the scribe read about the guards' conspiracy, the king suddenly realized he had never rewarded Mordecai.

Just then, the king heard footsteps approaching. Haman came, seeking permission to hang a certain Jew. "Haman," said the king, "How should I honor someone who has pleased me?"

Haman tried his best not to smile. Surely the king was thinking of him. So he said, "If it pleases the king, dress him in a royal robe and have him led through the city on your horse."

"Very well. Go at once to the official Mordecai, who sits at the gate, and bestow upon him the honor you have named. Lead him throughout the city and announce my tribute."

Haman was stunned. In disbelief, he left the palace to carry out the king's order. Later that morning, Haman delivered a royal robe to Mordecai. Then he led him throughout the city, declaring, "Here is what the king does for the man whom he delights to honor!"

Haman's closest friends stared in amazement. From that moment on, even his advisors were predicting his fate: "Your downfall started with Mordecai—you cannot stand against him."

Later Haman joined the king at Esther's banquet. This time, Esther answered the king's question. "O King," she said, "please spare my life and my people's lives, for we are in danger!"

With tears, Esther explained how she and all her people would be killed. When the king heard her story, he glared at Haman, then he stormed outside in a rage. Haman rushed toward the queen and fell to his knees. "Please, I beg you—have mercy. . . ." When the king returned and saw Haman there, clinging to Esther, he ordered that Haman be hung on his own gallows.

Once Haman was taken, the king sat down with Esther and asked her about her family. When he realized that Mordecai had raised her, King Xerxes appointed him to replace Haman.

As the king's new chief official, Mordecai immediately wrote laws to protect the Jews. Then he established a new holiday for their people. From that time on, the Jews celebrated the "Feast of Purim," a holiday to help them always remember their deliverance, even today.

TBC 175

Homeward Bound

TBC Book One, Chapter 176
Ezra 7 - 10

A long journey lay ahead of Ezra. He was one of the finest Jewish teachers in Persia and one of King Artaxerxes' favorite scribes. But the king knew what Ezra wanted most—to go to Jerusalem to study and to teach. As usual, the king granted him his request.

King Artaxerxes authorized a letter giving him permission to go to Jerusalem. And he issued a decree, announcing that other Jews in Babylon could join him. It would take four months to travel there. But the king knew that Ezra's trip could accomplish a great deal. In the long run, it would also serve his kingdom, for he gave Ezra the authority not only to teach the people God's Law, but also to appoint judges.

A great many Jews responded to the king's invitation. Thousands of Israelites met with Ezra to prepare for the trip back to their homeland. In his journal, Ezra wrote: "Before we left, we gathered together to fast and pray for a safe journey. I was ashamed to ask the king for soldiers to protect us, for I had told the king the hand of God is on everyone who looks to him."

Ezra appointed twelve priests as leaders, with other Levites to assist them. Then he divided among them the gold and silver given by the king, along with gold and bronze furnishings for the temple. It was their job to guard them and deliver them safely.

As they journeyed toward Jerusalem, Ezra realized that God's favor must certainly still rest upon him. Even though they had no soldiers with them to protect them, their whole group arrived safely in Jerusalem. No bandits had tried to overtake them. After resting for three days, they offered sacrifices and praised God.

It was evident to those in Jerusalem that King Artaxerxes had given great authority to Ezra. The king had sent one of their own people to teach them and to appoint judges in the land. It was important that they cooperate with him. So some of the men came to him and said, "Many of our people, including the priests, Levites, and other leaders, have married Gentile women."

Immediately Ezra tore his robe and pulled hairs from his head and beard. After grieving for their sin, Ezra began to pray: "O my God," he said, "I am so ashamed. From the days of our forefathers, we have sinned. Our sins brought captivity and humiliation. But you have graciously left us a remnant and given us favor with the Persian kings.

"But now, what can we say? You warned our forefathers not to marry with the people who lived here. Shall we once again disobey you and make you angry? This time, perhaps you might destroy us altogether. O Lord, you are righteous. But we are guilty."

Ezra wept as he prayed. Meanwhile, a large group of people gathered. They too wept bitterly. Then one man came forward and spoke directly to Ezra.

"We have been unfaithful," he said, "but there is still hope. If you think it best, we will send away our foreign wives and children."

So Ezra called the leaders together. He made them take an oath to send away the foreign wives. Then they sent a proclamation throughout Judah. In three days, all the Israelites were to meet in Jerusalem. Those who did not come would be cut off from the community.

The people all came, but it rained miserably that day. Ezra called out to them: "You have been unfaithful to God. Now confess your sin and separate yourselves from the foreign wives."

The people agreed they must do this. But they knew that carrying this out was not that simple. It could not be done in a single day, and they sent leaders to tell that to Ezra.

Ezra listened. They were right. It would take time to do the right thing and to do it orderly. So the family heads met with each tribe to judge each case. And within three months, the pagan wives were gone. The people had kept their pledge to the Lord.

TBC 176

It All Began on the Wall . . .

TBC Book One, Chapter 177
Nehemiah 1:1 - 6:19

> I went out at night, taking only a few men. I had not told anyone what I planned to do. . . .

Thirteen years after Ezra had led thousands of exiles back to Jerusalem, the Lord's favor rested on yet another Jewish man who served the king of Persia. Nehemiah, the king's cup bearer, heard voices below the palace wall and realized, *Those men are speaking Hebrew.* The men had just returned from Jerusalem, and Nehemiah wanted to hear news from his homeland.

"How are the exiles who returned?" he asked. "How is Jerusalem?"

"They have no protection," one of the men answered. "The city wall is in shambles."

When Nehemiah heard this, he sat down and wept. For days he fasted and prayed.

"O Lord," he said, "please hear your servant's prayer. I confess we have sinned. But remember your promise to the remnant who obeys you. Please grant my request to the king."

That prayer marked a turning point for Nehemiah. Remarkable things began to happen. He kept a journal to chronicle his experiences, and this is what he recorded:

I brought the king his wine as usual. But never before had I been sad in his presence. When he asked me, "What's wrong?" I grew alarmed.

I answered, "The city of my forefathers lies in ruins. Its walls have been burned down."

"What is your request?" the king asked.

Silently I prayed to God. Then I answered, "If it pleases the king, and if your servant has found favor in your sight, send me to that city in Judea so I may help the people rebuild its wall."

The king asked, "How long would the journey take? When would you return?"

I paused then named a certain time. When it was apparent that the king planned to grant my request, I also asked that letters be sent to various officials. So letters were written to guarantee my safe passage and to secure the governor's help in getting timber.

Guarded by the king's soldiers, I made my journey to Jerusalem. I went first to the governor of the Trans-Euphrates region and gave him the king's letters. When the officials Sanballat and Tobiah heard that I came to help the Israelites, they were upset.

Three days after I arrived, I went out at night, taking a few men with me. I had not told them, nor anyone else, what God had placed on my heart about rebuilding the wall. Instead, I simply circled around the city, examining the wall from gate to gate.

The next day, I met with the officials in Jerusalem and told them how God had answered my prayers, how the king of Persia had sent me to help them build up the wall.

The men were surprised but then excited. One of them replied, "Let's start building!"

We organized the people by district and assigned each one part of the wall. Steadily we made repairs, for the people were working whole-heartedly. Then came Sanballat and Tobiah, the region's governors. They tried to discourage us by ridiculing our work.

But the wall was soon rebuilt to half its former height. When Sanballat, Tobiah, and some neighboring people saw our progress, they plotted to attack us. When I learned of their plans, I divided the workers into two groups, one to stand guard and the other to build.

Meanwhile, we experienced a famine. It had grown so bad that people began to borrow money and grain. Wealthy Israelites took advantage of the situation. They charged huge lending rates and took everything the people owned. So I called the people together and then addressed the problem.

"Stop doing this!" I said to the wealthy merchants. "This is not right before God."

After 52 days, we completed the wall. All during that time, Sanballat and our other enemies tried to stop us. They sent me letters trying to lure me away to meet with them. But I knew what they were scheming. So their plans failed. By the time we completed the wall, even our enemies realized the source behind our accomplishment—it was done with the help of God.

TBC 177

From Sorrow to Celebration

TBC Book One, Chapter 178
Nehemiah 7:1 - 13:30

The two brothers gazed at what God helped them accomplish. Nehemiah then turned to his brother and said to him, "Now that Jerusalem's wall and gates are completed, you are in charge. Do not open the gates at dawn; wait till people are awake." This would protect them from surprise attacks.

Now Nehemiah could turn his attention to other matters. The city was now well protected, but few people lived there because the houses had not been rebuilt. So Nehemiah summoned all the exiles to meet in Jerusalem. Each family would record where they were living.

Thirteen years had passed since Ezra the scribe had first arrived to teach the people the Law of God. And this particular day marked a special occasion. All the Israelites gathered in Jerusalem. Today they would hear Ezra read aloud from God's Book of the Law.

The people stood while Ezra read. Often he would pause; this gave the Levites a chance to explain to each small group what those words meant. As they listened, they all began to weep. And the more they heard, the more they wept.

Finally, Nehemiah called out, "Do not be sad this day. God wants you to celebrate!"

They learned that they were to celebrate the Feast of Booths every year during their harvest. Like their forefathers who left Egypt, they were to build huts out of branches. The huts served to shelter each family during the celebration. This symbolized God's protection.

For seven days they feasted, praising God. Each day Ezra read from God's Law. After the celebration ended, they confessed their sins as a nation. Once more they sent away pagan wives.

Nehemiah prayed, giving praise to God. And the people joined him in praising the Lord.

Then Nehemiah presented a scroll with the promises they made before God. They vowed not to intermarry, not to buy or sell on the Sabbath, and not to neglect giving tithes.

Nehemiah's next goal centered on rebuilding Jerusalem's population. First, the leaders of the province settled there. Then each tribe drew lots to see which families would move to the city. Some people volunteered to move, in spite of the danger.

Now that the families had resettled in Jerusalem, they would dedicate the wall and celebrate its completion. At the tops of the wall, Nehemiah positioned the leaders and two large choirs. Ezra led the procession as people sang and played musical instruments.

Nehemiah ruled as governor over Judah for 12 years. Then he returned to Persia to serve King Artaxerxes. A number of years later, he received permission to return to Jerusalem. But when he arrived, he could hardly believe what had happened while he was gone.

Eliashib, the high priest, had become friends with Tobiah and Sanballat, enemies of the Israelites. He even gave Tobiah a room among those located near the temple. The people had become so disgusted with what was happening that they stopped tithing. Soon the teaching and worship also stopped. And that was not all.

The people did not think twice about working on the Sabbath. When Nehemiah returned to Jerusalem and saw their utter disregard for the Sabbath, he rebuked them. Then he posted his own men as guards to make sure no one entered the city with merchandise on the Sabbath.

But what wrenched his heart the most was when he heard the children. Countless men had married foreign women, even the priests. Half of their children could not even speak Hebrew.

Nehemiah was so angry he called down curses on those men. "Don't you realize it was because of marriages like these that King Solomon sinned?" Then he made those families take a vow: There would be no more inter-marriages. As for the priests, new men were appointed.

Nehemiah's strong words penetrated many hearts, and the people repented. This time, with God as their witness, they would keep their vows.

TBC 178

A Conversation with God

TBC Book One, Chapter 179
Malachi

Shortly before Nehemiah returned to Persia, hard times began to fall upon the people of Judah. But no one knew why. Now that the temple was built, the people had expected to prosper. They fulfilled the mission God had given them. Wasn't it right to expect blessing? Instead, they suffered from famine. What the people did not realize, however, was that they were all drifting away from the Lord—and they didn't even know it. So the Lord sent them yet another prophet.

The prophet pretends God is having a conversation with his people, and it goes like this:

"I have loved you," says the Lord.

"How have you loved us?" they ask.

"Weren't Esau and Jacob brothers?" the Lord says. "Yet I chose to love Jacob. Today, Esau's inheritance is a wasteland.

The Lord continued, saying to them, "A son honors his father, and a servant honors his master. But where is my honor? You priests have despised me.

" 'How have we despised you?' you ask.

"By sacrificing crippled and diseased animals. Try offering those to your governor!

"It would be better that you shut the temple doors than to make offerings on my altar. For I will not accept your offerings. My Name will be honored among all the nations. But you have despised my Name by letting the people give the worst of their animals.

"If you priests continue to dishonor me, I will curse both you and your descendants. A priest ought to uphold my Law and teach others to obey it. Instead, you disobey me and cause others to do the same. So I will humiliate you before the people.

"The Israelites are all of one family, with one Father, are they not? Then why do you break faith by marrying outside that family? A detestable thing has happened in the land. Your men marry pagan women. And yet they continue to bring offerings to the Lord.

"And that is not all you do. You flood my altar with tears, asking, 'Why isn't God pleased with my sacrifice?' It is because you break your marriage vows. I hate divorce. Stop trying to cover your actions by saying that Moses gave you permission."

You can almost hear the Lord sigh as he says, "You weary me with your words.

" 'How have we wearied you?' you ask.

"By saying, 'The pagans are good in God's eyes. Look at how he has prospered them.'

"Then you say, 'Where is the proof that God is just?'

"Let me tell you something: When you least expect it, the Lord you are seeking will come. But when he does, who will be able to endure it? For when he comes, he will purify his people, just as gold and silver must be refined in the flames of the fire. I the Lord will bring judgment against those who take advantage of others and do not fear me.

"You have not given me your full tithes and offerings. If you give me your full tithe, watch what I will do. I will prosper your crops. But you have said, 'What good has it done to follow God's laws? God has blessed those who do not keep his requirements.' "

But those who truly feared the Lord began to talk among themselves. . . . And the Lord heard their conversation. Then he ordered that their names be written on a scroll, for they honored him. "They will be mine," the Lord said. "In the day of judgment, I will spare them.

"My judgment will burn like a furnace against every arrogant and evil person. But I will heal those who uphold my Name.

"Before that day, I will send the prophet Elijah. He will turn the disobedient back to me, or else I will strike the land with a curse."

TBC 179

SHARON DONOHUE is a free-lance journalist and former magazine editor. She began her career in Chicago as an editor for *Moody Monthly*, a Christian family magazine, then served as Managing Editor of *Marriage Partnership* and as Editor of *Today's Christian Woman*, publications of Christianity Today, Inc.

Sharon majored in Bible at Multnomah University (formerly Multnomah Bible College) and earned a B.S. in journalism from the University of Oregon. After moving from Chicago, she pursued a master's degree in education and taught English and social studies for 15 years.

Made in the USA
Middletown, DE
01 August 2020